*Enjoy your cookbook!*

*Shaké*

# Legacy Of Love

*Family Cookbook*

*A Collection of Favorite International Recipes*

*by*

*Shaké Bazoian*

Additional copies of Legacy of Love Family Cookbook may be obtained by inquiring at:

legacycookbook@bazoian.com

ISBN : 978-0-615-24232-3

Copyright © 2008 All rights reserved. No part of this book may be reproduced in any form, without written permission of the author.

Limited edition
October 2008

Printed in China
by China Offset and Litho Co. Ltd.

# Introduction

Good recipes are handed down in families from generation to generation and shared with friends within every culture throughout the world. Along the way, as recipes cross generations and cultures, ingredients may be added or removed, while modern-day short-cuts are added and the recipe is adapted to suit individual tastes.

This book is a compilation of the best of the best recipes I have accumulated from generations in my family as well as from many different cultures which I have visited. Many of the recipes have been revised or improved upon over the years. I do not claim originality to all the recipes in this book but can vouch for the authenticity and tastiness of all of them.

In this book, I have attempted to pull together everything learned over the years from my mother, mother-in-law, sisters, friends, relatives and the best of chefs I have been fortunate to have taken cooking classes from - Jean Francois Meteigner of L'Orangerie and presently La Cachette; Roy Yamaguchi of 385 North and later Roy's; Wolfgang Puck of Spago; Juachim Caula of St. Moritz Confectionery; Celestino Drago of Celestino's and Sharon Hoy. The writing of this book was only possible because of the generosity of my friends and family members who shared their favorite recipes with me and of my husband, children, and grandchildren who offered me their continued love, support and encouragement in writing this cookbook.

My love of cooking and baking began out of necessity. I was married at a young age in Beirut, Lebanon and came to the United States to start my married life and raise a family. I was clueless about cooking. I knew how food should taste if prepared properly but did not know how to cook myself. I had watched my mother cook, never using a recipe but simply tasting the food and adding whatever spice the food needed. As a young school girl, I was not interested in learning to cook. When I realized I was on my own and had a husband to feed, I started sending letters to my mother in Beirut and asking for help. "Please send recipes. I don't know how to cook".

I started out slowly, following my mother's recipe for simple rice pilaf. The Armenian recipe below is in my mother's handwriting and became a staple for the many Armenian dishes I would later learn to cook.

Once I had learned the basics, I became interested in learning how to bake pastries.

My mother-in-law made the best pies, well known in our family for having incredibly light and flaky pie crusts. The first recipe she gave me (original handwritten recipe to the right) was for Pecan Pie, assuring me it would be the easiest pie to try for the first time.

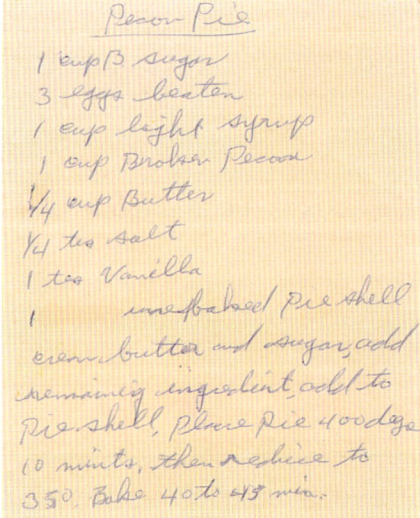

She also gave me the recipe for her pie crust along with a personal demonstration of how to make that famous flaky pie crust. Try as I have, I still cannot make it like she did. She had that magic touch! I am forever, grateful, however, for the recipes and wisdom she passed on to me and for all of the baked goodies she shared with me and my family.

As I grew in my marriage and my cooking abilities developed, I was able to use my opportunities traveling with my husband around the world to bring home new recipes, flavors, and ideas. We have enjoyed sampling local foods in foreign countries and bringing those flavors home. This cookbook contains ethnic recipes I have acquired abroad and have simplified or modified to pass on to others.

All of the recipes in this book have been used during the past 45 years. I have tried to simplify preparations by creating step-by-step instructions. Some people consider cooking and baking a profession, some consider it as a hobby, and some think it is a form of art. I believe that cooking and baking can be a rewarding craft that anyone can learn. This book has been designed to encourage even the most novice or timid cook to experiment and create fancy ethnic dishes with straightforward instructions, tips and pictures for each recipe.

My hope is that, as the years go by, my daughters, grandchildren and generations to come will use this book to make dishes which will remind them of their childhood favorites and the many, many happy times we have had and will have together - cooking, baking, tasting, entertaining and sharing fun times with our friends and extended families.

# Acknowledgements

My passion for cooking would have resulted in nothing more than some occasional good meals for family and friends but for the love, support and generosity of the many individuals who have shared recipes with me and who have encouraged me to compile and refine all the recipes in this book. Many of these individuals also stood dutifully and anxiously by my side ready and willing to sample all of the dishes I prepared while writing this book. I dedicate this book to all of those individuals and am so grateful for the support they have given me.

I must specially acknowledge and thank the following people:

- My mother Araxie, for my highly developed taste buds and an introduction to the finest foods at an early age.

- My mother-in-law Ethel, for teaching me the American way of preparing Middle Eastern dishes and for the many old country recipes she passed down to me.

- My daughters, Suzanne and Kathy for their hours of editing and proof-reading of this book.

- My son-in-laws, Eric and Tom for their eagerness in trying new recipes and giving me both positive feedback and constructive criticism.

- My grandchildren, Taylor, Matthew and Christine for making me feel like a celebrity chef who can do no wrong in the kitchen.

- My nephew Allen, for all of the technical support and for being, at all hours, just one telephone call away to help me with my computer challenges.

- Most importantly, I thank my husband, Haig for his love and enthusiastic support of my idea to write this book, which has been unwavering from beginning to end.

The journey I have been on in writing this cookbook has been enormously rewarding for me as my self-confidence has continued to grow hearing from my grandchildren that "Grandma, you are the world's greatest cook" and the best "*caker baker*". I know that I have accomplished my objective when young children think that a broccoli casserole or a spinach dish is yummy. I am thankful and satisfied that my passion has turned into a cookbook for all to share and that the process of writing the book led to many happy tummies and big smiles.

# Table of Contents

Introduction …………………………………………………..…..………3

Acknowledgment …………………………………………..…………….5

Spice Description ………………………………………….…..……....6

Appetizers and First Courses ……………………..……...……..9-44

Beverage………………………………………………………..…………..45-55

Soups………………………………………………………………….…...56-65

Salads……………………………………………………..…………..66-93

    Dressings …………………………………………..……………90-93

    Jello Molds………………………………………………..…………94-97

Seafood and Shellfish ………………………………....………….....98-113

Meats……………………………………………………………….……114-148

    Beef, 114-129; Lamb, 130-143; Pork, 144-146; Veal, 147-148

Poultry………………………………………………………….…...…149-163

Pasta……………………………………………………………….……164-170

Potato, 171-175; Rice, 176-186; …...……………...………….171-186

Snacks & Sandwiches……………………………………..………..187-196

Sauces and Marinades……………………………....………..…….197-211

Vegetables…………………………………………………….....………212-233

Breads ……………………………………………………………..234-242

Cakes ……………………………………………………………….243-275

Cookies…………………………………………………………………..276-326

Candies, 327-339; Jams & Jellies 340-343 …………………….327-343

Desserts…………………………………………………………….344-365

Measurements and Temperature Equivalent ……………..………367-369

Index …………………………………………………………………….366

# Spice Descriptions

### Ajvar
Ajvar is a thick blend of roasted red peppers and eggplant. It is sold in jars in Middle Eastern grocery stores. Available in mild or hot.

### Cumin
Cumin is the seed of a small plant. It has a spicy-sweet aroma. Its flavor is pungent, powerful, sharp and slightly bitter. Cumin is freely available in the West, although it is not a traditional European spice. It is found in every grocery store in the spice isle.

### Mahlab
Mahlab is the kernel of a black cherry. The kernels are small and pear-shaped with a light brown skin. They are sold in Middle Eastern stores either in whole kernels or pulverized. They are used in a number of Lebanese and Middle Eastern cookies and biscuits.

### Mastic
Mastic is a resin, the hardened sap from a tree. It appears as pea-sized globules, known as tears. They are rounded, pear-shaped, sometimes oblong, with a brittle, crystalline texture. The resin is semi-translucent, pastel yellow or faint green at its best, white mastic being inferior. It has a piney bouquet and a cedar taste. Although well known in the Balkans and the Middle East, mastic is not widely available elsewhere.

### Ma' Zahr
Ma'Zahr is orange blossom water. It is distilled from macerated Seville orange blossoms. Ma'Zahr is used in most Middle Eastern sweets very sparingly. It is very fragrant and has a slightly bitter taste.

### Sumac
Sumac is a less widely known spice. It is used in pulverized form to add a sour flavor in salad dressings, marinades, or is rubbed onto meat, fish or chicken before broiling. It has a pleasant lemony taste which enhances flavor and has a dark red color.

### Tahini
Tahini is sesame seed paste. It is used quite often in Mediterranean dishes and pastries. It is available in Middle Eastern stores. It comes in jars or in cans.

### Turmeric
Turmeric is the underground stem of a ginger-like plant. It is usually available ground, as a bright yellow, fine powder. It has an earthy and slightly acrid bouquet, and the flavor is warm and aromatic with a bitter undertone.

### Zahtar
Zahtar is a Middle Eastern blend of dried thyme, ground sumac, and toasted sesame seeds. The primary ingredient in the mixture is thyme. Zahtar is available in Middle Eastern or specialty stores.

# Appetizers and First Courses

## Artichoke-Chili Dip

*A simple and classic popular dip. You can use a hot plate or a fondue-like set-up to keep it warm.*

### Ingredients
1 (14 oz) can artichoke hearts packed in water
1 (4 oz) can chopped Ortega chilies
1 cup grated parmesan cheese
1 small onion, chopped
1 cup mayonnaise
Tortilla chips, corn chips, crackers, or breadsticks for dipping

### Preparation
1. Preheat oven to 350°F before baking.
2. Drain and chop the artichoke hearts.
3. Mix all the ingredients and put the mixture in an 8-inch round baking dish.
4. Bake at 350°F for 20 minutes until heated through.
5. Serve warm with tortilla chips, corn chips, crackers, or breadsticks.

Makes 2½ - 3 cups

### Tips
- *You may prepare dip ahead of time and refrigerate. Bake when ready to serve.*

# Artichoke-Spinach Dip

*This dip is one of the most popular dips. A version of this recipe is in most restaurants' menus.*

## Ingredients
1 (14 oz) can artichoke hearts
    packed in water
1 (10-13 oz) pkg frozen spinach
1 cup mayonnaise
1 cup Parmesan cheese
2¼ cup grated Jack cheese
Salt and pepper to taste
Assorted crackers or chips for serving

## Preparation
1. Preheat oven to 350°F before baking.
2. Drain and chop artichoke hearts.
3. Thaw and squeeze the excess water out of the spinach. Consistency of this dip depends on how much moisture is squeezed out of the spinach. If it looks too dry, add 1-2 Tbsp of milk.
4. Mix all ingredients together and transfer to a baking dish.
5. Bake for approximately 20 minutes until the cheese melts and bubbles.
6. Serve with assorted crackers or chips.

Makes 4-5 cups

## Tips
- *May be prepared one day ahead and chilled until baking time*
- *If you have any left over dip, the next day you may use it by tossing with cooked noodles and thinning it with the water in which the pasta was cooked.*

# Spanakopita (Spinach Turnovers)

*This is a Greek specialty that is a very popular appetizer at parties. Prepared in advance and frozen makes a handy last minute appetizer and a snack.*

## Ingredients
12 oz fresh baby spinach leaves
1½ tsp salt
1 large onion, chopped
¼ cup Extra-virgin olive oil
¼ cup chopped parsley
2 Tbsp chopped fresh oregano
8 oz feta cheese, crumbled
¼ tsp black pepper
2 eggs, slightly beaten
1 pkg frozen filo dough, thawed
2/3 cup clarified butter

## Preparation
1. Wash and chop spinach. Sprinkle with salt and rub with hands to wilt them. Leave for 1 hour then squeeze well to get rid of the excess liquid and place in a large mixing bowl.
2. Heat ¼ cup olive oil in a skillet and sauté the onion until soft. Set aside to cool.
3. Mix together with the spinach onion, parsley, oregano, feta cheese, black pepper and eggs.
4. Open filo dough package and cut the stack of sheets into four strips lengthwise. (2-2½ inches wide).
5. Working on one turnover at a time; stack three strips on top of each other buttering each layer with a brush dipped in clarified butter. Place a tablespoon of spinach filling at one end of the stacked strips and fold one corner over the filling making a triangle. Continue folding in triangles (flag-fashion) until the strip is all folded. Brush top with butter. Place on a tray.
6. Repeat with remaining dough and spinach filling. Arrange all in a tray cover loosely and freeze. After they are frozen, arrange them in a Tupperware with wax paper between each layer. (You can prepare them to this point and freeze them until ready to use at a later date).
7. When ready to bake, preheat oven to 400°F, place frozen turnovers on a tray and bake for 20 minutes or until golden brown. Serve warm or at room temperature.

Makes 34-36 turnovers

## Tips
- *To keep filo dough crisp, be sure the spinach is squeezed dry.*
- <u>*Clarified butter:*</u> *In a saucepan, melt sweet butter over low heat. Skim the milk solids off the top and carefully pour the clarified butter into another container without disturbing the remaining milk solids and water that is in the bottom of the pan. Clarified butter keeps up to 6 months in the refrigerator.*

# Spinach-Cheese Swirls

*This is the perfect appetizer for the hostess who wants to be out of the kitchen greeting guests.*

## Ingredients
1 sheet frozen puff pastry, thawed
½ cup shredded Jack cheese
¼ cup grated Parmesan cheese
¼ tsp garlic powder
2 Tbsp chopped green onion
1 (8-10 oz) pkg frozen spinach, thawed and well drained
1 egg for egg-wash
1 Tbsp water

## Preparation
1. Preheat oven to 400°F before baking.
2. In a medium bowl mix Jack and Parmesan cheeses, garlic powder, onion and drained spinach. Set aside.
3. In another small bowl beat the egg with one tablespoon water, and set aside.
4. Unfold puff pastry sheet on a lightly floured board and cut lengthwise in half. Brush with egg wash. Spread half of the spinach-cheese mixture on one piece.
5. Start from the long side of the dough and roll like jelly roll. Repeat the same with the other half.
6. Cut into ½ inch slices and arrange on cookie sheet 2 inches apart. Brush tops with egg-wash.
7. Bake for 15 minutes or until golden brown.

Makes 40-50 swirls

## Tips
- *Frozen puff pastry is very easy to use. It is found in the frozen food section in most grocery stores.*
- *The swirls can be made earlier in the day and refrigerated.*
- *The best way to thaw out frozen puff pastry is to take it out of the freezer the night before and place it in the refrigerator. It usually takes 6-8 hours to thaw in the refrigerator. Thawed pastry is good for up to 2 days in the refrigerator. For quick thaw, take frozen pastry out of the box and wrap in plastic wrap and let it thaw at room temperature. It will take 30-40 minutes.*

# Black Olives and Feta Cheese Swirls

*This finger food could be part of an assortment of appetizers made well in advance of your party.*

## Ingredients
1 sheet frozen puff pastry, thawed
1/3 cup crumbled Feta cheese
1/3 cup chopped Kalamata olives
1 tsp finely chopped Jalapeno pepper
2 Tbsp finely chopped green onions
1 small tomato chopped
    (without the seeds)
1 egg for egg-wash
1 Tbsp water

## Preparation
1. Preheat oven to 400°F before baking.
2. In a medium bowl mix crumbled feta cheese, chopped Kalamata olives, pepper, onions, and tomato. Set aside.
3. In another small bowl beat the egg with one tablespoon water, and set aside.
4. Unfold puff pastry sheet on a lightly floured board and cut lengthwise in half. Brush with egg wash. Spread half of the olive and cheese mixture on one piece.
5. Start from the long side of the dough and roll like jelly roll. Repeat with the other half.
6. Cut into ½-inch slices and arrange on cookie sheet 2 inches apart. Brush tops again with egg-wash.
7. Bake for 15-18 minutes or until golden brown.

Makes 40-50 swirls

## Tips
- *Frozen puff pastry is found in the frozen food section in most grocery stores.*
- *The swirls can be made earlier in the day and refrigerated.*
- *The best way to thaw out frozen puff pastry is to take it out of the freezer the night before and place it in the refrigerator. It usually takes 6-8 hours to thaw in the refrigerator. Thawed pastry is good for up to 2 days in the refrigerator. For quick thaw, take frozen pastry out of the box and wrap in plastic wrap and let it thaw at room temperature. It will take 30-40 minutes.*
- *If you wish to kick up the heat, add more chopped jalapeno pepper to the mixture.*

# Parmesan Cheese Twists

*Simple, easy, light and flaky, as well as irresistible. Prepare in advance and serve at room temperature.*

## Ingredients
1 pkg frozen puff pastry, thawed
1 cup Parmesan cheese
1 tsp seasoned pepper
½ tsp red pepper flakes
1 tsp garlic powder
1 tsp oregano
½ tsp salt
1 Tbsp dried chopped parsley
1 egg for egg-wash
1 Tbsp water

## Preparation
1. Preheat oven to 375°F before baking.
2. Line baking sheets with parchment paper.
3. In a small bowl combine Parmesan cheese, seasoned pepper, red pepper flakes, garlic powder, oregano, salt and parsley flakes.
4. In a small bowl, beat the egg with one tablespoon of water for the egg-wash.
5. Unfold pastry sheets onto cutting board, brush with egg-wash, and sprinkle with ¼ of cheese mixture on each sheet and lightly press into pastry. Turn over the pastry dough and repeat the same on the other side.
6. Cut each sheet lengthwise in half, then into ¾ inch strips. Twist and place on greased cookie sheet.
7. Bake for 12 minutes or until puffed and golden brown.
8. Cool and serve at room temperature.
   <u>Note</u>: If you want to serve it in the next day or two, put them in a warm oven to crisp them. Cool, then store in an air-tight container. They will stay nice and crisp, otherwise they get soft.

Makes 48 twists

## Tips
- To make a variety of twists, use one of the two packaged pastry sheets for the Parmesan cheese flavor and reduce the ingredients by half. Use the other sheet by creating your own mixture of spices. Better yet, sprinkle a sugar and cinnamon mixture following the above instructions.
- You may use a pizza cutter for cutting into strips. Much easier.
- You may prepare them in advance and freeze them before baking. When ready to serve, bake them frozen for 15 minutes or until golden brown.

# Seasoned Pita Chips

*Prepare several days in advance and you have an interesting and tasty chip to serve with any dip. It is good even on its own.*

## Ingredients
3 (6-inch round) pita breads
¼ cup olive oil
1 clove garlic, slice into quarters
¼ tsp freshly ground pepper
¼ tsp paprika
¼ tsp cayenne pepper
¾ tsp crushed oregano
¼ cup grated Parmesan cheese

## Preparation
1. Preheat oven to 375°F before baking.
2. In a small pan heat the oil, garlic, pepper, paprika, cayenne pepper and oregano until garlic is fragrant. Remove garlic from the oil and discard.
3. Separate each pita bread into two rounds. Arrange on a baking sheet. Brush rough sides with the olive oil mixture and then sprinkle parmesan cheese all over.
4. With a clean kitchen shear, cut each pita round into eight wedges. Spread wedges seasoned side up in a single layer, on a baking sheet.
5. Bake for 8-10 minutes or until golden brown and crisp.
6. Cool on a wire rack. Store in an airtight container to be used later.

## Tips
- *For variation, instead of oregano use thyme or finely chopped chives, or instead of the spices above, use any dry salad dressing seasoning mixed with oil.*
- *Use pesto sauce thinned with olive oil. Brush on the bread and then sprinkle parmesan cheese and bake.*
- *For sweet version, brush with melted butter and sprinkle with cinnamon and sugar mixture. Omit Parmesan cheese.*
- *Will keep for up to 2 weeks in an airtight container. Briefly re-crisp them in a hot oven for a few minutes.*

# Savory Parmesan Cheese Cookies
*Wonderful, simple, easy, light and flaky cookies make a great accompaniment with pre-dinner drinks. Prepare in advance and serve at room temperature.*

## Ingredients
1¾ cup flour
¾ cup grated Parmesan cheese
   plus 2 Tbsp for topping
½ tsp crushed garlic
1 tsp salt
½ tsp cayenne pepper
1 cup unsalted butter

## Preparation
1. Preheat oven to 350°F before baking. Line baking sheets with parchment paper.
2. In a food processor combine flour, Parmesan cheese, garlic, salt, and cayenne pepper. Pulse a couple seconds to mix.
3. Cut butter into small pieces, add to the flour and pulse until mixture comes together. Form dough into a ball. Divide in half and roll each half into 12-inch logs. Refrigerate for 30 minutes. (At this point you can keep it refrigerated for several days or freeze it for several weeks until ready to use).
4. Remove from refrigerator and slice into 1 inch slices. Place on cookie sheet 1½-inches apart; flatten them with your hands into 2-inch rounds. Sprinkle tops with the 2 tablespoons of Parmesan cheese and if you like them spicy, more cayenne pepper.
5. Bake for 20 minutes or until golden brown. Cool and serve at room temperature.

Makes 28-30 cookies

## Tips
- *You may also bake them and keep them in an air-tight container in the freezer for several weeks.*

# Herbed Cheese

*I often call this cheese homemade "Boursin". In 1957 a French cheese maker, Francois Boursin, created Boursin cheese. This delicious soft cheese is very similar to the store bought "Boursin". Preparation takes minutes. Use in a wrap, omelets, or over grilled steak.*

## Ingredients
1 (8 oz) pkg cream cheese
½ cup sour cream
2 Tbsp plain yogurt
2 Tbsp butter
1½ tsp minced garlic
1½ tsp minced chives
1½ tsp minced parsley
½ tsp cayenne pepper
¼ tsp black pepper
Salt to taste
Assorted crackers for serving

## Preparation
1. Combine all the above ingredients in a food processor or blender and blend until mixture is very smooth and creamy.
2. Place in a serving bowl, cover with plastic wrap, and refrigerate. Or keep it in air-tight container in the refrigerator. It will keep for one week.
3. Serve at room temperature with crackers.

Makes 2 cups

## Tips
- *You can create your own variety of flavors both sweet and savory. Instead of parsley and chives feel free to use your favorite herbs like thyme, dill, hot pepper flakes, mint, basil etc.*
- *Instead of spices sweeten with jams or jellies and use it on bagels and English muffins.*

# Shankelish

*This is a homemade spicy yogurt cheese which is quite popular in Middle Eastern countries.
It is used in salads also baked as a topping on bread.*

## Ingredients
16 cups regular yogurt
   [2 (64 oz) tubs]
2 Tbsp salt
½ cup water
1 Tbsp salt
2 Tbsp Chili pepper flakes
¾ cup pure zahtar (ground thyme)

## Preparation
1. On a stove top combine yogurt, salt, and ½ cup water. Cook on medium heat until yogurt curdles, approximately 35-45 minutes.
2. Line a colander with cheese cloth and drain the mixture for 3-4 hours until it resembles cottage cheese.
3. Transfer the contents to a mixing bowl and add 1½ tablespoons salt and the chili pepper. Knead all together until mixture holds together. You may add a little water if the mixture is too dry.
4. Form into tennis ball size balls and place on a tray, lined with paper towels, to dry 3-5 days. Change the wet paper towels daily. To expedite the drying of the shankelish you may put the tray in the sun only one hour a day.
5. After it is dry, wet the balls by hand and roll them in pure zahtar. Wrap individually in plastic wrap and refrigerate or freeze. Use as needed as an appetizer or baked on bread.

Makes 6 shankelish balls

## Tips
- *Shankelish keeps very well in the freezer for several months.*
- *See recipe for Shankelish salad on (page 19), and Shankelish bread on (page 242).*
- *Zahtar sold in Middle Eastern stores are a mixture of ground sumac and ground dried thyme. Often they are mixed with sesame seeds as well.*

# Shankelish Salad as an Appetizer
*This is a treat for those who have a taste for Middle Eastern food.*

## Ingredients
1 ball Shankelish (recipe on page18)
1 medium tomato, chopped fine
1 small onion, chopped fine (optional)
3 Tbsp extra virgin olive oil
Pita bread or lavash, cut into
    wedges or squares.

## Preparation
1. In a mixing bowl combine the above ingredients and toss lightly.
2. Serve with pita or lavash bread wedges.

## Tips
- *Another form of presentation is to chop the shankelish and spread it on a plate, sprinkle the chopped onion on top, then the chopped tomatoes. Drizzle with olive oil.*
- *If you are out of shankelish, a quick fix would be to use crumbled feta cheese mixed with Zahtar.*

# Hummus

*This is one of the most popular Middle Eastern dips, traditionally served with pita bread. It is served as an appetizer, or as a side dish with fish or grilled meat. The convenience of canned chickpeas and a food processor makes this easy to prepare. Vegetarians' delight - healthy and addictive.*
*Once you have made this at home, you will never resort to store bought versions.*

## Ingredients
1 can (15.5 oz) garbanzo beans
    drained and rinsed
4 Tbsp tahini (sesame seed paste)
3 Tbsp lemon juice
1 clove crushed garlic (optional)
2-4 Tbsp water as needed
¾ tsp salt
2 Tbsp Extra-virgin olive oil
Paprika for garnish
Cumin for garnish
Pita bread wedges for serving

## Preparation
1. In a food processor with the steel blade, puree chickpeas, tahini, lemon juice, and garlic. To acquire the right dip consistency, add one tablespoon of water at a time. Hummus should have the consistency of sour cream. Adjust seasoning.
2. To serve, spread the dip in a 2-inch deep bowl. Drizzle with Extra-virgin olive oil, and sprinkle paprika and/or cumin to your taste.
3. Serve with pita bread wedges.

Makes 1½ cups

## Tips
- *If you don't have a food processor, a blender works well too.*
- *Can be made a day in advance, cover and refrigerate.*
- *Sesame seed paste is found in most specialty and Middle Eastern grocery stores. It comes in cans or jars. Often the oil separates from the pasty part, so make sure to stir tahini before measuring.*
- *It is important to use Extra-virgin Olive Oil as it enhances the flavor of Hummus.*
- *Some people like to sprinkle the top with toasted pine nuts. That is tasty too.*

# Baba Ghanoush

*This dish is a Middle Eastern specialty. It is a mixture of roasted eggplant, tahini and lemon juice. Traditionally it is served as an appetizer or as an accompaniment with fish dishes, garnished with pomegranate seeds. Roasting the eggplant is the secret to this tasty dip. Baked eggplant does not give you the smoky flavoring. Even if you don't like eggplant, you will love this dish.*

## Ingredients
2 large eggplants
3 Tbsp tahini (sesame seed paste)
2 Tbsp lemon juice
1 clove crushed garlic (optional)
¾ tsp salt
2 Tbsp Extra-virgin olive oil
Mint leaves to garnish
Pomegranate seeds (optional)
Pita bread, cut into wedges

## Preparation
1. Place eggplant under the broiler or on BBQ, turning it several times until it is all charred and blistered. Remove from fire and let it cool to room temperature.
2. Cut eggplants in half lengthwise and with a spoon remove the pulp and place in a bowl or food processor. If the eggplants have large dark seeds, remove them as they are unpalatable and will give the dip a bitter taste.
3. Add tahini, lemon juice, garlic and salt. Pulse until mixture is smooth or if you do not like it too smooth, mix by hand. Adjust seasoning.
4. Spread the dip in a 2-inch deep bowl. Drizzle with Extra-virgin olive oil, sprinkle with pomegranate seeds, and garnish with mint.
5. Serve with chips or pita bread wedges.

Makes 2 cups

## Tips
- *With a fork poke the eggplant before cooking to prevent it from bursting.*
- *If you don't have a food processor, a blender works well too.*
- *Eggplant tastes best when it is grilled on charcoal or gas barbeque.*
- *Sesame seed paste is found in most specialty and Middle Eastern grocery stores. It comes in cans or jars. Often the oil separates from the pasty part, so make sure to stir tahini before measuring.*
- *It is important to use Extra-virgin olive oil as it enhances the flavor of baba ghanoush.*

# Mouhamara

*This is a killer dip. It is a Middle Eastern dip made with roasted red peppers. For quicker and easier preparation, use mild "Ajvar" which is a thick blend of roasted red peppers and eggplant. Being a spicy dip, it is also good with roasted or grilled meat, such as lamb or chicken kebabs.*

## Ingredients

1 (19 oz jar) Ajvar, mild or hot
1 cup soft white bread crumbs
1 cup walnuts, finely ground
1 cup water
2 Tbsp Extra-virgin olive oil
1 tsp cumin
½ tsp allspice
2-3 tsp Aleppo crushed red pepper
1½ Tbsp pomegranate molasses
1 tsp salt
2 drops red food coloring (optional)
Pita bread wedges or corn chips
    for dipping

## Preparation

1. In a mixing bowl, combine all ingredients except the pita bread, and mix thoroughly. Cover and refrigerate.
2. Serve mouhamara as a dip at room temperature with pita bread triangles or corn chips.
3. When serving grilled chicken or meat, serve mouhamara on the side as a sauce to enhance food flavors.

Makes 3 cups

## Tips

- *Ajvar, Aleppo pepper, and pomegranate molasses are found in specialty and Middle Eastern markets or international food isles of well stocked supermarkets. If you cannot find pomegranate molasses, you may substitute lemon juice.*
- *Ajvar comes mild or hot. If you need an extra kick, increase the amount of dried crushed red pepper or buy the hot Ajvar.*
- *If you cannot find Ajvar, puree 3-4 roasted red peppers, and follow the recipe adjusting spices.*
- *Sometimes red food coloring is needed to enhance the appearance of the mouhamara.*

# Guacamole (Avocado Dip)

*The simplest and most delicious dip! Nothing beats the fresh taste of avocados in guacamole. Great with margaritas!*

## Ingredients
2 ripe avocados
1 tsp minced jalapeño pepper
1 small tomato chopped
2 Tbsp minced onion
1-2 Tbsp fresh lemon or lime juice
½ tsp salt
2 Tbsp chopped cilantro for garnish
Tortilla chips or Fritos for serving

## Preparation
1. Remove skin and seeds and mash avocados with a fork in a medium bowl.
2. Seed and remove the veins of the jalapeno pepper before mincing.
3. Mix in remaining ingredients, except tortilla chips and cilantro, and adjust seasoning.
4. Garnish with cilantro and serve with tortilla chips.

Makes 2½ cups

## Tips
- *For a tastier guacamole, use the Hass avocados - the burley brown ones. The vibrant green avocadoes are not as tasty.*
- *To ensure ripe avocados for your party, purchase them 3-4 days ahead, put them in a paper bag and let them ripen at room temperature.*
- *You can prepare guacamole a few hours in advance and prevent it from turning brown by placing the avocado seeds back into the prepared guacamole, cover with plastic wrap and refrigerate. Remove the seeds before serving.*
- *To spice up guacamole, add ¼ tsp red pepper sauce or increase the minced jalapeño.*

# 7-Layer Mexican Dip

*Another classic crowd-pleasing, quick-fix recipe with south of the border flavors.
Great served with margaritas.*

## Ingredients
1 (16 oz) can refried beans
½ pkg taco seasoning mix
½ cup sliced green onions
¾ cup sour cream
1 (2 oz) can pitted sliced black olives, drained
1 cup shredded Jack cheese or Cheddar cheese
1 cup chunky salsa, or fresh tomato salsa
1 avocado, peeled and chopped
3 Tbsp chopped cilantro
Tortilla chips or Fritos for dipping

## Preparation
1. Mix beans with taco seasoning. Spread onto the bottom of a 9-inch pie pan or serving dish.
2. Layer with the onions, sour cream, olives, cheese, and salsa. Cover and chill for several hours.
3. Right before serving, toss avocado with cilantro and spoon on top of salsa.
4. Serve with tortilla chips or Fritos.

Makes 6 cups

## Tips
- For variation you may wish to add ground beef, flavored with taco seasoning. Spread on top of the beans then continue layering with the remaining ingredients.
- Another variety would be to add shredded cooked chicken over the beans and then layer with the remaining ingredients.

# Pigs in a Blanket

*Everybody's old time favorite! Adults love them as much as children do at their parties. This will be the first appetizer to disappear from the appetizer table. It's our 7-year old grandson Matthew's favorite thing to eat any time of the day.*

## Ingredients
2 pkgs refrigerated crescent roll dough
1 pkg all-beef cocktail franks
Ketchup for dipping
Honey mustard for dipping

## Preparation
1. Preheat oven to 375°F before baking.
2. Remove dough from package and cut between perforations. Cut each triangle into four smaller triangles and wrap around each small frank.
3. Place wrapped franks on an ungreased baking sheet and bake 10-12 minutes until dough is puffy and golden.
4. Serve warm with ketchup and honey mustard for dipping.

Makes approximately 40-45

## Tips
- *If you cannot find cocktail franks, you can always cut regular hot dogs into smaller pieces.*
- *May be prepared in advance and refrigerated. Bake before guests arrive.*
- *For variety you may use other flavored sausages. Just split them in half and quarter them.*

# Crab Stuffed Mushrooms

*Crab stuffed mushroom caps make a delicious appetizer for any party. The filling can be prepared ahead of time and refrigerated.*

## Ingredients
12 white mushrooms,
   (2" in diameter)
1 tsp lemon juice
4 Tbsp butter
4 Tbsp chopped shallots
1 clove garlic, crushed
1 Tbsp flour
½ cup chicken broth
½ tsp salt
¼ tsp black pepper
¼ tsp cayenne pepper
¼ cup heavy cream
2 Tbsp chopped parsley
½ cup lump crab meat
2 Tbsp Parmesan cheese
2 Tbsp bread crumbs

## Preparation
1. Preheat oven to 350°F before baking.
2. Wipe the mushroom caps with a damp paper towel. Remove the stems from the mushrooms and chop them very fine. Sprinkle mushroom caps with lemon juice.
3. In a frying pan melt the butter and sauté shallots, chopped mushroom stems, and garlic. Add flour and sauté for another minute. Gradually add the chicken broth until the sauce thickens, add the spices and the cream and continue cooking for a few minutes longer. Add the parsley and crab meat. Adjust seasoning. Remove from heat. Mix in the Parmesan cheese. Let it cool.
4. Spoon stuffing into mushroom cavities and arrange on a greased baking dish. Sprinkle the tops with bread crumbs and a little Parmesan cheese. Bake for 20 minutes.

Makes 12 mushrooms

## Tips
- *For variety, you may use ground chicken, but try to sauté it with the shallots until cooked, or use cooked chicken and grind it to add to the mixture.*
- *Easier version and equally delicious filling: 8 oz crabmeat, 8 oz cream cheese, ½ cup garlic croutons, finely chopped. Mix them all together, fill in the mushrooms, sprinkle top with Parmesan cheese and lightly sprinkle with paprika.*

# Rice Stuffed Grape Leaves (Yalanchi Sarma)

*Yalanchi Sarma is made with olive oil and makes a wonderful appetizer dish. Prepare a day in advance, arrange on serving platter, cover and refrigerate until party time.*

## Ingredients

1 jar preserved grape leaves
7 medium size onions, chopped
2 cups rice, rinsed and drained
1¾ cup olive oil
¼ cup lemon juice
1 cup chopped fresh tomatoes
2 Tbsp chopped parsley
2 Tbsp chopped fresh mint
2 Tbsp tomato paste
2 tsp salt
½ tsp black pepper
¼ tsp red pepper flakes or cayenne
1½ cups water for the rice
1¾ cups hot water for cooking sarmas

## Preparation

1. Place chopped onions in a 4-quart saucepan and over low heat let it sweat to release its juices.
2. Add to the saucepan rice; 1½ cup olive oil (reserve the other ¼ cup for cooking juice), lemon juice, tomatoes, parsley, mint, tomato paste, salt, pepper, cayenne pepper and water. Bring to a boil. Reduce heat, cover the pan and simmer for 15-20 minutes until all the liquid is absorbed. The rice will not be cooked completely. Set aside to cool.
3. <u>Assemble Sarma:</u> Rinse the preserved grape leaves in cold water and squeeze out the excess water. Cut and discard the long stems. Spread, one leaf at a time, on a plate with the shiny side down. Place 1 tablespoon of the rice filling along the stem side. Bring the two sides of the leaf over the filling and starting from the stem side roll to wrap. The average size of each sarma will be approximately 3-inches long and ¾-inch in diameter depending on the size of the leaves. Repeat with the rest of the leaves until all the rice filling is used.
4. Line the bottom of the pan with a few extra grape leaves to prevent the bottom layer from sticking to the bottom of the pan. Arrange sarmas, side-by-side, in layers in the pot. Cover with an inverted plate for weight to keep them in place while cooking.
5. Pour 1¾ cups of hot water and the reserved ¼ cup olive oil over the sarmas and bring to a boil. (During cooking the olive oil will give a shine to the sarmas. Reduce heat to low, cover the pan and simmer for 45-50 minutes until the grape leaves are soft. Drain any remaining liquid. Most of the liquid should be absorbed while cooking. Let them cool completely in the pan before transferring to a serving plate.

Makes 75-80 sarmas

## Tips

- *Preserved grape leaves are sold in Middle Eastern grocery stores.*
- *To avoid tears when chopping onions briefly place them in the freezer before chopping.*

# Fried Chicken Fingers

*Marinate chicken fingers earlier in the day to save last minute chores in the kitchen. Serve as an appetizer with a dipping sauce.*

## Ingredients
1 lb chicken breasts or tenders
1 tsp salt
½ tsp pepper
½ tsp garlic powder
½ cup buttermilk
1 egg slightly beaten
½ cup seasoned bread crumbs
½ cup flour
½ tsp baking powder

## Preparation
1. Cut the chicken into ½-inch strips.
2. Salt and pepper chicken strips and add garlic powder; cover them with the buttermilk mixed with the egg, and let marinate for an hour.
3. In a plastic bag mix bread crumbs, flour and baking powder.
4. Take the chicken strips out of the marinade and drop them in plastic bag with bread crumbs. Shake the bag until chicken strips are coated with the crumbs.
5. In a skillet over medium high heat, heat ½ cup vegetable oil. Fry the chicken in batches for 4-5 minutes or until golden brown on all sides. Drain on paper towels.

Makes 2-3 servings

## Tips
- *If you do not have buttermilk handy around the house, mix ½ cup of milk and 1½ teaspoons of vinegar or lemon juice and let it sit for 5 minutes then marinate the chicken.*

# Chicken Quesadillas with Mango Salsa

*Quesadillas are crisp thin irresistible pan-grilled sandwiches. They are usually made with flour tortillas filled with cheese and maybe some vegetables, chicken or shrimp. They are usually pan-grilled with just a touch of oil, served warm with guacamole, salsa and sour cream.*

## Ingredients
8 (9-inch) flour tortillas
1 tsp butter or oil
3 cups grated Jack cheese,
   or Cheddar cheese
2 cups cooked shredded chicken
¼ cup chopped cilantro

### Mango Salsa
2 large ripe mangos
1 small red onion, diced
1 small jalapeno pepper,
   finely chopped
2 Tbsp lime juice
¼ cup chopped cilantro
¼ tsp salt

## Preparation
1. Peel and dice mango into half inch cubes. Place in a bowl. Add diced onion, jalapeno pepper, lime juice, and salt. Toss gently. Set aside.
2. Melt 1 tsp of butter or oil in a large heavy skillet over medium high heat.
3. Place a tortilla on a work surface, sprinkle 1/3 cup shredded cheese on the tortilla, then sprinkle half a cup of shredded chicken over it, 1 tablespoon of chopped cilantro, and another 1/3 cup of shredded cheese. Top with another tortilla and lightly press with the palm of your hand. Gently place tortilla on the heated skillet and cook for 2 minutes until cheese starts melting and the bottom tortilla starts browning. With the help of a wide spatula flip over and brown the other side. Remove from the skillet and place on a tray. Keep warm in a low temperature oven while you prepare more. Repeat the same with the rest of the tortillas.
4. Transfer quesadilla to plate and cut into 6 wedges, serve with mango salsa.
5. Serve soon after cooking, eat while still crisp.

Makes 4 servings

## Tips
- *You may wish to use one tortilla at a time folded in half.*
- *For variety for quesadilla filling, spread 2 tablespoons of any Mexican bean dip, top with your choice of chopped vegetables; onion, mushroom, bell pepper, olives, avocado etc. Top vegetables with grated cheese then top with another tortilla and grill.*
- *To make several quesadillas at a time, arrange quesadillas on a buttered baking sheet and bake in a preheated oven 375° F for 6-8 minutes or until cheese melts and the bottom starts browning. Flip over to brown the other side. Serve with guacamole, salsa and sour cream.*

# Baked Quesadillas

*When frozen, these baked quesadillas can be heated to make a handy lunch or snack item anytime.*

### Ingredients
10 Carb balance fajita flour tortillas
1 egg, slightly beaten for egg wash
White sesame seeds
Black sesame seeds (optional)
Vegetable oil

*Filling*
10 oz Jack cheese grated
1 egg, slightly beaten
¼ tsp black pepper

### Preparation
1. Preheat oven to 375°F before baking.
2. Mix grated cheese, 1 slightly beaten egg and black pepper. Set aside.
3. Brush a baking sheet with vegetable oil.
4. Lay out tortillas and brush one side with vegetable oil. Flip them over.
5. Place 2 tablespoons of the cheese mixture in one half of each tortilla, brush the edges with egg-wash, fold over and press the edges together.
6. Brush the top with egg-wash and sprinkle with sesame seeds.
7. Prick top with a fork for air vent. Bake for 15-18 minutes until they start browning. Serve warm.

Makes 10

### Tips
- *Carb-balance tortillas seem to be flakier and tender when baked then the regular flour tortillas.*
- *You may freeze them after baking. They keep well in the freezer. Heat before serving.*
- *For variety, you may mix a small can of chopped Ortega chilies, and/or chicken into the filling.*

# Vegetarian Samosa

*Samosas are traditional Indian pastries: homemade dough filled with meat or vegetables then fried. I prefer the light and crisp version made with filo dough and baked. These healthy and delicious vegetable pockets are a good snack anytime of the day.*

## Ingredients
½ pkg filo dough (14 sheets)
3 medium size potatoes
2 Tbsp butter
1 large onion, diced
1 tsp cumin
2 tsp ground coriander
1 tsp salt
½ tsp black pepper
¾ tsp crushed red pepper
¾ cup frozen peas
1/3 cup frozen corn
¼ cup chopped cilantro leaves
2 Tbsp lemon juice
Clarified butter or vegetable oil for assembling and baking samosas

## Preparation
1. Preheat oven to 375°F before baking.
2. Boil the potatoes until fork tender. Cool. Peel and dice into half inch cubes.
3. In a skillet melt 2 tablespoons of butter and sauté diced onion until tender; add the spices and cook 2 minutes longer. Add diced potatoes, frozen peas, corn, chopped cilantro and lemon juice. Mix well and adjust seasoning.
4. Cut filo dough in half lengthwise and fold each piece in half lengthwise.
5. Using one strip of filo dough at a time, lightly brush with melted butter. Place 2 tablespoons of mixture at one end and fold pastry diagonally over the filling to form a triangle. Continue folding over and over until the entire strip has been used and the pastry has formed a triangle. Place triangles seam side down, 2 inches apart on a baking sheet coated with cooking oil. Use the remainder of the dough the same way. Brush tops of samosas with melted butter or vegetable oil spray. (At this point you can freeze them for later use).
6. Bake for 15-20 minutes or until golden brown.

Makes 28 samosas

## Tips
- *Clarified butter:* In a saucepan melt sweet butter over low heat. Skim the milk solids off the top and carefully pour the clarified butter into another container without disturbing the remaining milk solids and water that are in the bottom of the pan. Clarified butter keeps up to 6 months in the refrigerator.
- Samosas freeze well. Arrange unbaked samosas on a tray and freeze. After they are frozen, store them in a freezer plastic bag or in an air-tight plastic container. Use wax paper between layers to prevent them from sticking to each other.
- If baking frozen samosas, increase baking time by 5-8 minutes.

# Meat Samosa

*I prefer the baked version made with filo dough instead of the traditional homemade dough which is fried. These healthy, light, crisp, and delicious meat pockets are a good snack anytime of the day. Great for lunch served with a salad.*

## Ingredients
½ pkg filo dough (14 sheets)
½ lb ground beef
2 Tbsp butter
2 bunches scallions, chopped
1 clove garlic, minced
¼ tsp ginger
¼ tsp cloves
Pinch of cardamom
½ tsp salt
½ tsp black pepper
2 Tbsp chopped cilantro leaves
Clarified butter or vegetable oil for assembling and baking samosas

## Preparation
1. Preheat oven to 375°F before baking.
2. In a skillet melt the butter and sauté diced onion until tender; add garlic, spices and cook 2 minutes longer. Add the ground beef and cook until browned. Add chopped cilantro, and mix well; adjust seasoning. Drain excess liquid.
3. Cut filo dough in half lengthwise and fold each piece in half lengthwise.
4. Using one strip of filo dough at a time, lightly brush with melted butter. Place one tablespoon of mixture at one end and fold pastry diagonally over the filling to form a triangle. Continue folding over and over until the entire strip has been used and the pastry has formed a triangle. Place triangles seam side down, 2 inches apart on baking sheets coated with cooking oil. Use the remainder of the dough the same way. Brush tops of samosas with melted butter or vegetable oil spray. (At this point you can freeze them for later use).
5. Bake in preheated oven 375°F for 15-20 minutes or until golden brown.

Makes 28 samosas

## Tips
- *Clarified butter: In a saucepan melt sweet butter over low heat. Skim the milk solids off the top and carefully pour the clarified butter into another container without disturbing the remaining milk solids and water that are in the bottom of the pan. Clarified butter keeps up to 6 months in the refrigerator.*
- *Samosas freeze well. Arrange unbaked samosas on a tray and freeze. After they are frozen, store them in a freezer plastic bag or in an air-tight plastic container. Use wax paper between layers to prevent them from sticking to each other.*
- *If baking frozen samosas, it will take an extra 5-8 minutes of baking time.*

# Puff Pastry Dough Cheese Beoreks

*I don't think it is ever possible for me to have a dinner party without serving these delicious cheese turnovers. Advance preparation makes these beoreks the perfect accompaniment for a soup or salad or as a side dish on a buffet table. Make them smaller, and you can serve them as an appetizer. We always have a supply handy in our freezer.*

## Ingredients
1 pkg Puff pastry dough squares, (12 5x5-inch squares)
1 egg, for egg-wash
1 Tbsp water
Sesame seeds to sprinkle on top

*Filling*
10 oz. Jack cheese grated
1 egg, slightly beaten
¼ tsp black pepper

## Preparation
1. Preheat oven to 400°F before baking.
2. Mix grated cheese, slightly beaten egg and black pepper. Set aside.
3. Thaw the puff pastry dough at room temperature.
4. With a rolling pin, enlarge the 5x5 inch square to 5x6 or 5x6½-inch squares.
5. Cut dough in half horizontally to make two 5x3-inch rectangles.
6. Place 1 tablespoon of the cheese mixture in one half of each puff pastry rectangle, brush the edges with water, fold over and press the edges together. Reinforce edges with a fork dipped in flour. Prick the tops with a fork for air vent. At this point, if you wish, you may freeze beoreks until time to use.
7. Before baking, brush the top with egg-wash and sprinkle with sesame seeds.
8. Bake for 18-20 minutes, or until they are puffed and start browning. Serve warm or at room temperature.

Makes 20 beoreks

## Tips
- *If you cannot find puff pastry squares in your store, buy the puff pastry sheets, and cut them.*
- *The beoreks keep well in the freezer. If frozen, brush with the egg-wash before baking.*
- *For variety, you may mix in the filling a small can of chopped Ortega chilies or some chopped parsley and onion.*
- *When using frozen beoreks, take them out of the freezer half an hour before baking, brush the tops with the egg-wash right before baking.*

# Fried Cheese Beoreks

*If you are not watching your weight and you do not have a cholesterol problem, you must try these tasty cheese turnovers. Preparing the dough can be labor intensive, so I use prepared won ton or egg roll skin which makes preparation fast and easy.*

## Ingredients
1 pkg large size won ton skins or egg roll dough
1½ lb Akawi cheese, grated or Jack cheese
1 bunch Italian parsley, only the leaves
1 medium size onion, chopped fine
2 eggs, slightly beaten
¼ tsp black pepper
Vegetable oil for frying

## Preparation
1. In a large bowl combine grated cheese, parsley leaves, onion, eggs and pepper. Mix well.
2. In the center of each won ton skin place 3-4 tablespoons cheese mixture lengthwise.
3. With a brush, wet the edges of the dough and bring the two edges to the center overlapping to seal.
4. Fill a 14-15 inch large frying pan with vegetable oil ½-inch deep and heat to 375°F. Fry 2 beoreks at a time turning them once until they are golden brown on both sides. Drain on paper towel. Serve warm or at room temperature.

Makes 16 beoreks

## Tips
- *Akawi cheese is found in Middle Eastern markets. If you cannot find Akawi cheese, substitute Jack cheese.*
- *Use the smaller won ton skins, fold into triangles and serve them as appetizer.*

# Mock Sou Beorek

*Popular in the Middle East, Sou beorek can be an extremely labor intensive dish if you have to make your own dough and boil it. Well, this is an imitation of the real Sou Beorek. An easier version and quite tasty. It is best enjoyed warm.*

## Ingredients
1 lb Ricotta cheese
1 lb Jack cheese, grated
1 lb Armenian string cheese, grated
1 pkg frozen Filo dough, thawed
¾ cup clarified butter
½ tsp black pepper
½ cup chopped parsley (optional)
5 eggs
3 cups milk

## Preparation
1. Mix together ricotta cheese, grated Jack cheese, and grated string cheese.
2. Slightly beat 3 eggs with ½ teaspoon black pepper and add to the cheese. (If using parsley, add to the cheese). Mix thoroughly.
3. Butter the bottom of a 1-inch deep 12x16-inch pan. Layer 1/3 of the filo dough and brush each sheet with a little clarified butter.
4. Sprinkle half of the cheese mixture; use the next 1/3 of the filo dough brushing each layer with butter.
5. Spread the rest of the cheese mixture, and use the rest of the filo dough brushing each layer with butter.
6. With a sharp and wet knife, cut the beoreks into squares.
7. Beat the remaining 2 eggs with 3 cups of milk and a little salt and pepper to taste. Pour over the beoreks.
8. Bake in a preheated oven 375°F for approximately 45 minutes, or until top browns. Cool 5 minutes to let the cheese set, then serve.

Makes 32-40 beoreks

## Tips
- *Reheat leftovers in the oven for best results.*
- *Armenian String cheese is found in Middle Eastern grocery stores. Mozzarella cheese can be substituted for it.*
- **Clarified butter**: *In a saucepan melt sweet butter over low heat. Skim the milk solids off the top and carefully pour the clarified butter into another container without disturbing the remaining milk solids and water that are in the bottom of the pan. Clarified butter keeps up to 6 months in the refrigerator.*

# Marinated Olives

*Olives are tastier when marinated. They are colorful and attractive when presented with chopped onion and fresh thyme or tarragon. The red pepper flakes add a bit of heat. Advance preparation enhances the flavor. Adds variety to an assortment of appetizers at a party*

## Ingredients
1 cup cured green olives drained
1 cup Kalamata olives
1 small red onion chopped
3 Tbsp fresh thyme
　　or tarragon leaves
2 Tbsp Extra-virgin olive oil
2 Tbsp lemon juice
　　or pomegranate syrup
½ tsp crushed red pepper

## Preparation
1. Mix all ingredients together.
2. Serve at room temperature with pita bread wedges.

Makes 2 cups

## Tips
- Green olives are an acquired taste, if you do not like them you may use only Kalamata olives.
- You may prepare ahead of time, and before serving add the onions, and thyme.
- For variety, you may add Feta cheese cubes and cherry tomatoes.

# Parsley Frittata (Ejjeh)

*There are special frying pans for frying these frittatas which makes them thicker, but I prefer the conventional frying pans and thinner frittatas.*

## Ingredients
3 cups chopped parsley
1/3 cup chopped fresh mint
¼ cup diced onion
8 eggs, well beaten
1 Tbsp flour
½ tsp black pepper
1 tsp salt
1 clove crushed garlic (optional)
Vegetable oil for frying

## Preparation
1. Beat the eggs with salt and pepper. Add the remaining ingredients except the oil.
2. In a frying pan, pour some oil to cover the bottom of the pan and heat it. Drop the egg mixture one tablespoon at a time, spreading it in the pan like a pancake. You can cook 3-4 at the same time depending on the size of the frying pan. Brown one side, then flip over to brown the other side. Drain on paper towel. If needed, add more oil to the pan and continue cooking.
3. Serve at room temperature, as an appetizer, a sandwich, or as a side dish on a buffet table.

Makes 40-45 ejjehs

## Tips
- *Save leftover ejjehs in a covered container and they will keep well in the refrigerator for several days.*

# Lentil Patties (Merjemekli Kufteh)

*This is an Armenian meatless dish which is very popular during the Lenten Season.
Kuftehs are hand-shaped patties, easy to prepare, delicious, and very healthy.*

## Ingredients
2 cups split red lentils
5-6 cups water
2 cups fine bulgur,
   (cracked wheat #1)
1½ tsp Aleppo red pepper
2 tsp salt
4 Tbsp butter
1 large onion, minced
1 tsp cumin
1 cup finely chopped green onion
1 bunch flat leaf parsley,
   chopped fine

## Preparation
1. Pick through the lentils for any stones or other grains, and then rinse them.
2. Bring lentils and 5 cups of water to a boil and simmer until lentils are soft, adding more water if necessary.
3. Stir in bulgur, red pepper and salt. Cover the pan and let it stand for 30 minutes until bulgur is softened.
4. Meanwhile, sauté onions in butter until soft and they start turning pink; mix the onion and the butter into the lentils.
5. Reserve 1/3 cup of chopped parsley and ¼ cup of chopped green onions to sprinkle on top of the finished kuftehs.
6. Add cumin, the remainder of the parsley and the green onions. Mix well.
7. When cool enough to handle by hand, knead to make it all stick together. Adjust seasoning. Do not over knead. Take a handful of the mixture in your hands and shape them into patties (kuftehs), occasionally dipping your hands in warm water to prevent stickiness.
8. Arrange on a platter and sprinkle on top with reserved green onions and parsley.

Makes 18-20 medium size kuftehs

## Tips
- *If you don't want to use your hands shaping the patties, try shaping them into ovals by using two soup spoons, or using an ice cream scoop.*

# Twice Baked Cheese Soufflés

*This recipe was given to me by my friend, Ann Cheals, in England. After spending a day sight-seeing with her and her husband Max, she served this soufflé at dinner as a first course and we went - Wow!*
*Make soufflés ahead of time, freeze and have them ready for a dinner party without last minute work. These individual soufflés are delicious and make a great elegant first course or with a light salad make a lovely luncheon entrée.*

## Ingredients
2 cups milk
1 cup flour
1 bay leaf
¼ tsp cayenne pepper
3-4 peppercorns
¼ tsp cayenne pepper
¾ tsp mustard
1 onion, quartered
1 stick butter
3 cups grated Gruyere cheese
6 large eggs, separated
½ tsp salt
¼ tsp pepper
1½ cup cream
½ cup Parmesan cheese

## Preparation
1. Preheat oven to 400°F before baking.
2. Grease and flour 8 ramekins or custard dishes. Set aside.
3. Bring milk to a boil with bay leaf, peppercorns, cayenne, mustard and onion. Remove from heat, let cool for 10 minutes and strain.
4. Meanwhile, melt the butter, add the flour and cook over medium heat for 1 minute. Remove from heat and gradually stir in the hot milk, return to the heat and stir until the mixture boils and thickens.
5. Remove from heat, stir in the cheese and mix until cheese is melted. Add the egg yolks, salt and pepper and mix well.
6. Beat the egg whites until stiff and fold in the mixture.
7. Fill the ramekins ¾ full and place them in a deep pan and fill pan halfway with boiling water. Bake for 20-22 minutes or until puffed and golden. Remove ramekins from pan and cool.
8. Remove soufflés from ramekins and freeze individually.
9. Two hours before baking, take frozen soufflés out of the freezer. Preheat oven to 400°F. Put soufflés in a greased oven-proof dish. Pour the cream over the top, sprinkle with Parmesan cheese and bake for 20 minutes or until golden brown. Serve with exotic salad greens drizzled with lemon vinaigrette.

Makes 8 individual soufflés

## Tips
- *Frozen soufflés keep well in the freezer for 6 weeks.*
- *To prevent cheese from sticking to a grater, spray the grater with cooking oil before grating.*

# Fried Halloumi Cheese (Saganaki)

*Halloumi cheese is a delicious, white semi-firm goat milk cheese. It has a unique nutty flavor.
Fried and served with a salad makes a perfect first course to any meal.*

## Ingredients
1 (8 oz) pkg Halloumi cheese
2 cups frisée (curly endive)
2 cups mixed baby salad greens,
    or chopped Romaine lettuce
2 Tbsp lemon juice
1 tsp water
½ tsp mustard
3 Tbsp olive oil
1 tsp dried oregano
½ tsp black pepper

## Preparation
1. Slice the cheese into 1/3-inch thick slices.
2. Heat a non-stick frying pan, spray with vegetable oil, add cheese slices and sauté for about 45 seconds on one side until it browns, then turn to the other side.
3. Whisk lemon juice, water, mustard, olive oil, oregano and pepper. Drizzle over salad greens. Top with fried cheese slices. Serve immediately.

Makes 4 servings

## Tips
- *You may purchase Halloumi cheese in any Middle Eastern or Greek grocery stores.*

# Cheese Fondue

*This dish was originated in Switzerland and is a very popular dish in ski resorts. It is a fun and easy way to entertain friends. Bread cubes are dipped in a melted cheese pot. To do it right, you must swirl the bread on the bottom of the fondue dish to prevent the cheese from sticking to the bottom of the pan. If you lose your bread in the pot, you must buy a bottle of wine to share with your company.*
*This dish is usually served with white wine.*

## Ingredients
2 cups grated Emmenthaler cheese
1½ cups grated Gruyere cheese
¾ cup grated Jack cheese
1 clove garlic
½ cup dry white wine
1 Tbsp cornstarch
1 Tbsp unsalted butter
1/8 tsp black pepper
Dash of grated nutmeg
¼ cup kirsch liqueur
1-2 French baguettes,
   cut into bite size pieces

## Preparation
1. Combine the cheeses together and set aside.
2. Rub a clove of garlic cut in half inside a heavy saucepan. Discard the garlic.
3. Combine the wine and the cornstarch, stir until the cornstarch is dissolved. Set aside.
4. Melt the butter in the saucepan, and add the wine-cornstarch mixture. When the wine is hot but not bubbling, add a handful of the cheese mixture and stir until the cheese is melted. Continue adding cheese until all the cheese is used up and the mixture is smooth.
5. Add the pepper and nutmeg, stir, add the kirsch and mix well.
6. Transfer to a fondue pot over a votive candle or very low flames to keep the cheese melted.
7. To eat fondue, spear a bread cube with a fondue fork piercing the crust last. Dip the bread in melted cheese and swirl to coat with melted cheese. It is important to swirl to keep the cheese fondue in motion and prevent sticking to the pan. Transfer the bread to your own plate and use your dinner fork to eat. (No double dipping!)
8. On the side, serve a basket of bread cubes, boiled potatoes, and steamed broccoli.

Makes 2-4 servings

## Tips
- *To prevent cheese from sticking to a grater, spray the grater with cooking oil before grating.*
- *If the cheese separates, re-blend by adding 1 teaspoon cornstarch dissolved in 1 tablespoon of wine.*
- *Leftover cheese can be used in pasta dishes the next day.*

# Smoked Salmon and Avocado Timbale

*We had this dish as a first course on a Silverseas cruiseship on our way to New Zealand. It was so good and the presentation so attractive, I had to come home and try to recreate it. Success!*
*This timbale is drum-shaped layers of lettuce, salmon, and avocado.*

## Ingredients
1 cup chopped salad greens
½ cup chopped smoked salmon
½ cup chopped avocado
¼ cup chopped tomato
1 Tbsp capers
1½ tsp lime juice
Extra-virgin olive oil

## Preparation
1. Place a dariole mold in center of your serving plate. (A dariole mold is a small cylindrical mold (3-inches in diameter). If you do not have one, use a well washed tuna can opened on both sides.)
2. Fill the bottom of each mold with ½ cup chopped salad greens, top with ¼ cup chopped smoked salmon. Over the salmon layer ¼ cup chopped avocado. Drizzle avocados with lime juice, and sprinkle over it one tablespoon of chopped tomatoes.
3. Gently lift the mold. Drizzle Extra-virgin olive oil around the timbale, and sprinkle a few capers around the plate.
4. Serve as a first course.

Makes 2 servings

## Tips
- *A knife carefully slipped around the side of the timbales will make unmolding easier.*
- *Make sure you use Extra-virgin olive oil to drizzle. It enhances the flavor of the dish.*

# California Rolls

*Sharon Hoy, a Chinese Chef, taught me all about Chinese cooking. She also taught me to make California Rolls. You don't have to be a Japanese sushi chef to be able to make California Rolls.*

## Ingredients
6 cups cooked Cal-Rose rice
8 pieces toasted seaweed sheets
3 Tbsp toasted sesame seeds
½ cup mayonnaise
8-10 long pieces crab legs
    or imitation crab sticks
1-2 avocados sliced into ½-inch strips
1 cucumber sliced lengthwise into
    thin strips
1 Sochi mat (woven bamboo mat)
Soy sauce
Wasabi paste
Pickled ginger (optional)

### *Vinaigrette*
¾ cup white vinegar
½ cup sugar
1 Tbsp salt

## Preparation
1. Place vinegar, sugar, and salt in a saucepan over low heat stirring until sugar and salt dissolve.
2. With a wooden spoon, fluff the cooked rice separating the grains, and stir in vinaigrette dressing.
3. On a bamboo mat, lay seaweed sheet shiny side down. Spread ¾ cup rice on seaweed sheet leaving a one inch uncovered border at one end.
4. Sprinkle sesame seeds over rice mixture.
5. Spread one teaspoon mayonnaise in the center, across the width of rice covered seaweed. Arrange crab, avocado, and cucumber strips over mayonnaise.
6. Holding the bamboo mat, roll the upper half of the rice covered seaweed sheet over the filling - making sure the rice covers the center filling. Continue to roll until the sushi roll is sealed. Hold for a few seconds to seal the edge. Squeeze lightly.
7. Unwrap the bamboo roll. Slice and serve with soy sauce, wasabi paste and pickled ginger, if desired.

Makes 8 rolls, each sliced into 8 pieces

## Tips
- *Wasabi is powdered dried Japanese horseradish. Use sparingly since it is very pungent.*
- *Wasabi paste as well as seaweed sheets, soy sauce and pickled ginger are found in all well stocked grocery stores.*

# Falafel

*Falafels are spicy dried broad bean and garbanzo bean fritters. Sold by street vendors in the Middle East, falafels have gained a lot of popularity in the States as a healthy vegetarian dish.*

## Ingredients
1 cup dried broad beans (fava beans)
1 cup dried garbanzo beans
1 medium sized onion, chopped
2 cloves garlic, crushed
½ cup finely chopped fresh parsley
½ cup finely chopped cilantro
½ tsp cumin
½ tsp powdered coriander
1½ tsp salt
½ tsp black pepper
½ tsp red pepper flakes
1 tsp baking soda or baking powder
Vegetable oil for frying
Tahini Sauce (Taratour, page 207)

## Preparation
1. Soak fava beans in 3 cups of water for 2 days, changing the water the second day.
2. Soak the garbanzo beans in 3 cups of water for 24 hours.
3. Drain the beans. In a food processor, process the beans, onion, and garlic for 1 minute scraping down the sides of the bowl, as needed.
4. Add chopped parsley, cilantro, cumin, salt, pepper, pepper flakes and baking soda. Process for 10 seconds until everything is well distributed. Let it rest for 30 minutes for the flavors to blend.
5. Shape 1 tablespoon of mixture into a disc half-inch thick and place on a parchment paper lined tray. (The falafels can be refrigerated at this point for several hours).
6. In a deep frying pan or a Dutch oven, over medium-high heat, raise the vegetable oil temperature to 375°F.
Fry 6-8 falafels at a time, for 5-6 minutes, turning them to brown evenly. Remove from oil and drain on paper towel.
7. Serve as an appetizer with Tahini Sauce (Taratour, page 207)

Makes 24 falafel patties

## Tips
- *Falafel makes great sandwiches served in pita bread with sliced tomatoes and Tahini Sauce.*

# Beverages

*Smoothies are good any time of the day. They are light, cool, refreshing and nutritious. It takes only a minute to prepare making them a perfect treat. You can go wild in your combinations of fruits, juices, and/or vegetables; you don't have to stick to only using yogurt in it, you can use frozen yogurts and ice creams as well. Kids love them.*

## Strawberry Banana Smoothie

### Ingredients
6 large strawberries, frozen
1 small banana
½ cup orange juice
1 (6 oz) container light strawberry banana yogurt
1 Tbsp honey
Strawberry and mint leaves for garnish

### Preparation
Rinse strawberries, remove stems and freeze until firm. Cut bananas into 1 inch pieces. Combine the fruits, yogurt and honey in a blender and blend until smooth. Pour into chilled glass, garnish with fresh strawberry and mint leaves. Serve immediately.

## Mango Apricot Smoothie

### Ingredients
¾ cup chopped fresh mango
¼ cup apricot nectar
1 (6 oz) container lemon yogurt
1 Tbsp honey
Mint leaves for garnish

### Preparation
Combine all the ingredients in a blender and blend until smooth. Pour into chilled glass, garnish with mint leaves. Serve immediately.

# Raspberry Smoothie

## Ingredients
1 cup fresh raspberries
1 small banana
1 (6 oz) container raspberry yogurt
¼ cup cranberry juice
2 Tbsp honey
Raspberries and mint leaves for garnish

## Preparation
Freeze the raspberries until firm. Slice the bananas into 1-inch pieces. Combine the fruits, yogurt, cranberry juice, and honey in a blender and blend until smooth. Garnish with raspberries and mint leaves. Serve immediately.

# Blackberry Smoothie

## Ingredients
1 cup frozen blackberries
1 small banana
1 (6 oz) container vanilla yogurt
1/3 cup grape juice or orange juice
1 Tbsp honey
Mint leaves for garnish

## Preparation
Slice the bananas into 1-inch pieces. Combine the fruits, yogurt, juice, and honey in a blender and blend until smooth. Garnish with mint leaves. Serve immediately.

# Cantaloupe Smoothie

## Preparation
1 cup cubes of cantaloupe
1 (6 oz) container lemon yogurt
1 Tbsp honey
Cantaloupe pieces and mint leaves for garnish

## Preparation
Chop the cantaloupe into 1-inch pieces.
Freeze the cantaloupe until firm.
Combine cantaloupe, yogurt and honey in a blender and blend until smooth. Garnish with cantaloupe balls and mint leaves.
Serve immediately.

# Peach Smoothie

## Ingredients
1 (6 oz) container peach yogurt
1 cup frozen chopped peaches
½ cup peach sorbet
¼ cup milk
¼ tsp cinnamon
Slice of fresh peach and/or
    mint leaves for garnish

## Preparation
In a blender blend all ingredients until smooth. Garnish with mint leaves.

# Pineapple Smoothie

## Ingredients
1 (6 oz) container lemon yogurt
½ cup pineapple juice
1 cup pineapple chunks
1 Tbsp honey
4-5 ice cubes
Strawberry, pineapple chunk and mint leaves
    for garnish

## Preparation
In a blender combine all ingredients and blend. If more sweetness is required, add some honey. You may use a scoop of lemon sorbet, or ice cream instead of the ice cubes.

# Gazpacho Smoothie

### Ingredients
½ cup bottled tomato juice
½ cup fresh tomato chunks
¼ cup bell pepper chunks
1 Tbsp chopped onion
1 tsp fresh lemon juice
¼ tsp salt
¼ tsp pepper
Celery or grape tomato for garnish

### Preparation
Peel and cut tomatoes into ½ inch cubes and freeze them. Combine frozen tomatoes, and the rest of the ingredients in a blender and blend until smooth. Garnish with grape tomatoes, and celery. Serve immediately.

# Bloody Mary Smoothie

### Ingredients
8 oz tomato juice
1 cup fresh tomato chunks
¼ cup chopped celery
¼ cup chopped tomato
1 tsp Worcestershire sauce
1 Tbsp lemon juice
2 dashes of hot pepper
¼ tsp salt
¼ tsp sugar
1½ oz vodka
Celery with the leaves left on for garnish

### Preparation
Peel and cut tomatoes into ½ inch cubes and freeze them. Combine frozen tomatoes and the rest of the ingredients in a blender and blend until smooth. Garnish celery stick.
Serve immediately.

# Classic Pimms Cup # 1

*Haig's favorite drink.  Reminds him of his college trip to England.*

## Ingredients
2 oz Pimm's #1
6-8 ice cubes
4 oz lemon soda
Cucumber slices
Celery stalk with the leaves left on for garnish

## Preparation
1. Pour the Pimm's into a highball glass, or Pimm's mug add the ice cubes, cucumber and celery stalk.
2. Pour the lemon soda.  Serve.

# Classic Margaritas

*My favorite drink! Great with Mexican appetizers and dinners.  Easy to prepare for a group.*

## Ingredients
1 lime cut into wedges
Coarse salt (optional)
2 cups ice cubes
1 (6 oz) can frozen limeade, thawed
¾ cup tequila
¾ cup triple sec or other orange liqueur

## Preparation
1. Rub lime slices around the rim of 4 glasses.
2. Dip rims of glasses into salt if desired.
3. Combine ice and limeade, tequila and triple sec in a blender and blend until smooth.  Pour into glasses and garnish with lime slices.

Makes 4 servings

# Lemon Shandy

*Who knew lemonade and beer could taste so good. In Spain, while looking for a light alcoholic drink at a bar, I was introduced to a drink I liked called Lemon Shandy.*

## Ingredients
1 cup prepared lemonade
Chilled beer mugs
2 bottles chilled beer

## Preparation
1. Fill the mugs with 1/3 cup lemonade or to taste, and top off with chilled beer.

Makes 3-4 servings

# Appleized Tea

*A lovely summer luncheon drink. This iced tea does not need any sugar. The sweetness from the apple juice sweetens it naturally*

## Ingredients
4 cups brewed tea
4 cups apple juice
Apple slices for garnish
Lemon wedge for garnish

## Preparation
1. Fill a pitcher with brewed tea and stir in the apple juice.
2. Fill a glass with ice cubes and pour appleized tea over it.
3. Garnish with an apple slice and a lime wedge.

# Classic Sangria

*A very pleasant fruity wine drink that is of Spanish origin.*

### Ingredients
2 large juicy oranges
1 large juicy lemon
¼ cup sugar
¼ cup triple sec
1 (750 ml) bottle of Merlot wine
Ice cubes
Mint leaves for garnish

### Preparation
1. Wash and slice the oranges and lemon into rounds.
2. In a large pitcher add the orange and lemon slices, add the sugar and with a wood spoon mash the fruits to release their juices and dissolve the sugar. Stir in triple sec and wine; refrigerate for at least 2 hours or overnight. Before serving, add plenty of ice cubes and stir to distribute the fruits and pulp. Serve immediately.

# Champagne Sangria

*You can use white wine instead of the champagne for a White Sangria*

### Ingredients
1 orange, sliced into thin rounds
1 cup seedless white grapes
1 small green apple, cut into wedges
8-10 strawberries, blueberries or raspberries
1 bottle champagne or sparkling wine
¼ cup triple sec
¼ cup sugar
Ice cubes
Mint leaves for garnish

### Preparation
1. Wash and slice the orange into rounds. Prepare the other fruits, and slice the apple into wedges.
2. In a large pitcher add the orange slices and the sugar. With a wood spoon mash the orange to release its juices; add triple sec and mix until sugar is dissolved. Add grapes, apple wedges and strawberries and let stand for 10 minutes. Before serving, add the champagne and plenty of ice cubes, stir to distribute the fruits. Serve immediately.

# Festive Punch

*A great punch to serve at big parties.*
*For the adults, mix vodka or rum in the punch.*

## Ingredients
8 cups guava nectar
4 cups pineapple guava juice
1 (12 oz) can frozen lemonade
1 (6 oz) can frozen orange juice
1 (12-14 oz) frozen strawberry, pureed
10 oz club soda
4 cups lemon lime soda
Mint leaves for garnish

## Preparation
1. Mix the first five ingredients together.
2. Add club soda and lemon lime soda just before serving.

## Tips
- *To keep the punch cold during the party, instead of ice cubes, I usually freeze orange juice in a jello mold and before guests arrive I unmold the frozen juice and place it in the punch bowl. When ice cubes are used to keep the punch cold, they melt and dilute the punch, but the frozen orange juice enhances the flavor.*

# Mimosa

*The Grand Marnier kicks it up a notch in this classic cocktail. A great drink for brunch.*

## Ingredients
3-4 oz champagne
1½ tsp Grand Marnier
¼ cup fresh squeezed orange juice, chilled

## Preparation
1. Fill a champagne glass half full with champagne.
2. Add 1½ tsp Grand Marnier and orange juice.

# Best Hot Chocolate
*Made with real chocolate and milk.*

### Ingredients
4 oz chocolate, Baker's sweet works well.
2 cups low fat milk
½ tsp vanilla
Cinnamon Stick

### Preparation
1. Chop the chocolate into small pieces.
2. In a 1-quart saucepan heat the milk and add the chocolate. Stir until chocolate is melted. Do not boil.
3. Add vanilla and whisk to create a little foam. Pour into mugs and serve with a cinnamon stick.

Makes 2 servings

# Hot Spiced Cider
*This is the perfect non-alcoholic warming drink at parties during the cold season. As you simmer the cider, the whole house smells festive with the smell of cinnamon and clove.*

### Ingredients
4 cups apple cider or apple juice
1 cup orange juice
¼ cup lemon juice
4 cinnamon sticks
10 cloves
Additional cinnamon sticks for garnish

### Preparation
1. Combine all the ingredients together and refrigerate.
2. Half an hour before the guests arrive, heat the cider, reduce the heat and simmer on low heat until ready to serve. Garnish with a cinnamon stick.

Makes 5-6 cups

# Hot Buttered Rum

*A popular drink in ski resorts. I was introduced to this drink in 1965 on my first trip to Mammoth Ski resort. The waiter's tray tipped and the hot buttered rum was on my lap. Believe me it was hot!*

## Ingredients
1/3 cup dark brown sugar
½ stick butter, room temperature
2 Tbsp honey
¼ tsp cinnamon
1/8 tsp nutmeg
Dash of cloves
1/3 cup spiced rum
1 cup boiling water
2 cinnamon sticks

## Preparation
1. In a 4 cup measuring cup mix the first 6 ingredients with a hand held blender.
2. Add rum and boiling water, stir until the butter is dissolved.
3. Divide mixture into 2 mugs and garnish with cinnamon sticks and serve.

Makes 2 servings


# Hot Port

*I was introduced to this drink one cold November night in Dublin, Ireland in a pub. It was delicious and it certainly warmed me up.*

## Ingredients
6 oz port wine
4 oz boiling water
2 tsp sugar
Lemon twists
Dash of nutmeg

## Preparation
1. Heat wine in a saucepan or in the microwave.
2. Place one teaspoon of sugar in each mug, add boiling water and warmed wine.
3. Serve with sprinkle of nutmeg and a lemon twist.

Makes 2 servings

# Limoncello

*This recipe was published in the LA Times newspaper shortly after we returned from a trip to Italy where the drink was very popular. Of course I had to try to make it.*
*It is a refreshing after dinner drink.*

### Ingredients
12 lemons
2 (750 ml) bottles 100-proof vodka
2 cups water
2 cups sugar

### Preparation
1. Remove the yellow part of the lemon peel with a sharp peeler, avoiding the bitter white pith.
2. Put the peels in a jar, add 1 bottle vodka and seal tightly. Steep until peels lose their color; for at least 2 weeks.
3. Put the water and sugar into a 3-quart saucepan and boil until the syrup turns clear. Let it cool.
4. Strain the vodka from the peels and mix with the remaining bottle of vodka and syrup. Put the liqueur in bottles, seal tightly and let the liquids marry for at least 1 week before using.
5. For drinking the Limoncello straight, store it in the freezer.

# Coffee Liqueur

*This home-made liqueur was quite popular in the sixties. I think we all tried to make it.*

### Ingredients
1 cup sugar
1½ cup water
2 Tbsp instant coffee powder
1 tsp vanilla extract
20 fl oz vodka

### Preparation
1. In a 2-quart saucepan put sugar, water, instant coffee and vanilla and bring to a boil. Simmer for 5 minutes. Skim off the foam and let it cool.
2. Mix together coffee syrup and vodka and pour into bottles. Seal tightly and let the liquids marry for at least a weak. Serve straight or over ice.

# Soups

## Cold Cucumber Yogurt Soup (Tzatziki)

*To the Greeks it is known as Tzatziki, to the Armenians Jajek, to the Americans Yogurt Sauce.
This refreshing soup uses the classic combination of cucumber and yogurt. Very refreshing.
It can also be served as a dip or sauce by adjusting the amount of cucumber and water. (See tips below)*

### Ingredients
1 cup chopped cucumbers
1 small clove crushed garlic
½ cup water
½ tsp salt
1 tsp lemon juice
2 cups plain yogurt
2 Tbsp chopped fresh mint
   or 1 Tbsp crushed dried mint

### Preparation
1. Remove the seeds from the cucumber and chop to measure ½ cup. Save the rest for garnish.
2. In a blender or food processor, place the chopped cucumbers, garlic, water, salt, lemon juice, and yogurt. Blend for a few seconds. Add the mint and blend for another second. Do not over blend.
3. Adjust the seasoning. If needed, add more water to obtain the desired soup consistency.
4. Refrigerate for several hours to blend the flavors.
5. Serve cold. Garnish with diced cucumbers and julienne cut mint leaves. Drizzle with olive oil.

Makes 2 servings

### Tips
- *As a dip:* increase cucumber to 2½ cups and eliminate the water.
- *As a sauce:* Use 2 cups of cucumber and add a little water to desired consistency. As a sauce it is good with pork, Lamb Kebab and Sini Kufteh.

# Cold Papaya Champagne Soup
*This is a lovely refreshing first course soup. Tasty and colorful.*

## Ingredients
3 papayas, seeded and quartered
2 cups orange juice
2 limes
4 Tbsp honey
1 cup champagne
1 Kiwi and strawberry for garnish

## Preparation
1. Peel, seed and quarter papayas
2. In a blender blend papaya, orange juice, the juice from 2 limes and honey. Chill until ready to serve.
3. Before serving, mix in cold champagne.
4. Serve chilled, garnished with sliced kiwis, strawberries, and mint leaves.

Makes 6 servings

## Tips
- *Save the papaya seeds to make Papaya Seed salad dressing (Page 93).*

# Cold Cantaloupe Soup
*This soup made with over-ripe melon make a cooling summer appetizer.
Serve as a first course or as dessert with a dollop of ice cream.*

## Ingredients
1 medium ripe cantaloupe
¼ cup whipped cream
¼ cup sugar
½ cup honey
½ tsp cinnamon
2 Tbsp Grand Marnier
Mint leaves for garnish

## Preparation
1. Cut melon into cubes, reserve a few cubes for garnish. Puree the rest in a blender or food processor.
2. In a bowl whisk whipped cream, sugar, honey, cinnamon and Grand Marnier, blending all together. Add pureed cantaloupe and mix well. Adjust sweetness.
3. Chill the soup in a covered container. To serve, garnish with chopped cantaloupe or strawberry with mint leaves and serve in a chilled bowl.

Makes 4 servings

## Tips
- *If the cantaloupe is very sweet, reduce the amount of honey and/or sugar.*

# Cold Strawberry Soup
*A cool summer soup served as a first course or as a light dessert served with a dollop of cream or ice cream and accompanied with a cookie.*

## Ingredients
4 cups quartered strawberries
½ cup orange juice
3 Tbsp sugar
1 cup plain yogurt
½ cup champagne or sweet wine
Mint leaves and strawberry for garnish

## Preparation
1. In a blender or food processor, process the first three ingredients. Transfer to a bowl.
2. Whisk in the yogurt. Adjust sweetness. Refrigerate.
3. Before serving, add champagne and mix. Serve in chilled bowls garnished with a slice of strawberry and mint leaves.

Makes 5-6 servings

## Tips
- *To serve this soup as a dessert, top with a scoop of vanilla ice cream and serve with cookies.*

# Gazpacho

*Preparing this soup is a breeze. It also takes the place of a fresh salad, since basically it is a liquid salad. I prefer hand-chopping the vegetables vs. chopping them in a food processor so the colors of the vegetables stay vibrant. It looks more appetizing.*
*On a hot summer eve, a sandwich and a cold cup of gazpacho is just the right light supper.*

## Ingredients
1 cup diced ripe tomato
¼ cup diced each red
   and green bell peppers
1 cup diced cucumber
¼ cup diced white onion
1 clove garlic, minced
3 Tbsp red wine vinegar
1 tsp salt
2½-3 cups tomato juice
½ tsp hot pepper sauce
2 Tbsp Extra-virgin olive oil
Diced avocado and/or croutons
   for garnish

## Preparation
1. In a large bowl combine all diced vegetables, vinegar, salt and pepper. Let it stand for 5-10 minutes to let the vegetables give out their juice.
2. Stir in tomato juice and hot sauce. Adjust seasoning. Cover and refrigerate.
3. Serve cold, drizzled with a teaspoon of olive oil and garnished with diced tomatoes, croutons, or diced avocado.

Makes 4-5 serving

## Tips
- *Before mixing the soup, keep a tablespoon of any of the diced vegetables to use for garnish.*
- *I freeze the extra tomato juice in an ice cube tray. To keep the soup cold when it is served, instead of ice cubes I drop one of the frozen tomato cubes in each soup bowl.*

# Yogurt Soup with Stuffed Kibbeh

*My husband's favorite soup. He can eat this soup everyday and not get tired of it.*

## Ingredients
30-36 Stuffed Kibbehs (page 138)
2-3 lbs cut up chicken
1 celery stalk
1 carrot
1 small onion quartered
4 cups plain yogurt
1 egg
½ cube butter
2 tablespoon dried crushed mint

## Preparation
1. Follow preparation of the Kibbehs on page 138 up to step number 9. Refrigerate or freeze prepared kibbehs.
2. <u>Soup preparation</u>  In a large pot, cover chicken with water, add onion, celery, and carrot; bring to a boil on high heat. Reduce heat and boil chicken until tender, approximately 35-40 minutes.
3. Remove the chicken out of the broth. Cool, shred into pieces, and set aside.
4. Strain the broth into another pot. Bring to boil and drop the kibbehs in the broth. Boil for 8-10 minutes. (The broth in the pot should cover the kibbehs, if not, add canned broth or water). With a slotted spoon, remove boiled kibbehs and set aside.
5. In a large bowl, beat the yogurt with the egg, then gradually add 1 cup of hot broth. Add more hot broth until mixture has reached the desired soup consistency. Return the soup to the pot and start heating on low flames. <u>Do not boil</u>.
6. Meanwhile in a small frying pan, melt the butter. Add dried mint and sauté for a few minutes. Pour into the yogurt soup and stir. Add the shredded chicken. (At this point you can remove the soup from the heat and wait until serving time).
7. To serve, heat the soup and drop the pre-cooked kibbehs in the soup to heat. Garnish with fresh mint.

Makes 6-7 servings

## Tips
- *Kibbehs could be boiled and then frozen, or could be frozen uncooked and cook them when preparing the soup.*

# Basic Split Pea Soup

*How easy is this? You tell me. All you need is split peas, water or broth, an onion and butter.*

## Ingredients
3 cups split peas, picked over
6-8 cups water, chicken broth or
    vegetable stock
2 Tbsp butter
1 Tbsp olive oil
¼ tsp red pepper flakes
1 medium size onion sliced thin
Salt to taste
Croutons for garnish

## Preparation
1. Wash the peas, and cover with 6 cups of water. Bring to a boil. Skim off the foam and let it simmer, stirring occasionally until the soup starts thickening. Add the last 2 cups of water or broth and keep simmering on low flames until the peas are very soft and well blended with the liquid.
2. In a frying pan, melt the butter and olive oil, add the red pepper and sauté the onions until they start turning brown.
3. Stir in fried onion with the oil into the soup. Stir well. Add the salt and adjust seasoning.
4. Serve the soup garnished with croutons.

Makes 6 servings

## Tips
- *For variety, you may add chopped carrots with the peas. You can also add bacon or sausage slices to the soup.*

# Split Lentil Soup

*Split red lentils are faster cooking than other varieties of legumes. This is a very simple soup, it is earthy, light and very satisfying.*

## Ingredients
2 cups red split lentils, picked over
5-6 cups water and/or chicken broth
¼ cup short grain rice
2 Tbsp butter
1 Tbsp olive oil
¼ tsp red pepper flakes
1 tsp cumin (optional)
1 medium size onion sliced thin
1¼ tsp salt
Croutons and/or chopped parsley
    for garnish

## Preparation
1. Rinse the lentils and cover with 3 cups of water. Bring to a boil. Skim off the foam and let it simmer, stirring occasionally until the soup starts thickening. Add the rice and add the last 2-3 cups of liquid and keep simmering on low heat until the rice is cooked and the lentils are very soft and well blended with the liquid. (If you need a thicker soup, add only 2 more cups of liquid).
2. In a frying pan, melt the butter and olive oil add the red pepper, cumin, and sauté the onions until softened and they start turning brown.
3. Stir in the fried onion with the oil into the soup. Stir well. Add the salt and adjust seasoning.
4. Serve the soup garnished with croutons and/or chopped parsley.

Makes 6 servings

## Tips
- *For variety, you may add chopped carrots with the lentils. You can also add bacon or sausage slices to the soup.*
- *Left-over soup keeps well in the refrigerator up to a week.*
- *The lentils cook faster if you do not add salt to the lentils at the beginning of cooking.*

# Barley Mushroom Soup

*Such a simple and delicious soup, served with a sandwich, makes a wonderful meal to warm you up on a cold winter night. Use "pearled" barley for this soup as it cooks relatively quickly and retains its texture.*

## Ingredients
¼ cup butter
1 onion, chopped
2 cloves garlic, minced
2 large carrots, chopped
2 large celery stalks, chopped
1 lb mushrooms, sliced 1/3-inch thick
2/3 cup barley, rinsed
2 Tbsp flour
8 cups chicken broth
Salt and pepper to taste
Chopped parsley for garnish

## Preparation
1. In a Dutch oven, melt butter. Add chopped onion, garlic, carrots and celery and sauté until tender.
2. Add mushrooms and continue sautéing until mushrooms are softened. Add barley and continue sautéing for 2 more minutes.
3. Add flour to the pot and stir for 3 minutes until everything is well incorporated.
4. Gradually add 8 cups of broth. Bring to boil, reduce heat and cook about 45-60 minutes, until barley is cooked and the soup is thickened. Season to taste with salt and pepper.
5. Garnish soup bowl with chopped parsley.

Makes 6 servings

## Tips
- *If using Portobello mushrooms, with a spoon scrape out the gills before slicing, otherwise it will darken the color of the soup.*

# Creamy Cauliflower/Potato Soup

*A delicious, creamy and healthy starter soup to any meal without using any cream.*
*A cup of soup and a sandwich make a perfect meal.*

## Ingredients
3 Tbsp butter
1 cup chopped onion
1 head cauliflower florets (8 cups)
1 large baking potato, cubed ½ inch
5 cups chicken broth
½ tsp turmeric
Salt and pepper to taste
2 tsp lime juice
2 Tbsp chopped Italian parsley and
    croutons for garnish

## Preparation
1. In a Dutch oven, sauté onion in butter until it is softened, add cauliflower and potato and continue sautéing for a few minutes longer.
2. Add chicken broth and cook until cauliflower and potatoes are very tender.
3. In a blender or with a hand blender, puree cooked cauliflower. Return to pan and simmer for 5 minutes.
4. Add turmeric, salt and pepper to taste. Flavor the soup with lime juice.
5. Serve with croutons and chopped parsley

Makes 4-6 servings

## Tips
- *You can prepare broccoli soup the same way but eliminate turmeric.*

## Mediterranean Bean Salad

*This salad made with canned beans does not need anything more than lemon juice, onion and parsley. The combination of the 3 kinds of beans makes it an attractive colorful salad.
Perfect selection for a buffet table.*

### Ingredients
1 (15.5 oz) can garbanzo beans
1 (15.25 oz) can red kidney beans
1 (15 oz) can canellini or white
   kidney beans
¼ cup chopped parsley
¼ cup chopped onion
3-4 Tbsp fresh lemon juice
3-4 Tbsp Extra-virgin olive oil
¼ tsp black pepper

### Preparation
1. Drain and rinse the beans.
2. In a bowl, combine the rinsed beans and the rest of the ingredients and toss gently until coated with the dressing.
3. Serve on lettuce cups, or on chopped Romaine lettuce.

Makes 5-6 cups

### Tips
- *Keeps in the refrigerator covered for one week.*
- *Use any combination of your favorite beans in your pantry.*
- *For a shortcut, instead of lemon juice and olive oil, use prepared Italian Salad dressing.*
- *For variety, you may add ¼ cup Feta cheese crumbles.*
- *For the Holidays, you may substitute green garbanzo beans, found in the frozen food section in health food stores, and eliminate the canellini beans.*

# White Kidney Bean and Tuna Salad
*This is a classic Italian salad which is easy to prepare and makes a wonderful luncheon salad.*

### Ingredients
1 (15 oz) can white kidney beans drained and rinsed
1 (6 oz) can tuna, solid albacore drained and flaked
1/3 cup chopped roasted red pepper
1/3 cup chopped Kalamata olives
¼ cup chopped flat leaf Italian parsley
¼ cup chopped red onion

### *Vinaigrette dressing*
2 Tbsp capers chopped
½ tsp mustard
1 Tbsp balsamic vinegar
2 Tbsp fresh lemon juice
3-4 Tbsp Extra-virgin olive oil
Salt to taste
¼ tsp black pepper

### Preparation
1. In a small bowl, mix together the balsamic vinegar, lemon juice, mustard and capers. Whisk in olive oil, and add salt and pepper to taste.
2. In a bowl, combine the above ingredients and toss gently until coated with the dressing. Serve as-is on lettuce cups, or on chopped Romaine lettuce.

Makes 4 cups

### Tips
- *For a shortcut, instead of lemon juice and olive oil use prepared Italian Salad dressing.*
- *For variety, you may use garbanzo beans instead of white kidney beans.*
- *Roasted red peppers are sold in jars in the grocery stores.*

# Lentil Salad

*A nutritious and rich-in-fiber salad. For extra color and flavor, sprinkle chopped parsley over the salad.*

## Ingredients
1½ cup brown lentils
4 cups water
1 medium size white onion, diced
  or 2 scallions cut into thin slices
1 large tomato seeded and diced
1 tsp salt
½ tsp black pepper
3 Tbsp Cider vinegar
3 Tbsp Extra-virgin olive oil
2 Tbsp chopped parsley

## Preparation
1. Put the lentils in a large saucepan and cover with water. Bring the water to a boil, lower the heat, and simmer the lentils until they are soft but not mushy. Approximately 25 minutes. If needed, add more hot water.
2. Drain the lentils through a colander and reserve the liquid.
3. Place the drained lentils, diced onions, tomatoes, salt, and pepper in a large salad bowl and drizzle with vinegar and olive oil. If needed, add some of the reserved liquid. Adjust seasoning.
4. Garnish with chopped parsley.

Makes 4-6 servings

## Tips
- *Lentils cook faster without salt in the water. Season with salt after they are cooked.*

# Carrot Salad

*This is another tasty and colorful salad that adds variety to a buffet table. The vinegar balances the sweetness of the raisins. Advance preparation is a bonus.*

## Ingredients
6 cups grated carrots
3 Tbsp sugar
½ tsp salt
2 Tbsp white vinegar
½ cup sour cream
¼ cup mayonnaise
½ cup raisins

## Preparation
1. In a mixing bowl, dissolve sugar and salt with the vinegar.
2. Add sour cream and mayonnaise. Mix well.
3. Add raisins and carrots. Toss the salad. Chill for several hours before serving.

Makes 6 servings

## Tips:
- *Will keep for a week in the refrigerator in an air-tight container.*
- *Carrots with the tops attached tend to be sweeter and tender. To save time, you may clean the carrots a day ahead and store covered in water in the refrigerator. Drain well before using.*

# Potato Salad

*There are over one hundred versions of potato salads. This simple but delicious version tossed with lemon dressing complements far more dishes than just summer barbeques and is particularly good with fish.*

## Ingredients
2 large baking potatoes
1 small white onion, chopped
3 Tbsp chopped flat leaf parsley
¼ tsp black pepper
¾ tsp salt
3 Tbsp lemon juice
2 Tbsp Extra-virgin olive oil

## Preparation
1. Boil the potatoes until tender. Drain and cool. Peel and dice into 3/4 inch cubes. Makes approximately 3 cups.
2. Add onion, parsley, pepper, salt, lemon juice and olive oil. Toss gently to coat.
3. Taste and adjust seasoning.
4. Serve warm or at room temperature.

Makes 3 servings

# Oven Roasted Tri-Color Potato Salad

*I learned how to make this salad in a cooking demonstration at the Greenbrier Resort in West Virginia. At first I was impressed because it was so colorful. After tasting it, I loved the flavor too.*

## Ingredients
- 4 lbs mixed red, gold and purple potatoes
- 3 Tbsp Extra-virgin olive oil
- 2 Tbsp chopped herbs, cilantro, basil, thyme
- 2 cloves fresh garlic, crushed
- ½ tsp salt
- ½ tsp black pepper
- 3 stalks celery, sliced diagonally
- 6 green onions, sliced ¼-inch
- 2 roasted red peppers, diced ¼-inch
- 4-6 ounces mustard vinaigrette dressing (page 91)

## Preparation
1. Preheat oven to 425°F before baking.
2. Dice potatoes into 1-inch cubes.
3. Add olive oil, herbs, salt and pepper. Toss to coat. Spread onto a greased baking sheet and place in the oven for 40-45 minutes, or until potatoes are cooked and start browning.
4. Remove potatoes from the oven; while they are still warm, toss with the remaining ingredients.
5. Taste and adjust seasoning.
6. Serve warm or at room temperature.

Makes 6-8 servings

## Tips
- *If you toss the potatoes with the salad dressing first, while you chop the vegetables, the potatoes will absorb the dressing and it will be more flavorful.*

# Green Bean Salad

*A wonderful salad to serve with cold cuts. Especially good with fried eggplants.*

## Ingredients
1 lb fresh Italian string beans
1 small onion, chopped
¼ cup chopped flat leaf parsley
1½ Tbsp lemon juice
1½ Tbsp Extra-virgin olive oil
Salt and pepper to taste

## Preparation
1. Cut off the ends of string beans, and cut them into 1½-2 inch pieces. Place them in a pot and cover with water. Bring to a boil. Cook until beans are cooked but still firm. Drain. To achieve a good color, refresh very quickly in a bowl of cold water and ice cubes. Drain well before using in the salad.
2. In a salad bowl, mix string beans, chopped onion, chopped parsley, lemon juice, and olive oil.
3. Season with salt and pepper. Cover and refrigerate. May be served cold or at room temperature.

Makes 3-4 servings

## Tips
- *Perfect accompaniment served with cold cuts, fried eggplant or any grilled vegetables.*

# Greek Salad

*It is delicious! The intense, sweet, and pungent flavor of the balsamic vinegar is the perfect dressing for this salad. This is such a simple fresh vegetable salad that can be prepared in almost no time, if you have feta cheese and Greek olives handy.*

## Ingredients
4 cups chopped romaine lettuce
1 cup chopped cucumbers
1 cup chopped tomatoes
½ green bell pepper, chopped
1 small red onion, chopped
1 cup crumbled feta cheese
1 cup Kalamata olives, pitted

### *Balsamic Vinaigrette*
2 Tbsp balsamic vinegar
3 Tbsp Extra-virgin olive oil
½ tsp sugar
½ tsp dried oregano
Salt and black pepper to taste

## Preparation
1. Place chopped romaine lettuce in a large mixing bowl. Top with chopped cucumbers, tomatoes, onions, peppers, feta cheese and Greek olives.
2. In a small bowl, whisk together olive oil, vinegar, sugar and oregano; season with salt and pepper.
3. Drizzle the vinaigrette dressing over salad and toss gently.

## Tips
- *You may prepare salad dressing in advance, and assemble the salad vegetables in advance. Refrigerate both separately until just before serving.*
- *I usually chop the olives, saving a few for garnish. When the olives are chopped, the salad has a more even taste with every bite.*

# Fattoush

*This is a traditional Lebanese bread salad. It is quite popular in Middle Eastern countries. A good way to use stale pita bread. Our 5-year old granddaughter Christine's favorite salad.*

## Ingredients
2 pita breads
2 cups chopped lettuce
1 cup chopped parsley
¾ cup chopped green onions
1 cup diced cucumbers
½ cup chopped fresh mint
1 cup purslane leaves (ba'li)
7-8 radishes, thinly sliced
2 medium firm tomatoes diced

### Salad dressing
½ cup lemon juice
¾ cup Extra-virgin olive oil
1 Tbsp sumac
l clove crushed garlic
Salt to taste

## Preparation
1. Toast the pita bread in the oven until it starts browning. Cool. Cut into bite size pieces and set aside.
2. In a large mixing bowl, gently toss the vegetables.
3. Prepare the salad dressing by whisking all the ingredients together.
4. Pour over the prepared vegetable and bread. Toss lightly and adjust seasoning.
5. Serve immediately.

Makes 8 servings

## Tips
- *Purslane (ba'li) is sold in Middle Eastern produce markets.*
- *Sumac is sold in Middle Eastern grocery stores.*

# Cucumber Tomato Mint Salad

*Simplicity is the secret to this salad.*
*A classic flavor combination. Good with any meal.*

## Ingredients
1½ cup round sliced cucumbers
1 medium firm tomato diced, bite size
1 small white onion sliced, thin rounds
¼ cup fresh mint leaves (10-12)

<u>Salad dressing</u>
1½ Tbsp wine vinegar
3 Tbsp extra virgin olive oil
Salt to taste

## Preparation
1. If cucumber slices are too big, cut them in half or quarters.
2. Combine cucumber, tomato, onion and mint in a salad bowl.
3. In a small bowl, whisk together vinegar, olive oil and salt.
4. Pour dressing over cucumber mixture and toss to coat with the dressing.

Makes 2 servings

## Tips
- *Save time by preparing in advance. Put the dressing in the salad bowl, and top with the rest of the vegetables. Do not mix. Cover and refrigerate. Toss before serving and adjust seasoning. Can be prepared several hours in advance.*

# Tabouleh

*This delicious Mediterranean salad has become quite popular in recent years. The authentic tabouleh has very little bulgur and lots of fresh chopped herbs, tomatoes, and fresh squeezed lemon juice.*

## Ingredients

½ cup fine bulgur (cracked wheat # 1)
6 cups chopped flat leaf parsley
½ cup chopped mint leaves
½ cup chopped scallions
2 cups chopped fresh tomatoes
¾ cup chopped cucumber
1 small jalapeno pepper, chopped
¼ cup lemon juice
½ cup Extra-virgin olive oil
1½ tsp salt
½ tsp black pepper
¼ tsp red pepper flakes
Romaine lettuce leaves

## Preparation

1. Place cracked wheat in a large bowl. Add chopped vegetables over it. (You may prepare ahead of time to this point and mix the dressing just 20 minutes before serving).
2. If you do not want the heat from the jalapeno, either omit it or devein and seed it before chopping.
3. Add lemon juice, olive oil, salt and peppers and toss the salad. Adjust seasoning.
4. Serve with Romaine lettuce leaves.

Makes 6 (1 cup) servings

## Tips

- *The secret to this tasty salad is using fresh squeezed lemon juice and Extra-virgin olive oil.*
- *Prepare everything in advance. Add the salt, lemon juice and olive oil 20 minutes before serving. It will soften the bulgur and improve the flavoring.*
- *The most time consuming part is chopping the parsley. If you chop the parsley a day or two in advance, put it in a plastic container and cover with a dampened paper towel then plastic wrap, it will stay fresh and crisp.*

# Armenian Eetch Salad

*The first time I tried this salad was in Aleppo, Syria. My sister, Renee, gave me the recipe for it. Unlike Tabouleh, this salad is much grainier as it contains mostly bulgur. It is spicier and keeps longer in the refrigerator*

## Ingredients
3 white onions, chopped
1 jalapeño pepper, minced
4 medium size tomatoes, chopped
1 bunch parsley, chopped
2 cups fine cracked wheat (Bulgur #1)
3 Tbsp tomato paste
2 Tbsp pepper paste
1 tsp red pepper
1½ tsp salt
¼ tsp black pepper
1/3 cup lemon juice
¾ cup Extra-virgin olive oil
Romaine lettuce leaves

## Preparation
1. Sauté onions with 2 tablespoons olive oil until they look transparent. Add jalapeño and sauté for another minute. Add chopped tomato and stir until tomato has released its juices, approximately 4-5 minutes.
2. Add tomato paste, pepper paste, red pepper, salt and black pepper. Add lemon juice and remaining olive oil and mix together.
3. Add the bulgur, mix well and then add the chopped parsley. Mix thoroughly and adjust spices.
4. Let it cool and let bulgur absorb the flavors and soften. Serve with romaine lettuce leaves which can be used as a wrap.

Makes 8 servings

## Tips
- *Scoop desired amount of the salad in the fold of the romaine lettuce and eat.*

# Cole Slaw

*This is a versatile salad made from inexpensive ingredients that keep in the refrigerator for days and are readily available when you need them. The secret to this tasty Cole Slaw is to enhance its flavor by mixing and refrigerating it for a couple of hours before serving.*

## Ingredients
8-10 cups finely chopped cabbage
1 cup finely chopped red cabbage
1 carrot, shredded
2 Tbsp minced onion
½ cup buttermilk
1/3 cup sugar
½ tsp salt
1/8 tsp pepper
½ cup mayonnaise
2½ Tbsp lemon juice

## Preparation
1. In a large bowl combine buttermilk, sugar, salt, pepper, mayonnaise, and lemon juice, and whisk until smooth.
2. Add the chopped cabbages, carrots, and onions. Mix well.
3. Cover and refrigerate for 1 hour to enhance the flavor.

Makes 8 servings

## Tips
- *If buttermilk is not available, use ½ cup of milk with 1 tablespoon white vinegar. Let it sit for 5-10 minutes then use it.*
- *For this recipe, chop the cabbage, do not shred it.*
- *For variety to add sweetness, add a cubed apple and a handful of raisins.*
- *For a tangy salad, instead of mayonnaise use vinegar and oil and add a chopped tomato.*

# Oriental Chicken Cabbage Salad

*A wonderful salad that is quite popular on restaurant menus as a luncheon entrée. For a summer luncheon, this light and colorful salad is a treat. The crunchy ramen noodles, almonds, and cabbage, make this a salad you will want to dig into as soon as it is served.*

## Ingredients
6 cups shredded cabbage
3 scallions, sliced thin diagonally
1 pkg Top Ramen Noodles, broken into pieces (save the spice packet for the dressing)
¼ cup slivered almonds, roasted
2 cups cooked chicken, shredded
1 (12 oz pkg) won ton wrappers fried for topping for extra crunch (optional)

### Dressing
¼ cup sugar
½ tsp salt
½ tsp red pepper flakes
Saved packet of soup seasoning
1/3 cup white vinegar
3 Tbsp rice vinegar
¼ cup salad oil
3 Tbsp sesame oil

## Preparation
1. Whisk together sugar, salt, pepper, seasoning, and vinegar until dissolved. Gradually whisk in salad oil. Set aside.
2. If using won ton wrappers, cut them into strips and fry in hot oil. Drain on paper towel.
3. In a salad bowl, place the cabbage, scallions, noodles, almonds and the chicken.
4. Add the dressing and toss the salad. Top with the fried won ton strips.

Makes 4 servings

## Tips
- *In this salad the chicken should be shredded and not chopped. Tastes best served at room temperature.*
- *Instead of slivered almonds you may use toasted sesame seeds.*
- *You may want to mix 1 cup of shredded red cabbage with the green cabbage to make the salad more attractive.*
- *If you like ginger, a teaspoon of grated ginger in the dressing adds extra flavor.*

# Grilled Eggplant Salad

*This salad is best when made with char-roasted eggplant. The lemon vinaigrette makes this a delicious salad. When assembling the salad, toss lightly so the eggplant pieces don't get too mushy.*

## Ingredients
2 large eggplants
½ green bell pepper, cubed
1 large tomato
1 small white onion, sliced thin
8-10 fresh mint leaves
Juice of half a lemon
2 Tbsp Extra-virgin olive oil
Salt and pepper to taste

## Preparation
1. Poke eggplants with a fork to prevent them from exploding as they cook and create internal steam.
2. Grill eggplant either under the broiler, or on the charcoal grill until the skin is almost burned and the eggplant is cooked. Let it cool completely.
3. Cut the eggplant in half. With a spoon, scoop out the cooked eggplant and place in a bowl.
4. Cut the eggplant into bite size pieces. It will be mostly mushy and in long strips.
5. Add bell pepper, tomato, onion, and mint leaves.
6. Whisk together lemon juice, olive oil, salt and pepper. Pour over the salad.
7. Toss very gently so that the eggplant does not get mushier.

Makes 2-3 servings

## Tips
- *Eggplant tastes best when it is grilled on charcoal or gas barbeque.*

# Asparagus and Roasted Pepper Salad

*The asparagus should be cooked al dente. To achieve a good color, refresh very quickly in a bowl of cold water and ice cubes. They should be bright green and slightly crunchy.*

## Ingredients
2 lbs fresh asparagus
1 (8 oz) jar roasted red peppers
2 Tbsp pine nuts
2 Tbsp lemon juice
1 clove crushed garlic
2 Tbsp chopped basil
½ tsp salt
¼ tsp black pepper
1/3 cup Extra-virgin olive oil
2 Tbsp crumbled feta cheese

## Preparation
1. Remove the woody ends of asparagus.
2. Plunge the asparagus in boiling water and cook for 3 minutes. Drain and plunge into ice water. When cool, drain and pat dry with a paper towel. Arrange asparagus in serving dish. Set aside.
3. In a small bowl, whisk together lemon juice, crushed garlic, chopped basil, salt, pepper, and olive oil.
4. Drain roasted peppers and pat dry with a paper towel and dice them.
5. Add pine nuts to chopped pepper and toss gently with the dressing.
6. Spoon the pepper salad over asparagus, and sprinkle with crumbled feta cheese.

Makes 4-5 servings

## Tips:
- *Select medium thickness asparagus as they are more flavorful than the thin ones.*
- *An 8 oz. jar of roasted red pepper is equivalent to 2 fresh red peppers, roasted and peeled. (To prepare your own roasted pepper, cut the fresh pepper into large pieces. Place skin side up under a broiler. Broil until the skin is blackened and blistered. Place the grilled peppers in a plastic bag to sweat, then carefully peel away and discard the burned skin.)*

# Crunchy Broccoli Salad

*This salad tastes as good as it looks. It is very easy to prepare, nutritious and colorful. The mixture of crisp, chewy and sweet makes an interesting and tasty combination.*

### Ingredients
5 cups broccoli florets
1 small red onion, sliced
¼ cup raisins
1 (8 oz) can mandarin oranges, drained
¼ cup sugar
½ tsp salt
¼ tsp black pepper
1 Tbsp cider vinegar
½ cup mayonnaise
3 Tbsp bacon bits
¼ cup hulled dry roasted sunflower seeds

### Preparation
1. In a large bowl, toss broccoli, onion, raisins, and mandarin oranges.
2. In a small bowl, whisk together sugar, salt, pepper, vinegar, and mayonnaise.
3. Pour over salad and toss to coat. Cover and refrigerate for one hour or until well chilled.
4. Before serving, sprinkle with bacon bits and sunflower seeds.

Makes 5 servings

### Tips
- *You may want to blanch the broccoli for a more vibrant green color. Bring water to a boil and drop broccoli in boiling water. Within seconds broccoli gets a nice vibrant green color. Immediately drain and transfer into ice water. (If you blanch broccoli, make sure it is drained completely. Pat dry drained broccoli with paper towels.)*

# Mango and Hearts of Palm Salad

*This is a wonderful summer salad with tropical flavors. Very refreshing. The combination of sour lime juice, tangy and salty hearts of palm and sweet mango complement each other very well. Serve with fish, roast, or pan fried steaks and chops.*

## Ingredients
2 mangos, peeled, pitted, and sliced into ½-inch wedges
1 (14.5 oz) can hearts of palm, drained, and cut into 1-inch pieces
1 small red onion, sliced thin
Lettuce leaves
Mint leaves for garnish

### Lime Vinaigrette
1½ Tbsp lime juice
1 tsp water
1 tsp Dijon mustard
2 Tbsp Extra-virgin olive oil
½ tsp salt
¼ tsp black pepper

## Preparation
1. In a small bowl, whisk lime juice, 1 teaspoon water, mustard and olive oil. Set aside.
2. Peel mangos, and slice them into wedges, then cut them in halves. Slice hearts of palm.
3. In a medium bowl, combine sliced mangos, hearts of palm, sliced onion, and pepper. Drizzle with the lime vinaigrette dressing. Toss gently.
4. Line serving plate with lettuce leaves and top with mango salad.

Makes 4-6 servings

## Tips
- *If preserved hearts of palm are too salty, rinse and pat dry with a paper towel before chopping.*
- *I use 1 teaspoon of water in the dressing to cut down the sourness of the lime juice.*
- *If you like spicier food, chop a small jalapeño pepper and add to the salad mixture.*

# Grilled Lobster, Avocado and Mango Salad

*What a combination! It is delicious with the grapefruit vinaigrette. Makes four first course salads or two luncheon entrées. Using the lobster while it is still warm gives maximum flavor.*

## Ingredients

1 lb lobster tails
4 Tbsp Extra-virgin olive oil
Salt and pepper to taste
6 ounces fresh watercress
1 cup diced mango
1 avocado, diced
1 Tbsp fresh basil leaves, cut chiffonade

<u>Grapefruit Vinaigrette</u>
½ cup pink grapefruit juice
1 Tbsp honey
1 tsp minced shallots
½ tsp Dijon mustard
¼ tsp minced garlic
½ cup Extra-virgin olive oil

## Preparation

1. Preheat gas grill to high heat. Brush the lobster tails with olive oil and season with salt and pepper. Place the lobster tails on the grill and grill until the shells begin to turn red and the lobster is cooked through. Remove from heat and cool.
2. *<u>Prepare vinaigrette:</u>* In a small saucepan over medium high heat reduce ½ cup of grapefruit juice to half. Cool.
3. In a medium bowl, combine reduced grapefruit juice, honey, shallot, mustard and garlic. Whisk in the olive oil in little drizzles until emulsified. Season the vinaigrette with salt and pepper.
4. Remove lobster tails from the shells, and cut the meat into bite size pieces.
5. Remove the stems from the watercress. Use only the tender leaves and stems, approximately 2 cups loosely packed.
6. In a large bowl place the watercress, mango, avocado, basil chiffonade, and ½ cup of the vinaigrette; toss gently. Serve immediately.

Makes 2-4 servings

## Tips

- *You can prepare the vinaigrette ahead of time; if the oil is separated, just whisk it again before tossing the salad.*
- *You can also use boiled lobster tails instead of grilled.*

# Watercress, Blue Cheese and Walnut Salad

*The combination of these flavorings is magical - watercress, blue cheese, pear, and walnuts. A light vinaigrette dressing and a sprinkle of honey roasted walnuts completes the salad.*

## Ingredients
1 head lettuce
1 bunch watercress
½ small red onion, thinly sliced
1 pear, thinly sliced
½ cup crumbled blue cheese
¼ cup honey roasted walnuts
¾ cup Mustard Vinaigrette (page 91)

### Honey Roasted Walnuts
4 oz walnut halves
2 Tbsp honey
1 tsp sugar
¼ tsp salt

## Preparation
1. *Prepare honey roasted walnuts*: Cover a baking pan with aluminum foil and grease the foil. Mix honey, sugar, and salt and pour over the walnuts to coat them. Spread them on prepared pan. In a 350°F preheated oven, place the walnuts and bake 20-25 minutes until golden brown. Cool completely before using.
2. Tear the lettuce into bite size pieces and trim the stems from the watercress.
3. In a salad bowl, combine lettuce, watercress, sliced onion, and sliced pears. Toss with the dressing to coat. Sprinkle the top with candied walnuts and blue cheese. Serve immediately.

Makes 4 servings

## Tips
- *Use any kind of pear that is ripe but firm. Do not use over-ripe pears.*

# Balsamic Basil Vinaigrette

*This sophisticated vinaigrette is very flavorful and could be used in any salad that needs extra pizzazz.*

## Ingredients
¾ cup balsamic vinegar
2 Tbsp Dijon mustard
1½ tsp sugar or honey
1½ Tbsp chopped basil
1 Tbsp chopped flat-leaf parsley
½ tsp minced shallots
¼ tsp minced garlic
Dash of hot sauce
1 cup salad oil
Salt and pepper to taste

## Preparation
1. In a blender or food processor, blend all the ingredients, except the oil, until well combined.
2. With the motor running, add in the oil in a slow stream until the mixture is emulsified.
3. Adjust the salt and pepper seasoning. Store in an airtight container and refrigerate. Use as needed.

Makes approximately 2 cups

## Tips
- *Dressing will keep in the refrigerator for one week.*

# Raspberry Vinaigrette

*The sweetness of the honey and the tartness of the vinegar flavored with raspberries make a great combination.*

## Ingredients
4 Tbsp sugar or honey
¼ cup raspberry vinegar
¾ cup salad oil
1 Tbsp chopped shallots
¼ tsp salt
¼ tsp dry mustard
½ cup raspberries

## Preparation
1. Place all ingredients except fresh raspberries in a blender and blend thoroughly.
2. Add raspberries and blend slightly until raspberries are incorporated.

Makes approximately 1½ cup

# Mustard Vinaigrette
*A popular salad dressing that is good with most salads.*

## Ingredients
2 Tbsp white wine vinegar
1 Tbsp Dijon mustard
1 Tbsp fresh lemon juice
¼ cup extra virgin olive oil
¼ cup salad oil
Salt and pepper to taste

## Preparation
1. Whisk vinegar, mustard, lemon juice until well blended.
2. Gradually whisk in the oils. Season with salt and pepper.

Makes ¾ cups

# Lemon Vinaigrette
*Lemon vinaigrette is good with any vegetable salad.*

## Ingredients
3 Tbsp lemon juice
1 Tbsp water
1 tsp mustard
½ tsp salt
¼ tsp black pepper
1/3 cup Extra-virgin olive oil

## Preparation
1. In small bowl whisk lemon juice, water, mustard, salt and pepper.
2. Gradually add the olive oil and whisk until vinaigrette is emulsified.

Makes ½ cup

## Tips
- *Using water reduces tartness of the lemon and you use less olive oil.*

# French Dressing

*French dressing works well not only with mixed leaf salads but with chicken and meat salads as well. I like to keep the dressings on the light side, so I mix some water to reduce the tartness of the vinegar without adding extra olive oil.*

## Ingredients
½ cup water
½ cup red wine vinegar
½ tsp sugar
1 Tbsp lemon juice
1 Tbsp salt
1½ tsp black pepper
1½ tsp Worcestershire Sauce
½ tsp prepared mustard
1 small clove garlic, minced
2 cups salad oil

## Preparation
1. In a blender, blend all ingredients together except the oil. Gradually add the salad oil and blend until it is well emulsified.
2. Store in a covered jar in the refrigerator. Shake before serving.

Makes 3½ cups of dressing


# Tarragon Dressing
*An interesting twist to the French Dressing*

## Ingredients
1 cup French dressing
1 tsp chopped fresh tarragon

## Preparation
1. Mix the two together. Toss any salad with it.

# Papaya Seed Dressing

*This dressing with its piquant flavor is great on fruit salads or green salads. I like to serve this dressing on a green salad that is topped with cooked shrimp.*

## Ingredients
½ cup sugar
1 tsp salt
1 tsp dry mustard
1 small onion, minced
1 cup white wine vinegar
2 cups salad oil
2 Tbsp fresh papaya seeds

## Preparation
1. In a blender place sugar, salt, mustard, minced onion and vinegar. Turn on the blender and gradually add the salad oil.
2. When all is emulsified and well blended, add papaya seeds and continue blending until papaya seeds are the size of coarse ground pepper.

Makes 3 cups

# Honey Mustard Dressing

*A tasty dressing, sweet and tart. Serve on any salad.*

¼ cup vinegar
1 cup mayonnaise
1 tsp prepared mustard
1 tsp sugar
1 tsp minced shallots
½ cup honey
½ cup salad oil
Salt and pepper to taste

## Preparation
1. In a small bowl mix vinegar, mayonnaise, and mustard until smooth. Add sugar, shallots and honey.
2. Season to taste with salt and pepper. Gradually whisk in the oil until well blended.

Makes 2 cups

# Tri-color Raspberry Gelatin Mold

*This gelatin mold is a must at our Christmas Eve dinner party. Everybody's favorite. It is a little time consuming since you have to make it in three steps. I usually make it two days in advance, unmold it two hours before serving, and keep it refrigerated until the last minute.*

## Ingredients

*Top layer*
1 (6 oz) pkg raspberry gelatin
1½ cups boiling water
2 (10 oz) pkg frozen raspberries
1 tsp lemon juice

*Middle layer*
1 (6 oz) pkg lime gelatin
2 cups boiling water
1 cup cold water
2 (8 oz) containers lime yogurt
2 drops green food coloring (optional)

*Bottom layer*
1 (6 oz) pkg cherry gelatin
1½ cups boiling water
1 (16 oz) can crushed pineapple
1 (16 oz) can whole cranberries

## Preparation

1. *Prepare top layer.* Dissolve raspberry gelatin in hot water. Add frozen berries and lemon juice. Stir to thaw berries. Pour into bundt pan mold and chill until set.
2. *Prepare middle layer.* After top layer has set, dissolve lime gelatin in hot water, add the cold water and stir. Add the yogurt and the food coloring. Gently pour into the bundt pan over set raspberry gelatin. Chill until set.
3. *Bottom layer.* After the middle layer has set, dissolve cherry gelatin in hot water. Add pineapple with its juices and cranberry sauce. Let it thicken slightly then pour over the lime-yogurt layer. Chill overnight.
4. To unmold the gelatin, set the bundt pan in warm water for 30-40 seconds to loosen. Invert the serving platter over the mold and flip it over.

Makes 20-24 servings

## Tips

- *To make a smaller quantity, use a crystal bowl and layer the gelatin in the serving dish. Use smaller packages of gelatin and cut all other ingredients in half.*

# Strawberry-Lemon Gelatin Mold

*This gelatin mold can be served either as a salad or dessert. If using as a salad, use sour cream instead of the Cool Whip. If using as a dessert, use Cool Whip or even real whipped cream.*

## Ingredients

*First Layer*
1 (6 oz) pkg lemon gelatin
2 cups boiling water
1 (8 oz) container Cool Whip, thawed out in the refrigerator

*Second Layer*
1 (6 oz) pkg Strawberry gelatin
2 cups boiling water
1½ cup mashed fresh strawberries
Fresh strawberries and mint leaves for garnish

## Preparation

1. Dissolve lemon gelatin in 2 cups of boiling water. Let it cool to room temperature.
2. Whisk in thawed Cool Whip. Pour into a gelatin mold and refrigerate until set.
3. Dissolve strawberry gelatin in 2 cups of boiling water. Let it cool to room temperature.
4. Mix in mashed strawberries and gently pour over the set lemon gelatin in the mold. Refrigerate until set.
5. To serve, unmold the gelatin and garnish the serving dish with fresh strawberries and mint leaves.

Makes 16 servings

## Tips:
- *I usually prepare gelatin molds a day in advance and unmold when ready to serve.*

# Raspberry Gelatin Mold

*This gelatin mold is great for buffet tables. Great accompaniment to any chicken or meat dishes.*

## Ingredients
3 (3 oz) pkg raspberry gelatin
3 cups boiling water
2 (10 oz) pkg frozen raspberries, semi-thawed
1 (20 oz) can crushed pineapple
1 (16 oz) carton sour cream

## Preparation
1. Dissolve gelatin in hot water, add semi-thawed raspberries and crushed pineapple.
2. Pour half of the gelatin in a 9 x13-inch glass dish and refrigerate until set.
3. Remove from the refrigerator and spread sour cream over it. Gently pour the remaining gelatin over the sour cream. Refrigerate until set.
4. To serve, cut into squares and serve in the glass dish.

Makes 12-15 servings

## Tips
- *Any gelatin mold can be prepared a day or two in advance.*

# Cranberry Gelatin Mold
*This gelatin mold is best served on Thanksgiving Day with the turkey dinner.*

### Ingredients
3 (3 oz) pkg raspberry gelatin
4½ cups boiling water
2 cans whole cranberry sauce
1 envelope unflavored gelatin
½ cup walnuts, chopped fine
½ cup chopped celery
½ cup crushed pineapple
½ cup chopped apples

### Preparation
1. In a large bowl, dissolve raspberry gelatin and unflavored gelatin in boiling water.
2. Add the remaining ingredients and mix well.
3. Pour into a bundt pan and refrigerate until set.
4. Unmold before serving.

Makes 15-18 servings

### Tips
- *Prepare two days in advance and forget about it until party time.*

# Seafood and Shellfish

## Maple Syrup Glazed Salmon

*There are times when all we want is old fashioned plain fish fillets that are flavorful and easy to prepare. The simplest cooking method is the best and tastiest!*

### Ingredients
2 Tbsp olive oil
4 (6-8 oz) salmon filets
1 tsp salt
¼ tsp pepper

*Glaze*
½ cup maple syrup
¼ cup orange juice
¼ cup lemon juice
1 Tbsp minced garlic
1 Tbsp grated fresh ginger
1 Serrano chili cut in half
¼ tsp salt

### Preparation
1. In a small saucepan combine the maple syrup, orange juice, lemon juice, garlic, ginger, chili, and salt. Over medium heat, bring the mixture to boil and cook for 5 minutes or until it thickens. Discard the Serrano chili.
2. Rub the salmon with olive oil and season with salt and pepper.
3. Grill on medium hot grill turning fish once (4-5 minutes on each side) brushing frequently with the maple glaze. Remove from the grill and brush with additional glaze.
4. Serve with potato salad (page 74).

Makes 4 servings

### Tips
- *Salmon is easy to overcook watch carefully during the cooking process.*

# Fish Kebab

*This is an easy and fast preparation of fish kebab. Use your favorite fish combination skewered with vegetables and serve with rice pilaf and steamed vegetables*

## Ingredients
¾ lb salmon filet
¾ lb halibut filet
1 white onion
½ red bell pepper
½ green bell pepper
½ tsp salt
¼ tsp pepper
Lemon wedges
Plain Basmati Rice Pilaf (page 179)
Steamed vegetables

### Marinade
¼ cup lemon juice
2 Tbsp Extra-virgin olive oil
1 Tbsp fish seasoning (dry herbs)

## Preparation
1. Cut the fish into evenly sized chunks.
2. Cut the onion into quarters and separate the pieces.
3. Cut the peppers into evenly sized chunks.
4. Whisk together lemon juice, olive oil and fish seasoning.
5. In a bowl put the cubed fish and vegetables together, salt and pepper and pour over the marinade. Mix well. Let the fish and vegetables marinate at room temperature for 30 minutes before grilling.
6. Meanwhile if you plan to use wooden skewers, soak them in water for 30 minutes before using to prevent burning.
7. Thread the salmon on the skewers followed by onion and peppers, alternating with halibut.
8. Preheat the grill to medium high. Spray with cooking oil and place the skewers on the grill turning them frequently to assure even cooking. Brush with leftover marinade if necessary.
9. Serve with lemon wedges, basmati rice pilaf and steamed vegetables.

Makes 3 servings

## Tips
- *If using metal skewers, put on a light coating of oil before threading the fish and vegetables. They will slide off the skewer easier.*

# Grilled Shrimp with Pesto
*Easy as one, two, three. Voila! Dinner is ready.*

## Ingredients
1½ lb Black tiger shrimp,
   uncooked, peeled and deveined
½ cup prepared pesto sauce
   (page 206)

## Preparation
1. Soak bamboo skewers in cold water for 30 minutes to prevent them from burning on the grill.
2. Skewer the shrimps on the skewer wrapping them around each other as seen in the picture.
3. Brush with pesto sauce and let it marinate for 30 minutes.
4. Preheat the grill. Arrange the skewered shrimps on the grill. Grill about 2-3 minutes on each side. Do not overcook.
5. Serve with rice pilaf and extra pesto sauce on the side.

Makes 3 servings

## Tips
- *To save time, use commercially prepared pesto sauce which is readily available in the stores.*
- *To serve as an appetizer, you can skewer one or two shrimps on each skewer. After grilling, serve the shrimps on the skewers with extra pesto sauce for dipping.*

# Killer Shrimp

*Don't be intimidated by the long list of spices, they are all commonly used spices found in most kitchen pantries. This shrimp dish with its spicy broth is just spicy enough, flavorful, and easy to prepare. Serve with it lots of French bread to soak up the tasty broth. It will warm you up on a chilly night. To eat this dish, everyone peels their own shrimp at the table using their hands.*

## Ingredients
- 1 lb large uncooked shrimp with shells on
- 5 Tbsp butter
- 3 Tbsp olive oil
- 3 cloves crushed garlic
- 1 tsp Worcestershire Sauce
- 1 cup beer at room temperature
- ½ cup water
- French bread for dipping in the broth

### Seasoning
- 1 tsp black pepper
- 1 tsp red pepper flakes
- ½ tsp cayenne pepper
- ½ tsp salt
- ½ tsp crushed dried thyme
- ½ tsp crushed dried rosemary
- ¼ tsp crushed dried oregano

## Preparation
1. Rinse the shrimp in cold water and drain in a colander.
2. In a small bowl, combine dried seasoning and set aside.
3. In a large skillet over high heat, combine the butter and olive oil. When the butter is melted, add garlic, Worcestershire sauce and the mixed seasoning. Add the shrimp and cook the shrimp for 2 minutes until they start turning pink. Add the beer and the water and bring to a boil and cook for another minute or two. Remove from heat.
4. Serve immediately in bowls with the sauce and lots of French bread for dipping.

Makes 2 servings

## Tips
- *If you do not like this dish spicy, reduce the amount of cayenne and red pepper flakes.*
- *Make sure you have lots of paper napkins handy to wipe your hands.*
- *Plain cooked rice makes a great accompaniment in separate small bowls.*

# Curried Prawns

*The coconut milk and the spices complement the flavor of shrimp making it a very tasty dish.
Serve with basmati rice.*

## Ingredients
1 Tbsp butter
2 cloves garlic, crushed
1 lb medium size prawns,
 peeled and deveined
4 cardamom pods
4 cloves
1 Tbsp mustard seeds
1 onion, chopped
1 jalapeño pepper, finely chopped
4 tomatoes, diced
1 can coconut milk
3 Tbsp garam masala
1¼ tsp salt
2 tsp chili pepper
Plain basmati rice (page 179)

## Preparation
1. Melt the butter in a large pan, add garlic and stir for few minutes. Add prawns and sauté briskly until they change color. Remove shrimp to a plate and set aside.
2. In the same pan, add cardamom pods, cloves, and mustard seeds; sauté for 2 minutes to let the flavors out. Add chopped onion and jalapeño pepper and sauté for 5 minutes until onion is softened and starts browning.
3. Add diced tomatoes, coconut milk, garam masala, salt and chili pepper to taste. Bring to a boil, add sautéed shrimp and cook for 5-8 minutes.
4. Transfer to a serving dish and serve with basmati rice.

Makes 4 servings

## Tips
- *If you do not like the shrimp spicy hot, reduce chili pepper or eliminate jalapeno pepper.*
- *Garam masala is a mixed Indian spice found in specialty or Indian markets.*

# Orzo Shrimp Salad

*The salty and tangy feta cheese gives character to this salad. Often people think of orzo as rice because of its shape, but it is pasta and because of its size it cooks very fast.*

## Ingredients
5 cups boiling water
2 cups orzo pasta
¾ lb cooked shelled shrimp
2 cups blanched broccoli florets
¾ cup crumbled feta cheese

### Dressing
2 Tbsp lemon juice
1 tsp lemon rind
2 Tbsp rice vinegar
3 Tbsp Extra-virgin olive oil
Salt and Pepper to taste

## Preparation
1. Cook orzo in salted boiling water for 10 minutes, drain.
2. If using large shrimps, cut them into bite size pieces.
3. In a large salad bowl, mix orzo, shrimp, cooked broccoli, feta cheese,
4. Whisk together lemon juice, lemon rind, rice vinegar, and olive oil. Salt and pepper to taste.
5. Pour dressing over orzo and toss gently.

Makes 4-6 servings

## Tips
- *Try to prepare this salad a few hours ahead of time for the flavors to blend.*

# Kung Pao Shrimp (Spicy Shrimp with Peanuts)

*Authentic Kung Pao dish is usually spicy hot but you can control the heat. It should have a lot of zing. Serve with steamed rice.*

## Ingredients
4 Tbsp vegetable oil
1 tsp fresh crushed ginger
1 lb medium size raw shrimp, shelled and deveined
2-3 red dried chili peppers
2 tsp cornstarch
2 tsp water
2 green onions, sliced diagonally in 1-inch long pieces
1 Tbsp Hoisin sauce
½ tsp sugar
2 tsp sherry wine
1 Tbsp soy sauce
1 tsp sesame seed oil
¼ cup chicken broth
1 cup peanuts, roasted

### Marinade
1 Tbsp cornstarch
1 Tbsp dry sherry wine
½ tsp sugar
1 tsp crushed garlic
2 tsp soy sauce

## Preparation
1. Mix all the ingredients for the marinade and pour over the shrimp. Marinate for 10-15 minutes.
2. Cut chili peppers in half and shake out the seeds.
3. Mix 1 tablespoon of water with the cornstarch and set aside.
4. In a wok or large deep frying pan, heat 3 tablespoons of oil and sauté the chili peppers for 15 seconds. Remove peppers from the oil.
5. Stir-fry the shrimps for 2 minutes until they start curling and turning pink. Remove them from the wok.
6. Add the remaining 1 tablespoon of oil to the pan and sauté ginger for a few seconds then add the onions and sauté for 20 seconds.
7. Add Hoisin sauce, sugar, sherry wine, soy sauce, sesame oil, cornstarch mixed with water and chicken broth. Heat until sauce starts thickening, add shrimp and the red peppers. Stir-fry for 15 seconds and add the peanuts. Mix and serve immediately with steamed rice.

Makes 4 servings

## Tips
- *Don't eat the whole chilies in the prepared dish, they are extremely hot. If you can not find dried chilies in your store, use dried red pepper flakes.*
- *Authentic Chinese cooking suggests frying the nuts in oil. I prefer the roasted peanuts.*
- *You can control the heat in this dish by using less chili pepper.*
- *Hoisin sauce is found in most supermarkets.*

# Crab Stuffed Artichokes

*Artichokes cooked in advance and stuffed with the crab filling can be assembled ahead of time and chilled until cooking time. All it needs is crusty French bread.*

## Ingredients
6-7 artichokes
3-4 lemon slices
4 cloves garlic
1 tsp salt
French bread

### Filling
1 lb lump crab meat
2 cups Swiss cheese cut into ¼-inch cubes
¼ cup chopped red bell peppers
¼ cup chopped green bell peppers
1 small chopped jalapeño pepper (optional)
¼ cup chopped onion
½ cup mayonnaise
3 tsp lemon juice
1 Tbsp Worcestershire Sauce

## Preparation
1. *Prepare artichokes:* Cut the artichoke stems and discard. Trim off the leaf tips with kitchen shears. Place the artichokes cut side up in a saucepan and add lemon slices, garlic cloves, salt and a small amount of water. Bring to a boil cover and simmer for 30-35 minutes or until a leaf will pull out easily. Drain. Let it cool. Pull out the small center leaves, and gently spoon out the fuzzy choke leaving a good size cup in the center. Arrange the artichokes in a baking dish upright.
2. *Prepare the filling* Cube Swiss cheese and place in a mixing bowl.
3. Chop peppers and onion and add to the cheese.
4. Add mayonnaise, lemon juice, Worcestershire sauce, and crab meat. Toss gently.
5. Fill the center cavities of the artichokes. (At this point you can cover the artichokes with plastic wrap and refrigerate until baking time.)
6. Before baking, preheat oven to 375°F. Remove plastic wrap and cover the dish loosely with foil.
7. Pour 1-inch boiling water around the artichokes and bake for 35-40 minutes or until the cheese is melted and the filling is heated through.
8. Serve the artichokes with fresh crusty French bread.

Makes 6-7 servings

## Tips
- *Artichokes cook in a pressure cooker in 18-20 minutes while cooking on the stove top takes 50 minutes.*
- *May be prepared the night before or early in the morning and baked before serving.*

# Artichokes Stuffed with Shrimp Salad

*This is a fantastic luncheon or light supper meal. All it needs is crusty French bread or you might want to serve it with Cheese Beoreks*

## Ingredients
4 artichokes
2 cloves garlic
3 lemon slices
1 tsp salt
French bread

### *Filling*
1½ pound shrimp cooked,
   coarsely chopped
¼ cup chopped roasted red bell peppers
1/3 cup chopped green bell peppers
1 small chopped jalapeño pepper,
   (optional)
1 cup fresh cooked corn kernels
1 cup chopped celery
¼ cup chopped green onion
¼ cup mayonnaise plus more if needed
3 tsp lemon juice
2 Tbsp chopped fresh cilantro
2 Tbsp chopped fresh tarragon
¼ tsp black pepper
Salt to taste

## Preparation
1. *Prepare artichokes:* Cut the artichoke stems and discard. Trim off the leaf tips with kitchen shears. Place the artichokes cut side up in a saucepan and add lemon slices, garlic cloves, salt and a small amount of water. Bring to a boil cover and simmer for 30-35 minutes or until a leaf will pull out easily. Drain. Let it cool. Pull out the small center leaves, and gently spoon out the fuzzy choke leaving a good size cup in the center. Arrange the artichokes in a baking dish upright
2. *Prepare the filling:* Put all the chopped vegetables in a bowl; add the spices, mayonnaise, lemon juice, and chopped shrimp. Toss gently. Adjust seasoning. Cover and refrigerate.
3. Before serving, fill the center cavities of cold artichokes with the shrimp salad.
4. Serve the artichokes with fresh crusty French bread or Cheese Beoreks (page 33)

Makes 4 servings

## Tips
- *May be prepared the night before or early in the morning.*

# Crab Cakes

*A family favorite baked or pan-fried to golden brown. Make them smaller in size and they make wonderful appetizers. Serve with a small salad and it makes a nice first course. Serve with mashed potatoes and a side of vegetables and it becomes a dinner entrée. Also makes a great sandwich.*

## Ingredients
1 lb fresh lump crab meat
1 cup soft white bread crumbs
¼ cup chopped parsley
2 Tbsp grated white onion
1 Tbsp finely chopped red pepper
¾ cup mayonnaise
1 Tbsp Worcestershire sauce
1 tsp prepared mustard
¾ tsp salt
¼ tsp black pepper
2 Tbsp butter
1 cup Panko (Japanese bread crumbs)

## Preparation
1. Remove cartilage from crab meat. Squeeze the moisture out and pat with a paper towel.
2. In a bowl, mix bread crumbs, crab meat, parsley, onion and red pepper.
3. In another small bowl mix together mayonnaise, Worcestershire sauce, mustard, salt and pepper.
4. Pour mayonnaise mixture over crab meat mixture and fold lightly but thoroughly.
5. Form into patties, dip in Panko bread crumbs. Set aside. (You can prepare the patties to this point, cover and refrigerate until time to cook and serve).
6. Melt 2 tablespoons of butter in a frying pan and sauté crab cakes over medium-high heat until golden brown and heated thoroughly. Add more butter to the pan if necessary.

Makes 6 large or 10 small crab cakes

## Tips
- *If the bread used is old and dry, soften it with a little milk, or substitute mashed potatoes.*
- *Panko bread crumbs are sold in most grocery store in the Japanese food items' section.*

# Salmon Patties with Red Pepper Coulis
*Great for summer parties. Makes especially good sandwiches in a hamburger bun.*

## Ingredients
2 lb fresh salmon
1 carrot
1 small onion
10 peppercorns
1 tsp salt
½ tsp black pepper
½ cup finely chopped red onion
½ cup finely chopped red bell pepper
½ cup bread crumbs
2 Tbsp minced fresh basil
2 large eggs
1 tsp Worcestershire sauce
½ tsp hot pepper sauce
2 Tbsp butter

*Red Pepper Coulis*
1 large red pepper roasted
½ tsp rice vinegar
¼ tsp poppy seed
¼ tsp salt

## Preparation
1. *Prepare pepper coulis:* Cut the carrot into four pieces and quarter the onion.
2. In a shallow saucepan, place the salmon fillets, carrot, onion, peppercorns and salt, cover with water. Bring the water to a boil, reduce heat, cover the pan and poach the salmon for 12-15 minutes. Remove from the liquid and let it cool completely.
3. With a fork, flake the cold poached salmon making sure all of the bones have been removed.
4. In a mixing bowl, mix all the ingredients together. Adjust seasoning.
5. Form into patties in desired sizes.
6. Melt 2 tablespoons butter in a skillet over medium heat. Sauté patties until brown, about 5 minutes. Add more butter to the pan if necessary. Serve with Red Pepper Coulis.

Makes 4-6 patties

## Tips
- *Lemon Herb Mayonnaise (page 208) is another alternative for a sauce with the Salmon Patties.*
- *I prefer to serve the herbed mayonnaise when the patties are served as a sandwich.*
- *Mango salsa (page 29) is also good with Salmon patties.*

# Fried Rex Sole

*This is a very mild tasting fish and does not need anything else but salt and pepper.
Excellent pan-fried and served with the potato salad.*

## Ingredients
1 lb Rex sole fish
1 tsp salt
½ tsp pepper
½ cup vegetable oil for frying
1 cup flour for dredging

## Preparation
1. Rinse and paper towel pat dry excess moisture.  Season with salt and pepper.
2. In a frying pan over medium-high heat, heat the oil.
3. Dredge both sides of the fish with flour, shaking the excess flour.
4. Fry in the preheated oil, turning once, until it is golden brown.  Drain on paper towel.
5. Serve with potato salad (page 74) and lemon wedges.

Makes 2 servings

# Fried Red Mullet

*Red Mullet is a Mediterranean fish with very firm, lean flesh. Quite popular in the Mediterranean countries where it is known as "Sultan Ibrahim" but rarely available in the United States.
It is one of the most delicious fish with a unique nutty flavor.*

## Ingredients
1 lb fresh Red Mullet fish, cleaned
1 tsp salt
½ tsp pepper
¾ cup vegetable oil for frying
¼ cup olive oil for frying
1 cup flour for dredging
1 lemon cut into wedges

## Preparation
1. Rinse and paper towel pat dry excess moisture. Season with salt and pepper.
2. In a frying pan over medium-high heat, heat the olive oil and vegetable oil together.
3. Dredge both sides of the fish with flour, shaking the excess flour.
4. Fry in the preheated oil, turning once, until it is golden brown. Drain on a paper towel.
5. Serve hot with potato salad (page 74) and lemon wedges.

Makes 2 servings

## Tips
- *In the Middle Eastern countries, they serve with wedges of pita bread fried crisp in the same oil.*

# Fried Fresh Sardines

*Sardines are small soft-boned saltwater fish. Fresh sardines are available on a limited basis during the summer months. If you ask your store's fish department, they will try to get it for you when available. Sardines taste best grilled or fried.*

## Ingredients
1 lb fresh sardines, cleaned
1 tsp salt
½ tsp pepper
¾ cup vegetable oil for frying
¼ cup olive oil
1 cup flour for dredging
1 lemon, cut into wedges

## Preparation
1. Cut the heads off and clean the gut of the sardines. Rinse and paper towel pat dry excess moisture. Season the fish with salt and pepper.
2. In a frying pan over medium-high heat, heat the olive oil and vegetable oil together.
3. Dredge both sides of the sardines with flour, shaking the excess flour.
4. Fry in the preheated oil, turning once, until it is golden brown. Do not over-crowd the fish in the frying pan. Drain on a paper towel.
5. Serve with potato salad (page 74) and lemon wedges.

Makes 2-3 servings

## Tips
- *In the Middle Eastern countries, they serve with wedges of pita bread fried crisp in the same oil.*

# Fish Tacos

*Fish Tacos have gained great popularity in Mexican restaurants, and rightfully so because they are so festive, colorful, healthy, and yummy. What more can we ask for? Just a Margarita!*

## Ingredients

1½ lb fresh fish (Halibut, cod, mahi-mahi, or snapper)
Salt and pepper to taste
2 Tbsp mayonnaise
2 Tbsp sour cream
1 tsp lime juice
2 cups shredded cabbage
1 cup flour
¾ cups vegetable oil for frying
8 oz. Jack cheese, shredded
10 flour tortillas (one package)
Guacamole (page 23)
Tomato Salsa (page 197)
Sliced radishes, (optional)

## Preparation

1. In a medium size bowl, mix mayonnaise, sour cream, lime juice and a pinch of salt. Mix thoroughly; add shredded cabbage. Mix well and set aside.
2. Wipe the fish with a damp paper towel and slice to ½-inch thick strips. Sprinkle with salt and pepper. Dip the fish in flour, shake the excess flour and fry them in vegetable oil a few minutes on each side. Drain on paper towel.
3. Serve salsa, cheese, and guacamole, and cabbage with the tortillas and fish and let everyone assemble their own fish taco.

Makes 6 servings

## Tips

- *If you want to grill the fish instead of frying, feel free to do so. You get best results with the mahi-mahi fish for grilling. Use 1-inch thick filets cut into 1½-inch strips; marinate for 10 minutes in a marinade made with ¼ cup lime juice, 2 tablespoons chopped cilantro, 2 tablespoons oil and ½ teaspoon of salt.*
- *Thread each piece of fish on a skewer and grill until opaque and cooked through.*

# Paella Valenciana

*Classic Paella, which is a traditional Spanish dish, is a mixture of meats, seafood, vegetables and saffron flavored rice. First time we had it was in Toledo, Spain in 1963 on our honeymoon trip. It has unlimited varieties. It is usually cooked in flat-bottomed shallow pans which also make an attractive tableside presentation. This version of Paella is modified to our liking to please our grandchildren. They prefer more sausage and chicken then shellfish. Don't let the long list of ingredients intimidate you, preparation is easy.*

## Ingredients

1 lb Kielbasa sausage
1½ lb chicken tenders
1½ lb raw prawns, shelled
3 Tbsp olive oil
1 large onion, diced
1 red bell pepper, thinly sliced
4 cloves garlic, chopped
½ tsp crumbled saffron threads
½ tsp turmeric
½ tsp red pepper flakes
½ tsp black pepper
1 tsp paprika
1 tsp salt
1 cup peeled and diced tomatoes
½ cup white wine
2 cups long grain rice
4 cups chicken broth
2 cup frozen peas, thawed
3 Tbsp chopped Italian parsley leaves

## Preparation

1. Slice the Kielbasa sausage ½ thick, cut chicken tenders in half and peel the prawns; refrigerate until ready to use.
2. Heat the olive oil in a paella pan or a large deep frying pan with a lid. Sauté the chicken pieces until they turn white and are cooked through. Remove from pan and set aside.
3. In the same pan, sauté the chopped onion, pepper, and garlic until they are soft.
4. Add the sliced Kielbasa and cook, stirring until they are slightly brown.
5. Add the spices: saffron, turmeric, pepper flakes, black pepper, paprika and salt. Stir fry for a few minutes until the spices get aromatic.
6. Add the tomatoes and cook for 2-3 minutes. Add the wine and cook until the liquid is absorbed and the alcohol from the wine is evaporated. Add the broth.
7. Stir in the rice and bring the broth to a boil, reduce heat, cover the pan and let it simmer until the rice has absorbed most of the water. Add the chicken pieces and the peas and the prawns. Cover and continue cooking on very low heat until all the liquid is absorbed and the prawns turn pink. This will take approximately 8-10 minutes.
8. To serve, fluff the rice with a fork, transfer to a shallow bowl. Sprinkle with chopped parsley. Serve with a nice green salad and lemon wedges.

Makes 6-8 serving

## Tips

- *Clams and mussels could be added for a traditional version of Paella.*

## Meatballs

*This basic meatball recipe is very versatile. You can grill them; bake or fry them; cook in marinara or sweet and sour sauce; serve them as an appetizer, or make a dinner entree served with rice vegetables and a salad.*

### Ingredients
1 lb ground lamb
1 lb ground beef
½ cup bread crumbs
½ cup minced parsley
½ cup finely chopped onion
1 egg
1 tsp allspice
1¼ tsp salt
½ tsp ground black pepper
¾ cup vegetable oil for frying

### Preparation
1. Mix together the meat, bread crumbs, parsley, onion, egg, and spices.
2. Shape into walnut size balls and flatten them slightly.
3. Fry in heated oil a few minutes on each side, until they start browning.
4. Serve with mashed potatoes (page 172) or vermicelli pilaf (page 178), cooked vegetables and a salad.

Makes 60 (2-inch) patties

### Tips
- *You can use only beef or lamb. I like the combination of the two meats.*
- *You can cook and freeze the meatballs. Defrost and cook in your favorite sauce.*

# Meatball Stew (Daoud Pasha)

*These moist meatballs are hearty enough to serve with a salad and some crusty bread. It can also be served over rice or pasta.*

## Ingredients
2 lbs ground beef
½ cup bread crumbs
½ cup minced parsley
½ cup finely chopped onion
1 egg
1 tsp allspice
1¼ tsp salt
½ tsp ground black pepper
½ cup pine nuts, toasted
1 large onion sliced thin
1 (14½ oz) can crushed tomatoes
1 cup water
Chopped parsley for garnish

## Preparation
1. Preheat oven to 375°F before baking.
2. Mix together the meat, bread crumbs, parsley, onion, egg, and spices.
3. Shape into walnut size balls and place them in a baking dish.
4. Fry in preheated oil a few minutes on each side, until they start browning.
5. Pour out excess fat from the frying pan. Add sliced onions and sauté until they start turning brown. Remove from heat and sprinkle the onions over the meatballs. Then sprinkle the toasted pine nuts over the onions.
6. Pour the crushed tomatoes over the meatballs, and add 1 cup of water.
7. Bake uncovered for 40-50 minutes.
8. Serve over Vermicelli Rice Pilaf (page 178).

Makes 4-6 servings

## Tips
- *The leftovers keep well in the freezer. Can be reheated conveniently in the microwave.*

# Basic Meat Loaf

*Meat loaf is such an American classic. We all grew up eating meatballs and meat loaf.
A definite family favorite.
Serve with mashed potatoes to make a satisfying comfort meal.*

## Ingredients

½ cup fresh white bread crumbs
½ cup half and half
1 medium onion, minced
½ cup minced celery
¼ cup minced bell pepper
½ cup finely chopped mushroom (optional)
¼ cup chopped parsley
½ tsp crushed garlic
2 lbs mixed ground beef, pork and veal
1 egg
½ cup grated Parmesan cheese
½ tsp black pepper
¼ tsp cayenne pepper
¼ tsp of cumin
Dash of nutmeg
1½ tsp salt
½ cup ketchup

## Preparation

1. Preheat oven to 350°F before baking.
2. Soak the bread crumbs in half and half until all is absorbed.
3. In a frying pan, sauté minced onion, celery, pepper, mushroom, parsley, and garlic until vegetables are soft and liquid is absorbed. Cool slightly.
4. In a large bowl, mix together all the ingredients and shape into a loaf. (Do not over mix). Place in a baking pan.
5. Bake for 50-60 minutes basting occasionally with rendered pan juices.
6. The meat loaf is done when the thermometer inserted into the center reads 160°F and is slightly browned on top. Let stand 10 minutes before slicing.
7. Serve with mashed potatoes (page 172) and shitake mushroom sauce (page 203).

Makes 6-8 servings

## Tips

- *Over-mixing the meatloaf will make it tough. I usually mix the spices, ketchup, the egg and cooked vegetables with the soaked bread crumbs, and then I gently mix in the meat and Parmesan cheese.*
- *Left-over meatloaf makes great sandwiches the next day (page 193).*

# Beef Tacos

*It is easy to put together a tasty Taco dinner. Authentic tacos are often filled with slow-braised meats. The quick version is done by using ground beef and pre-mixed spices sold in the grocery stores. As for the toppings, use whatever pleases your taste buds.*

## Ingredients
1 lb. ground beef
1 pkg Taco spices and seasoning mix
2/3 cup water
12 taco shells
1 cup shredded lettuce
1 cup grated Jack cheese
Guacamole *(page 23)*
Fresh tomato salsa *(page 197)*
Cilantro for garnish

## Preparation
1. In a skillet, brown meat until it is not pink anymore.
2. Stir in spices and seasoning and 2/3 cup water.
3. Bring to a boil; reduce the heat to low, simmer uncovered for about 10-15 minutes, stirring occasionally.
4. Wrap taco shells in foil and heat for 5 minutes, or until crisp. Place on a plate to serve.
   In separate bowls, place the meat mixture, shredded lettuce, shredded Jack cheese, guacamole, tomato salsa, and chopped cilantro leaves. Let everyone assemble their own taco.

Makes 12 tacos

## Tips
- *The same ingredients could be used to prepare a tostada.*
- *You may use ground turkey, chicken, or pork instead of beef.*

# Chili con Carne

*On a cool day, a bowl of chili topped with crumbled crackers and grated cheese makes a satisfying lunch or dinner. I like to serve this dish either with rice and a salad or just salad and cornbread.*

## Ingredients
1 large onion, minced
2 lb ground beef
1 (8 oz) can tomato sauce
2 cups water
1 jalapeno pepper, minced
1 tsp garlic powder
1 tsp celery seeds
½ tsp cayenne pepper
1 tsp cumin
1 bay leaf
4 Tbsp chili powder
¼ tsp basil
2 tsp salt
1 (15 oz) can red kidney beans, rinsed and drained.
French bread for serving

## Preparation
1. Spray the cooking pan with oil. Sauté minced onion until slightly wilted, add the ground beef and cook until meat browns.
2. Add tomato sauce, spices, and water. Bring to a boil. Reduce the heat and simmer uncovered, until the sauce is desired thickness, about 30-40 minutes. Add kidney beans during the last 10 minutes of cooking. Adjust seasoning.
3. To serve, top with grated cheese and serve with crusty French bread, rice or cornbread.

Makes 5 cups

## Tips
- *For a quick fix of Chile con Carne, use the store bought chili mix and follow the package cooking directions.*
- *Special Cornbread (page 234) makes a really good accompaniment to the chili dish.*

# Crock Pot Beef Stew

*Not many dishes can compete with a slow cooked beef stew. This hearty stew has lots of flavor and no fuss. Fix it in the morning and go to work. Come home in the evening to a wonderful home cooked meal. It tastes even better the next day.*

## Ingredients
1 leek, chopped and washed
2 lb of cubed steak or stewing meat
Flour for dredging
2 Tbsp vegetable oil
3 carrots cut into 2-inch pieces
2 celery stalks cut into 2-inch pieces
2-3 potatoes cut into 2-inch pieces
8 oz fresh mushroom, optional
1 can of beef broth
1 pkg beef stew seasoning
1 can cream of mushroom soup
French bread

## Preparation
1. Cover the bottom of the crock pot with the chopped leek.
2. Coat beef cubes in flour. Heat the oil in a large skillet and brown the meat on all sides. Add into the crock pot on top of the chopped leeks. Layer carrots, celery, potatoes and mushroom.
3. Discard excess oil from the skillet, deglaze skillet with ½ cup water scraping the brown bits from the bottom of the pan. Add the beef broth, mushroom soup and seasoning mix. Pour mixture over the vegetables in the crock pot.
4. Cover crock pot and cook on high for 1 hour, lower heat and cook 6-7 hours.
5. Serve with crusty French bread.

Makes 4-5 servings

## Tips
- *If you do not use potatoes in the stew, rice makes a good accompaniment.*
- *The gravy is delicious and does not need to be thickened.*
- *Entire dish can be prepared the day before and reheated at the time of serving with excellent results.*
- *Instant potatoes are a good stew thickener.*

# Brisket Roast

*This recipe is absolutely great! If prepared this way it will be very tender with a great flavor. The marvelous thing about the roast is that it tastes better the next day when all the flavors are infused into the meat. The convenience of preparing the roast ahead of time makes this recipe the best for entertaining large groups of people.*

## Ingredients
1 (4-6 pound) Beef brisket
1 onion quartered and sliced thin
1 pkg Lipton's Onion Soup mix
3 Tbsp Worcestershire sauce
1 can beef broth

## Preparation
1. Preheat oven to 400°F before roasting.
2. Place half of the sliced onions on a large piece of heavy-duty aluminum foil, and sprinkle with half of the onion soup mix. Place the brisket fatty side up on top of the onion and sprinkle the rest of the onion slices and onion soup mix. Drizzle with the Worcestershire sauce. Fold over the sides of the foil and place brisket in a roasting pan. Before sealing the foil, pour the beef broth over the brisket and seal the foil.
3. Place the brisket in the preheated 400°F oven for half an hour then reduce the heat to 275°F. Bake for 5-6 hours.
4. Let it cool completely in the pan. Remove brisket from the foil onto a carving board and strip off all the fat. Slice the brisket across the grain into ½-inch slices and arrange the slices in a baking dish for reheating.
5. Skim the fat off the juices in the pan and pour over the sliced brisket. If not using immediately, cover with plastic wrap and refrigerate. Next day, remove plastic wrap, cover the dish with foil and re-warm the brisket in a 350°F preheated oven for 30 minutes.

Makes 8-10 servings

## Tips
- *The leftover brisket, shredded with a fork and soaked in its juices, makes great sandwiches the next day.*
- *This roast freezes so well, that when reheated you cannot tell if it was made one day or two weeks ago. The secret is to save its juices and freeze it in its juice so the flavors are infused in the meat.*

# Braised Short Ribs

*A flavorful dish you'll find satisfying particularly on a chili night. It is wonderful to come home after a day of work or running errands knowing that a bubbly comfort meal is waiting for you. Cooking slowly with low heat ensures tender and juicy meat..*

## Ingredients
4 lbs short ribs without bones
2 Tbsp tomato paste
Salt and Pepper
¾ cup flour for dredging
2 Tbsp vegetable oil
1 onion chopped
2 cloves crushed garlic
¾ cup red wine
1 can of beef broth
2 tsp cumin (optional)
½ tsp red pepper flakes
3 carrots cut into 2-inch pieces
2 celery stalks cut into 2-inch pieces
8 oz fresh mushrooms (optional)
2-3 potatoes cut into 2-inch pieces
French bread for serving

## Preparation
1. Season ribs with salt and pepper. Rub with tomato paste and dredge in flour.
2. In a frying pan, heat the oil and brown the meat. Transfer the ribs to a Crock Pot.
3. In the same frying pan, sauté chopped onion and crushed garlic until onion is transparent. Add the wine and deglaze the pan. Cook until the wine is reduced to half. Add a can of beef broth and bring the liquid to a boil. Add cumin and red pepper. Pour over the meat in the Crock Pot.
4. Layer the carrots, celery, potatoes and mushrooms over the meat.
5. Cover. Cook on medium to high heat for 3-4 hours until the meat is very tender.
6. Serve with crusty French bread.

Makes 6-8 servings

## Tips
- *Leftovers taste just as good the next day.*

# 7-Bone Roast

*7-bone roast is a chuck section cut. The crosscut bone is shaped like a "7" which gives its name. My husband, Haig, claims he used to make this roast in his young bachelor days, and all his friends raved about it. Since we have been married he has promised to cook it for me one day, 45 years later I am still waiting.*

## Ingredients
4-5 lbs 7-bone roast (chuck cut)
4 cloves garlic, sliced in half
1½ tsp salt
½ tsp black pepper
2 Tbsp tomato paste
2-3 Tbsp flour
2 Tbsp vegetable shortening
1 (14 oz) can beef broth
1 lb small potatoes
½ lb carrots, peeled

## Preparation
1. With a sharp knife poke some holes in the roast and insert the garlic pieces. Salt and pepper both sides of the roast.
2. Rub both sides with tomato paste and sprinkle with flour.
3. Heat an electric skillet at 400°F, melt the shortening and sear the roast on both sides. Reduce heat to 225°F. Add beef broth, cover skillet and let the roast cook for 1 hour, basting occasionally. If needed, add more broth or water. After one hour carefully turn over the roast to the other side, add potatoes and carrots to the skillet and continue cooking for another hour until the meet is fork tender and the potatoes are done.
4. Remove the roast to a carving board, and the vegetables to a plate; cover with foil to keep warm. Reserve the juice for serving as gravy over the meat. If it is too juicy, increase the heat to reduce to desired consistency.
5. Serve the roast with the roasted potatoes and carrots on the side.

Makes 6-8 servings

## Tips
- *If you do not have an electric skillet, you can use a Dutch oven, following the above instructions.*

# Seared Beef Tenderloin with Mushroom Sauce

*An elegant meat dish that requires very little time to prepare with very successful results.
Extraordinarily easy way to impress your guests.*

## Ingredients
1¼ lb beef tenderloin
3 Tbsp butter
3 Tbsp olive oil
1 onion chopped
2 cloves crushed garlic
1 cup sliced mushrooms
1 tsp lemon juice
2 tsp Worcestershire sauce
Salt and pepper to taste
¼ tsp red pepper flakes (optional)
½ cup red wine
1 Tbsp butter
1 Tbsp olive oil
2 Tbsp chopped parsley for garnish

## Preparation
1. Cut the beef tenderloin steak into half inch slices. Set aside.
2. Heat a frying pan on the stove over medium heat. Melt the 3 Tbsp butter and 3 Tbsp olive oil. Add the onions and garlic, sauté for a few minutes. Add the sliced mushrooms, lemon juice, Worcestershire sauce, salt, pepper and red pepper. Cook stirring until the mushrooms are tender.
3. Remove from heat and set aside in a bowl. Cover to keep warm.
4. In the same frying pan, melt the remaining 1 Tbsp butter and 1 Tbsp olive oil. Cook the steaks over medium-high heat turning once , 3 minutes on each side for medium.
5. Move steaks to a plate and cover with foil to keep warm.
6. Add ½ cup of red wine to the pan drippings and deglaze. Add the pre-cooked mushroom sauce to the pan and heat it through. Pour over the steaks and serve immediately. Garnish the platter with freshly chopped parsley.

Makes 3 servings

## Tips
- *Usually when I bring home the tenderloin steaks from the store, I slice them in half and wrap individual slices in plastic wrap and freeze them. When ready to use, it thaws out quickly.*

# Individual Beef Wellington

*An elegant dish to serve to company with minimum last minute food preparation.*

## Ingredients
4 (1½-inch-thick) center cut fillet mignons
Salt and pepper to taste
1 Tbsp vegetable oil
½ lb mushrooms, chopped
1 Tbsp butter
2 Tbsp finely chopped shallot
2 tsp crushed garlic
1 Tbsp Dijon mustard
1 frozen puff pastry sheet, thawed
4 slices Parma ham
1 large egg for egg-wash

<u>Sauce</u>
1 (14 oz) can beef broth
1 Tbsp chopped shallots
1 tsp crushed garlic
5 Tbsp butter

## Preparation
1. Pat filet mignons dry and season with salt and pepper.
2. In a skillet, heat the vegetable oil and sear the filets on both sides. Set aside to cool.
3. In a heavy skillet, melt the butter and sauté the shallots and garlic. Add chopped mushrooms and cook the mushrooms over moderate heat until all the moisture is gone and they are browned. Set aside to cool.
4. On a lightly floured board roll out puff pastry sheet into 14-inch squares. Cut them into four squares.
5. Put one slice of Parma ham in the center of a square. Top with mushroom mixture. Spread a thin layer of mustard on both sides of the filet and place on top of mushrooms. Top with another layer of mushrooms and press down gently.
6. Brush egg-wash all around the edge of the puff pastry, then bring opposite corners of the pastry over filet overlapping them. Seal the seams with egg-wash. Press the other two corners over the filet and seal in the same manner. Press pastry around the filet to enclose completely. Repeat the same with the remainder of the filets.
7. Arrange beef Wellingtons on a non-stick baking pan and refrigerate for an hour before baking.
8. Preheat oven to 425°F. Brush the tops of the Wellingtons completely with the remainder of the egg-wash and bake for 25-39 minutes until pastry is golden brown. Remove from the oven and let it rest for 5 minutes before serving. Serve with the sauce.
9. <u>Prepare Sauce:</u> Use the skillet in which you browned the beef. Skim off all the fat from the pan keeping the meat juices. Add 1 tablespoon of butter and sauté the shallots and garlic. Then add the broth and over high heat reduce the broth to less than half. Remove the skillet from the heat and whisk in the remaining butter in small pieces. Season with salt and pepper.

# Beef Roulade

*This dish does take a little extra time for preparation but you can prepare it ahead of time, even a day in advance, leaving extra free time for side dish preparation. It is delicious with a great presentation.*

## Ingredients
1½ lb beef sliced ¼-inch thick
¼ cup chopped flat leaf parsley
1 small onion, finely chopped
2 cloves crushed garlic
1 tsp salt
½ tsp black pepper
2 carrots cut into strips
¾ cup flour for dredging
1 cup canned crushed tomatoes
1 cup beef broth
1 bay leaf
1 tbsp Worcestershire sauce

## Preparation
1. Pound the meat slices lightly with a mallet to even thickness.
2. Mix together chopped parsley, onion and garlic.
3. Salt and pepper the beef. Spread one tablespoon of parsley mixture on each piece of beef. Place one carrot strip at one end, roll the slices and tie with a string or reinforce with a toothpick. Repeat with the rest of the slices.
4. Dip the rolls into flour, shake excess flour and brown in a skillet in heated oil until all sides are browned.
5. Arrange roulades in a saucepan add bay leaf and Worcestershire sauce; cover with beef broth and crushed tomatoes. Bring the liquid to a boil, reduce heat and simmer for an hour or until the meat is tender.
6. Remove roulades from pan, remove the strings and/or toothpicks, arrange on a platter and spoon the gravy over it. Sprinkle with more chopped parsley. Serve with mashed potatoes (page 172) and cooked vegetables.

Makes 4 servings

## Tips
- *You can prepare the rolls early in the day and refrigerate before cooking it in the sauce.*
- *You can cook it in the sauce hours before serving, remove the strings or toothpicks, return beef rolls back into the pan and reheat before serving.*

# Beef Stroganoff

*The classic ingredients in this dish are beef, onion, mushrooms and sour cream served over noodles. The recipe is modified from the original recipe from the Greenbrier Resort restaurant in West Virginia.*

## Ingredients
1½ lb lean beef filet  
1 Tbsp paprika  
4 Tbsp olive oil  
1 medium onion, diced small  
8 oz mushrooms, sliced  
1 cup white cooking sherry  
¾ cup beef broth  
1 cup dairy sour cream  
2 tsp lemon juice  
Salt and pepper to taste  
8 oz dried wide egg noodles  
1 Tbsp butter  
1 Tbsp chopped fresh parsley  

## Preparation
1. Cut beef in ¼-inch strips; season with paprika.
2. Heat 1 tablespoon of the oil in a skillet, then sauté half of the beef very fast (4 to 5 minutes). Transfer to a bowl. Repeat with 1 more tablespoon of the oil and the remaining beef. Transfer to the bowl.
3. Add the remaining 2 tablespoons of oil to the skillet. Add the onions, mushrooms and sauté a few minutes. Transfer to the bowl.
4. Add sherry to the skillet; reduce to one-half its volume by boiling. Add beef broth and let it boil briskly (uncovered) for 5 minutes. Add tempered sour cream (see tip below), lemon juice, and salt and pepper to taste.
5. Now add the meat and mushrooms to the skillet and bring just to a boil (do not boil when meat is in the sauce otherwise the sauce will separate).
6. Cook the noodles according to the package direction. Drain. Add 1 tablespoon of butter and mix. The butter will prevent the noodles from sticking to each other.
7. Spoon the meat over cooked buttered noodles. Sprinkle with chopped parsley.

Makes 4-6 servings

## Tips
- *Temper the sour cream before adding to the hot sauce by spooning a few tablespoons of the hot sauce into the sour cream, and then stir the sour cream mixture into the skillet.*

# Skirt Steak

*This is an inexpensive cut of beef but it is very tasty and tender if prepared properly. You get the best results by grilling it outdoors on a gas or charcoal grill.*

## Ingredients
1 lb of skirt steak
½ cup of teriyaki sauce
2 Tbsp soy sauce
2 Tbsp pineapple juice

## Preparation
1. Cut the steak into three or four equal pieces. Place in a plastic bag and pour teriyaki sauce, soy sauce and pineapple juice over it. Marinate for an hour or up to 3 hours.
2. Heat the grill to medium high. Place the steaks on the grill and grill 2-3 minutes on each side.
3. Serve with twice-baked potatoes (page 173).

Makes 2-3 servings

## Tips
- *Slice across the grain into strips and serve on a salad for a luncheon entrée.*

# Skirt Steak Fajita

*The skirt steak is full of flavor. When marinated, it is the perfect cut for fajitas   Next time you are planning a Mexican Fiesta, consider making this dish.  You will not regret it.*

## Ingredients
¼ cup lime or lemon juice
1 Tbsp balsamic vinegar
1 Tbsp soy sauce
2 Tbsp vegetable oil
1 clove crushed garlic
1 tsp salt
1 tsp black pepper
2 lb skirt steak
2 Tbsp vegetable oil for grilling
2 large onions, sliced thin
2 bell peppers, sliced thin
2 jalapeño peppers, sliced thin
1 cup fresh cilantro leaves
1 cup prepared guacamole
   (page 23))
15-18 flour tortillas

## Preparation
1. Stir together lime juice, balsamic vinegar, soy sauce, oil, garlic, salt and pepper in a shallow dish.
2. Cut the skirt steak into 4-5 inch pieces and marinate at room temperature for 20 minutes.
3. In a heavy skillet, pan grill sliced onions with 1 tablespoon vegetable oil. Remove to serving plate.
4. In the same skillet, pan grill sliced peppers like the onions. Transfer to serving plate.
5. In the same skillet, grill the skirt steaks 6 to 10 minutes for medium rare. Transfer to cutting board and let stand 5 minutes before slicing diagonally into thin slices. Remove to serving plate.
6. Add cilantro, guacamole, and lemon wedges to the serving plate and serve with flour tortillas. Let guests build their own fajita. Arrange meat on the tortilla, add choice of topping, roll up and enjoy.

Makes 6 serving

## Tips
- *To heat tortillas, I place them in a cloth napkin and microwave for 20-25 seconds. The heated tortillas come out soft and warm as if they were just baked.*
- *If pressed by time, use store bought guacamole.*

# Korean Barbeque Ribs

*This dish known as 'Kalbi' is the signature dish of Korean cuisine. These are meaty ribs, marinated in a sweet and savory marinade and barbequed. My Korean friend Maggie taught me how to prepare this dish. Traditionally, these ribs are served with steamed rice and kimchi.*

## Ingredients
4 lbs Korean-style short ribs
3 Tbsp vegetable oil for grilling
½ cup toasted crushed sesame seeds
Steamed rice
1 (15 0z) jar Kimchi

### Marinade
1½ cups lite soy sauce
1/3 cup sugar
3 Tbsp sesame oil
7-8 cloves of garlic, crushed
1 Tbsp toasted crushed sesame seeds
4 green onions, sliced thin

## Preparation
1. Trim the excess fat and remove the silver skin.
2. Prepare the marinade by mixing soy sauce, sugar, sesame oil and garlic until the sugar is dissolved. Mix in green onions.
3. Put short ribs in one or two sealable freezer bags and pour marinade into the bags. Turn bags around several times to ensure all meat is covered with the marinade and refrigerate. Marinate for at least 4 hours, preferably overnight, turning the bags several times to ensure even marinating.
4. Heat the grill to medium-high before grilling the ribs. Brush the grill with oil to prevent the ribs from sticking to the grill. Remove the meat from the marinade and place on the grill turning them 2-3 times until the ribs are browned on both sides. This takes approximately 6-8 minutes.
5. Sprinkle tops with toasted sesame seeds. Serve with, steamed rice and kimchi.

Makes 4 servings

## Tips
- *Kimchi is spicy fermented cabbage. You can buy them in Asian markets.*
- *Korean style short ribs can be found in Asian markets. The cut is different than other ribs. It is cut across the bone. Because of their thin cut the meat cooks faster than other ribs so it requires constant attention.*
- *Korean style short ribs are also excellent prepared in a crock pot. The meat simply falls off the bones.*
- *If grilled without the bones, you can serve lettuce leaves so that the meat can be wrapped in the lettuce leaves with a little rice and kimchi and eaten like a taco.*

# Lamb Chops with String Beans

*The string bean stew called 'yakhnit loubieh' is a typical Lebanese dish served with rice. It is made with chunks of lamb meat. I use shoulder lamb chops because they are very flavorful, and a short simmer time makes the meat very tender.*

## Ingredients
1 lb string beans
1 lb shoulder cut lamb chops
2 Tbsp vegetable oil
1 chopped onion
1 (14 oz) can chopped tomatoes, or 4 ripe tomatoes peeled and chopped
2 cups water
1½ tsp salt
½ tsp pepper

## Preparation
1. Cut off the stems from the beans, wash and set aside. Cut any long ones in half.
2. Sauté the chops in the oil until they are brown. Add the chopped onion and continue sautéing until they become transparent and start changing color. Add the string beans and sauté a few minutes longer until they start changing color. (They turn darker green)
3. Add tomatoes, water, salt and pepper to taste. Bring to a boil. Reduce heat and let it simmer until the chops and the beans are tender. Approximately 30-35 minutes. Turn off heat.
4. Serve with rice pilaf (page 178).

Makes 4 servings

## Tips
- You can use 1 or 2 russet potatoes cut into quarters and drop in the pot to cook with the meat and beans.
- If you use potatoes, you do not need the rice pilaf. Just serve the dish with crusty bread.

# Lamb Stew with Green Peas

*Served with rice pilaf, this stew is a nutritionally balanced meal.*

## Ingredients
1 Tbsp vegetable oil
1 lb cubes of lamb or beef
1 medium onion, chopped
2 cloves garlic, sliced
1 (14.5 oz) can chopped tomatoes
   or 2 cups chopped fresh tomatoes
2 cups water
1 tsp salt
¼ tsp pepper
1 (16 oz) pkg frozen peas

## Preparation
1. Heat the oil in a pan and sauté the meat. Add chopped onion and garlic and sauté until onions are wilted and start changing color.
2. Add chopped tomatoes, water, salt and pepper and bring to a boil. Lower the heat and simmer until the meat is cooked. Approximately, 30-45 minutes.
3. Add frozen peas and bring to a boil and cook for 5 more minutes until peas are cooked. Turn off heat and adjust seasoning.
4. Serve with rice pilaf (page 178).

Makes 3-4 servings

## Tips
- *Can be prepared with fresh peas when they are in season but frozen peas work just as well.*
- *You can use 1 or 2 russet potatoes cut into quarters and drop in the pot to cook with the meat and peas.*
- *If you use potatoes, you do not need the rice pilaf. Just serve the dish with crusty bread.*

# Lamb Stew with Okra

*Lamb stews with vegetables are served regularly in Middle Eastern families.
They are usually served with rice pilaf*

## Ingredients
2 lbs okra
3 Tbsp vegetable oil
1 lb cubes of lamb or beef
1 medium onion, chopped
2 cloves garlic, sliced
1 (14.5 oz) can chopped tomatoes or,
　　2 cups chopped fresh tomatoes
1 tsp salt
¼ tsp pepper
2 cups water
2 tsp lemon juice

## Preparation
1. Remove the stem and hard caps of the okra by cutting them in a cone shape at their natural slant angle. Wash and drain the okra in a colander and spread them on a kitchen towel to dry completely.
2. Heat 2 tablespoons oil in a pan and sauté the okra for 2 minutes in two or three batches until they are bright green and crisp. Do not let them start browning. Set aside.
3. Heat remaining 1 tablespoon oil in a 4-quart pan and sauté the meat. Add chopped onion and garlic and sauté until they are wilted and start changing color.
4. Add chopped tomatoes, water, lemon juice, salt and pepper and bring to boil. Lower the heat and simmer
until the meat is cooked. Approximately 30-45 minutes.
5. Add sautéed okra and lemon juice, bring to a boil. Reduce the heat and cook until the okras are cooked. Turn off heat.
6. Serve with rice pilaf (page 178).

Makes 3-4 servings

## Tips
- *If you eliminate the meat, it makes a nice vegetarian meal.*

# Lamb Shish Kebab

*The most popular Middle Eastern dish - chunks of lamb marinated and barbecued on skewers with superb taste and great presentation. Add more color to this dish by using a variety of colored pepper - red, yellow, green - skewered in-between the lamb pieces.
Using different marinades gives variety to this dish.*

## Ingredients
1 (4-5) lb leg of lamb
2 large onions, sliced thin
¼ cup olive oil
2 tsp salt
½ tsp black pepper
½ tsp red pepper flakes
2 Tbsp Worcestershire sauce
2 Tbsp tomato paste
1 cup red wine

## Preparation
1. Have the butcher bone the leg of lamb and remove all visible outside fat. Cube the meat into 2-inch pieces, removing all fat and gristle. Use only solid lean pieces for the kebab.
2. Place cubed leg of lamb in a bowl. Add onions, oil, salt, pepper, red pepper flakes, Worcestershire sauce, tomato paste, and wine. Mix, cover and refrigerate the meat overnight.
3. Skewer the lamb cubes on bamboo or metal skewers. If using bamboo skewers, soak them in water before skewering the meat. It will prevent the skewers from burning on the grill.
4. Barbecue or grill on medium high heat turning frequently to cook the meat evenly for about 15-20 minutes until the outside is cooked and crusty. Do not overcook. Rice pilaf (page 178) or Bulgur pilaf (page 177) will be the best accompaniment to this dish.

Makes 4-6 servings

## Tips
- *Marinating the meat overnight makes it more flavorful. You may use a plastic bag to marinate meat.. It is easy to flip over the bag to evenly marinate the meat. Cleanup is easy; just toss the bag.*
- *You may want to alternate some button mushrooms and pieces of red and green peppers between the meat cubes. If using quartered onions skewer them separately; they take longer to cook.*
- *For a variety of flavors, you may use a different marinade that will give you the flavors of the Orient, or India. (See recipes under Sauces).*

# Lule Kebab

*Also known as Kafta Kebab, this dish is ground lamb combined with onion, parsley and spices; skewered and grilled.*

## Ingredients
2 lbs ground lamb
½ cup fresh white bread crumbs
½ cup finely chopped onion
½ cup minced parsley
2 Tbsp tomato paste
1 tsp allspice
1¼ tsp salt
½ tsp ground black pepper
1 tsp Aleppo red pepper flakes

## Preparation
1. Soak bread crumbs with water, and then gently squeeze to remove excess water.
2. Pulse onion in food processor until minced, add parsley and pulse until finely chopped.
3. In a mixing bowl, mix the meat with onion, parsley, tomato paste, soaked bread crumbs and spices.  Do not over mix.
4. Divide into 20 portions 1/4-1/3 cup each.  Form into a ball, then roll into 4-5 inch long cigar shapes.  Slide a skewer lengthwise through center of each; two per skewer.
5. Grill over medium high heat turning often until just cooked through; approximately 7 minutes.
6. Serve with Rice pilaf (page 178) or Bulgur pilaf (page 177).

Makes 4-6 servings

## Tips
- *For Lule Kebab, I personally prefer using half and half lamb and beef mixed together.*
- *If using wooden skewers, soak them in water for at least 30 minutes before skewering the meat to prevent burning, or wrap the tips of each wooden skewer with aluminum foil.*

# Greek Style Leg of Lamb Roast

*Cutting the leg of lamb into serving pieces before roasting makes serving this dish much easier.
Marinating overnight tenderizes the meat and simplifies preparation for the next day.*

## Ingredients
1 leg of lamb roast
Salt and pepper to taste
1½ tsp crushed oregano
6-8 cloves of garlic
1 bay leaf
1 stalk celery, chopped
1 large onion, sliced
1 large tomato, diced
3 Tbsp lemon juice
¾ cup red wine
3 Tbsp butter

## Preparation
1. Preheat oven to 425°F before roasting.
2. Cut the lamb into serving size pieces and trim off all the fat.
3. Mix the meat with salt and pepper and oregano. Pile into a mound in a roasting pan. (Piling the meet will keep the meat moist while roasting)
4. Stick garlic pieces and bay leaf in between the cut up pieces. Sprinkle top with chopped celery, sliced onion and tomatoes. Pour the wine and lemon juice over the mound.
5. Cover the pan and refrigerate overnight to marinate the lamb.
6. Before roasting dot with 2-3 tablespoons of butter. Roast uncovered for 20-25 minutes, then reduce the heat to 325°F. Cover the pan and roast for 3 hours basting the meat occasionally to keep moist.
7. Discard the vegetables before serving and serve with roasted potatoes (page 174).

Makes 6 servings

## Tips
- *Have the butcher bone the leg of lamb to make your work easier.*
- *If you wish to roast the potatoes with the lamb, during the last hour of roasting arrange the potatoes around the roast and continue roasting.*

# Leg of Lamb Roast

*Lamb meat has a distinct flavor and prepared with the proper spices, it is sure to please your guests. It is delicious done either medium or well. Because of the shape of the leg of lamb, remember when roasting to take into consideration that even if the thick center is cooked rare, the thinner edges will be well done.*

## Ingredients
1 (5-6 lb) leg of lamb roast
1½ tsp crushed oregano
Salt and pepper to taste
3-4 cloves of garlic cut into long slivers
2 cups red wine
3 Tbsp butter or olive oil
¼ cup water for the sauce

## Preparation
1. Preheat oven to 450°F before roasting.
2. Have the butcher remove the fell and trim some of the fat from the leg of lamb.
3. Rub the leg with crushed oregano, salt and pepper. Make small slits near the bone and insert slivers of garlic in them. Pour 2 cups of red wine over it. Drizzle with melted butter or olive oil. Let the lamb stand at room temperature for 3-4 hours.
4. Roast the lamb in a preheated hot oven for 15 minutes, reduce the heat to 350°F and continue roasting, basting frequently with the pan juices and butter.
   <u>Roasting guideline</u>: 15 minutes per pound for rare meat, or inner temperature 125°F; for medium rare inner temperature 130°F; for medium 135°F, for well done, cook longer.
5. Transfer the lamb to a plate and let it rest for 10 minutes before carving. Meanwhile, skim the fat from the pan juices, add ¼ cup water to the pan and cook the liquid over moderate heat, scraping the brown bits on the bottom and sides of the pan.
6. Serve the pan juices with the roast. Serve with roasted potatoes (page 174) and mint jelly (page 343).

Makes 6-8 servings

## Tips
- *Lamb meat is very tender when it is roasted to medium or medium rare.*
- *You can also roast the potatoes in the same pan during the last one hour of roasting time.*
- *You can also use store bought mint jelly.*

# Parsley Crusted Rack of Lamb
*This delicious lamb dinner is a 30-minute masterpiece. Easy to prepare and elegant to present.*

## Ingredients
2 racks of lamb
   (about 1½ lb each)
2 slices of white bread
1 tsp minced garlic
½ cup minced fresh parsley
Salt and pepper to taste
1 tsp Dijon mustard
2 Tbsp olive oil

## Preparation
1. Preheat oven to 475°F before baking.
2. Remove crust from bread and, in a food processor, pulse bread slices until crumbs are formed. Add minced garlic and minced parsley mix well and set aside.
3. Trim lamb rack of excess fat, and cut halfway down the bones between chops. This allows the meat to get crisper at the edges of each chop. Season with salt and pepper.
4. In a large skillet over high heat, heat the olive oil, add lamb rack and cook for 3 minutes until brown on all sides. Brush the mustard all over the rack, press crumb mixture on all sides and place, bone side up, in a roasting pan. Roast for 20 minutes, or until meat thermometer inserted in the meatiest parts reads 130°F for medium rare or 135°F for medium.
5. Remove from oven and let sit for 5-10 minutes to let the juices distribute in the meat. Slice in-between the bones and serve with mashed potatoes and cooked vegetables.

Makes 4 servings

# Stuffed Kibbeh

*This is virtually the national dish of Lebanon - one of the most labor intensive dishes. Well worth the effort as it is the healthiest and most delicious dish. Kibbehs can be served in a variety of ways.*

## Ingredients

<u>Meat Filling</u>
1 lb ground lamb or beef
½ cup pine nuts
3 large onions, chopped
1 tsp salt
½ tsp red pepper
½ tsp allspice
½ tsp cumin
½ tsp black pepper
¼ cup vegetable oil plus 2 Tbsp butter

<u>Kibbeh</u>
2 cups fine cracked wheat (Bulgur #1)
1 Tbsp red pepper paste
1 lb lean finely ground lamb or beef
1 Tbsp minced onion or onion juice
½ tsp cumin
Salt and pepper to taste
1½ cup water plus more if needed
Lemon wedges for serving

## Preparation

1. *Preparing filling*: In a frying pan, with a touch of oil, sauté the pine nuts until they start turning pink. Remove from pan and set aside.
2. In the same pan, wilt the chopped onions until they become transparent. Add the ground meat.
3. Add the salt and cook the meat until it has changed color and the liquid is absorbed.
4. Add the remaining spices and ¼ cup vegetable oil and 2 tablespoons butter. Stir for a few minutes. Let the flavors blend. Add pine nuts. Mix and adjust seasoning. Set aside to cool.
5. *Preparing Kibbeh*: In a mixing bowl, using ½ cup water, wet the bulgur to soften. Let soak for 10 minutes. Add the pepper paste and knead so the bulgur takes the pepper color.
6. Add the meat, onion juice, and cumin, salt and pepper, and knead by hand adding water as needed to make a smooth but sticky and pliable mixture. Dip hands in water to facilitate kneading. (A food processor could be used to obtain the same texture.)
7. Take a handful of mixture at a time, and divide into walnut size pieces.
8. Take each walnut size kibbeh into you left palm, and with the right hand forefinger make a hole in the center and gradually enlarge the hole by rotating kibbeh in you palm and thinning its walls. Fill the center with a teaspoon of filling and bring the opening together, closing over the filling. Roll in palm of your hands and shape into long pointed oval shapes. (They will look like mini footballs). At this point, if you wish, you can freeze them.
9. Deep fry kibbehs in vegetable oil until golden and crispy. Drain on paper towel.
10. Serve with lemon wedges as an appetizer or side dish. As a light entrée, serve with a tomato and cucumber salad (page 79), or cold yogurt soup (page 56).

Makes 36-40 kibbehs

## Tips

- *To bake the kibbehs, brush them with oil and arrange on a greased tray. Bake in a 350° F preheated oven until golden brown, turning them so they brown evenly.*
- *Kibbehs can be fried an hour in advance and kept warm.*

# Kibbeh be Saniyeh

*This is a very popular Middle Eastern dish. It is like the fried Kibbehs but layered and baked in a tray.*

## Ingredients

<u>Meat Filling</u>
½ cup pine nuts
1½ ground lamb or beef
2 cups chopped onion
1½ tsp salt
½ tsp cumin
2/3 tsp allspice
½ tsp red pepper
½ tsp black pepper
¼ cup vegetable oil plus 2 Tbsp butter
<u>Kibbeh</u>
3 cups fine cracked wheat (Bulgur #1)
1½ Tbsp red pepper paste
1½ lb finely ground lamb or beef
1 Tbsp onion juice or grated onion
1 tsp salt
½ tsp black pepper
¼ cup vegetable oil
¼ cup water

## Preparation

1. <u>Preparing filling:</u> In a frying pan with a touch of oil, sauté the pine nuts until they start to brown. Remove from pan and aside.
2. In the same pan wilt the chopped onions until they become transparent. Add the ground meat.
3. Add the salt and cook the meat stirring occasionally until all the released liquid is absorbed.
4. Add the remaining spices and ¼ cup vegetable oil and 2 tablespoons butter. Stir for a few minutes and let the flavors blend. Add the pine nuts. Mix together and adjust seasoning. Set aside to cool.
5. <u>Preparing Kibbeh:</u> In a mixing bowl using 1 cup water soak bulgur for 10 minutes.
6. Add the pepper paste and knead so the bulgur takes the pepper color.
7. Add the meat, onion juice, cumin, salt and pepper, and knead by hand adding water as needed to make a smooth but sticky and pliable mixture. Dip hands in water to facilitate kneading. (A food processor could be used to obtain the same texture.)
8. Grease the bottom of 8x12-inch baking pan or a large round pan. Use half of the kibbeh mixture and flatten it on the bottom of the pan 1/3 - ½ inch thick, wetting your hands occasionally to smooth the kibbeh. Spread the meat filling evenly over the kibbeh. Top with the remainder of the kibbeh and smooth the top. With a sharp knife, score the top into diamond shapes or any desired shape.
9. Drizzle with ¼ cup vegetable oil and ¼ cup water to keep it moist while baking. Bake in a preheated 375°F oven until the top starts browning (approximately 45-50 minutes).
10. Serve with tomato and cucumber salad (page 79) and/or yogurt tzatsiki (page 56).

Makes 8-10 servings

## Tips

- *May be served hot or cold.*
- *Freezes very well. First wrap in plastic wrap, then in foil.*

# Kafta in a Tray

*This dish is ground meat flattened in a tray, topped with potatoes and tomato slices, and then baked.*

## Ingredients
1 lb ground lamb
1 lb ground beef
½ cup fresh bread crumbs
½ cup minced parsley
½ cup finely chopped onion
1¼ tsp salt
½ tsp ground black pepper
3-4 red potatoes
3-4 firm tomatoes

## Preparation
1. Mix together the meat, bread crumbs, parsley, onion and spices.
2. Press the meat mixture in a non-stick baking pan to a ¾-inch thickness. Smooth the top by wetting hands with water to facilitate handling the meat.
3. Cut the potatoes like French fries. Parboil for 5 minutes. Arrange on top of the meat in the tray.
4. Slice the tomatoes into ¼ inch round slices and arrange them on top of the potatoes. Sprinkle with salt and black pepper and drizzle with a tablespoon of vegetable oil.
5. Bake in 350°F preheated oven for approximately 45 minutes or until the meat is cooked.

Makes 4-5 servings

## Tips
- *If you wish you may use only ground lamb or only ground beef.*
- *I often assemble Kafta in 2 smaller trays. Freeze one unbaked tray for later use.*

# Dolma and Sarma

*Another Middle Eastern dish. Preparation is time consuming but easy - well worth the effort. A mixture of different vegetables stuffed with a mixture of rice and ground meat makes this dish very special and flavorful. The Greeks call only stuffed grape leaves, 'Dolmades'; but the Armenians call the grape leaves Sarma, and the stuffed vegetables Dolma. My sister, Renee taught me how to make this dish.*

## Ingredients
9 small Japanese eggplants
6 squash
3 red peppers
3 medium size tomatoes
30 preserved grape leaves,
　rinsed and squeezed dry

*Stuffing Mixture*
2 cups rice
2¼ lb ground beef or lamb
1 onion, chopped
1 bunch parsley, chopped fine
½ bunch mint, chopped fine
3 tomatoes, chopped
¼ cup tomato paste
2 Tbsp green pepper, chopped
2½ tsp salt (adjust salt to your taste)
1 tsp red pepper flakes
½ tsp allspice
½ tsp black pepper

*Cooking Juice*
1 cup tomato juice
3 cups water
4 tsp lemon juice
2 Tbsp vegetable oil or butter

## Preparation
1. Cut off the stem ends of the vegetables. With a round potato peeler scoop out the insides of the vegetables. Rinse them and set aside.
2. *Prepare filling:* Combine the rice, meat, spices, chopped onion, parsley, mint, tomato, and tomato paste. Adjust seasoning.
3. Stuff the vegetables with the mixture and line them in a deep saucepan or Dutch oven.
4. Place one tablespoon of filling on each grape leaf at the stem end. Fold over the sides. Starting from the stem end, roll to enclose the filling. It will look like a sausage. Arrange them on top of the stuffed vegetables in the pan.
5. Invert a plate over the stuffed grape leaves so they stay in place while cooking.
6. Bring the cooking juice to boil and pour over Dolmas and Sarmas. Cook approximately 45 minutes until done. Drain liquid to prevent the vegetables from getting soggy.

Makes 10-12 servings

## Tips
- *Cooking stuffed vegetables and grape leaves together adds more flavor to the dish.*
- *This dish freezes very well. To obtain best results in reheating leftovers, steam them frozen.*
- *Preserved grape leaves are sold in Middle Eastern grocery stores. They are sold in jars in the brine.*

# Eggplants Stuffed with Meat

*The Arabic name for this dish is 'Sheikh el-Mehshi' which translates as 'the lord of stuffed vegetables'. The cooked eggplants need extra care transferring to a serving plate in order to keep their shapes. It has an attractive presentation and is usually served with plain rice pilaf.
I learned how to prepare this dish from my mother.*

## Ingredients

10-12 small thin eggplants (each about 3-4 inches long)
¼ cup vegetable oil
1 ½ lb ripe tomatoes peeled and diced
¼ tsp allspice
Pinch of black pepper
½ tsp salt

*Meat Filling*
3 Tbsp butter
1/3 cup pine nuts
1 medium onion, diced
½ lb ground lamb or beef
¼ tsp cinnamon
½ tsp allspice
¼ tsp black pepper
1 tsp salt

## Preparation

1. **Preparing filling**: In a skillet over medium high heat, sauté pine nuts until golden brown. With a slotted spoon, remove to a dish.
2. In the same skillet sauté diced onion until it starts browning. Add the ground meat and 1 teaspoon salt to it and continue sautéing until the meat turns brown, breaking the lumps with a wooden spoon. Add cinnamon, allspice and black pepper. Adjust seasoning if necessary, and add the pine nuts. Mix well and set aside the filling.
3. **Preparing eggplants**: Cut the stalk from the eggplants and trim the cap leaving ½-inch of cap. Peel off ½-inch strips of the skin lengthwise at intervals to give the eggplant a striped look.
4. In a skillet, pour ¼ cup of vegetable oil and fry the eggplants until all sides are browned. Carefully remove them with a slotted spatula to a paper towel lined pan to drain.
5. Place the eggplants in a baking dish. With a small knife cut a deep slit along one side of the eggplants and fill with 1-2 tablespoons of meat filling.
6. Season diced tomatoes with cinnamon, allspice, salt and pepper and spread evenly over the stuffed eggplants.
7. Preheat oven to 350°F and bake for 40 minutes until tomatoes are cooked and most of the liquid released by the tomatoes is evaporated.
8. With a spatula, carefully transfer eggplants to a serving plate and serve hot with plain rice pilaf.

Makes 5-6 servings

## Tips

- *This dish can be prepared up to step 6, up to a day in advance. Cover and refrigerate. Bake before serving. Also the leftovers reheat beautifully.*

# Squash Stuffed with Meat

*The Arabic name for this dish is 'Sheikh el-Mehshi' which translates as 'the lord of stuffed vegetables'. It has an attractive presentation and is usually served with plain rice pilaf.*

## Ingredients

10-12 small squash (the ones with pale green color) or zucchini
¼ cup vegetable oil
1½ lb ripe tomatoes peeled and diced or (15 oz) canned diced tomatoes
¼ tsp allspice
¼ tsp salt
1/8 tsp black pepper

### Meat Filling
3 Tbsp butter
1/3 cup pine nuts
1 medium size onion, diced
½ lb ground lamb or beef
¾ tsp salt
1/8 tsp cinnamon
¼ tsp allspice
¼ tsp black pepper

## Preparation

1. *Preparing filling:* In a skillet over medium heat, sauté pine nuts until golden brown. With a slotted spoon remove from the frying pan to a dish.
2. In the same skillet sauté diced onion until it starts browning. Add the ground meat and ¾ teaspoon salt to it and continue sautéing until the meat turns brown, breaking the lumps with a wooden spoon. Add cinnamon, allspice and black pepper. Adjust seasoning if necessary, and add the pine nuts. Mix well and set aside the filling.
3. *Preparing squash:* Cut the stems off the squash and discard. Using an apple corer or a melon ball maker, remove the pulps.
4. In a skillet pour ¼ cup of vegetable oil and fry the squash until all sides are barely browned. Carefully remove them with a slotted spatula to a pan lined with paper towel to drain.
5. Place the squash in a baking dish. Fill the cavities with the meat filling.
6. Season diced tomatoes with allspice, salt and pepper and spread evenly over the stuffed squash.
7. Preheat oven to 350°F and bake for 45-60 minutes until tomatoes are cooked and most of the liquid released by the tomatoes is evaporated, occasionally basting the squash.
8. With a spatula, carefully transfer squash to a serving plate. I like to serve it hot with plain basmati rice pilaf (page 179).

Makes 5-6 servings

## Tips

- *This dish can be prepared up to step 6, up to a day in advance. Cover and refrigerate. Bake before serving. Also the leftover reheat beautifully.*
- *The pale green color, short and round squash are usually found in Middle Eastern produce stores.*

# Pork Kebab

*This dish, known as Pork Souvlaki in Greece, is grilled on skewers and served with finely chopped Greek salad-type salsa that makes a great accompaniment.*

## Ingredients
2 lbs pork tenderloin cut into 1½-inch cubes
1 lime, juiced
1 lemon, juiced
¼ cup Extra-virgin olive oil
2 cloves crushed garlic
1 tsp salt
2 tsp dried oregano
1 tsp dried thyme
½ tsp cayenne pepper
½ tsp black pepper

## Preparation
1. To prepare the marinade, combine all the ingredients except the pork.
2. Put the pork in a plastic bag, and pour the marinade over it. Marinate the pork overnight.
3. Thread the meat on skewers leaving a little space between the cubes, so they cook thoroughly.
4. Lightly oil the grill, and grill the pork, turning occasionally, until the meat is cooked.
5. Serve the pork immediately over rice, with some mixed grilled vegetables and the Mediterranean Salsa (page 198).

Makes 4-5 servings

## Tips
- *For a quick meal, use pre-marinated pork roast, and cut into cubes, then grill.*
- *For a short cut, use any commercially prepared pork marinades.*
- *If you prefer non-Greek spices, use mango salsa, or yogurt sauce, or any other preferred salsa with the pork.*

# Slow Cooker Pork Roast

*The combination of ingredients may seem unusual but somehow it works well. This is a family pleasing meal. Spend a carefree day while your crock pot does the cooking for you.*

## Ingredients
2 Tbsp olive oil
2-3 lbs pork tenderloin
2 baking potatoes cut into 1-inch slices (optional)
1 medium size onion, diced
2 cloves garlic, diced
2 tsp dried thyme
2 cups chicken stock
2 Tbsp corn starch
¼ cup red wine vinegar
¼ cup sugar
½ cup port or sherry wine
1 cup pitted prunes
2 pears, cored and sliced into 1-inch slices

## Preparation
1. Heat the oil in a large skillet over medium high heat. Season the pork with salt and pepper and brown on all sides. Place browned pork roast in the slow cooker. Top with sliced potatoes.
2. Add chopped onion and garlic to the skillet. Cook and stir over medium heat for 2-3 minutes. Add thyme. Pour the onion mixture over the roast in the slow cooker.
3. In a small mixing bowl, mix ¼ cup of chicken broth with cornstarch; set aside.
4. In the same skillet in which the onion and garlic were cooked, combine vinegar and sugar and cook stirring constantly until the mixture thickens to syrup consistency. Add the wine and cook 1 minute more. Add the remaining chicken broth and the cornstarch mixture. Whisk until smooth and slightly thickened. Pour into the slow cooker.
5. Cover, cook on LOW for 8 hours, or HIGH for 4 hours. During the last 30 minutes of cooking, add prunes and pears.
6. If you have not used potatoes, then serve the roast with mashed potatoes or rice, and crusty French bread to dunk in the gravy.

Makes 4 to 6 servings

## Tips
- *Special Corn Bread (page 234) makes a good accompaniment served with this roast.*

# Barbequed Pork Ribs

*For this dish, I use baby back ribs. The ribs are smaller and the meat is more tender. Instead of using a rub and barbequing for a long time, which dries out the meat, I first boil the ribs until the meat is tender and then marinate it overnight. The next day barbecue for only 12-15 minutes.*

## Ingredients
1 whole rack of baby back ribs (about 3-4 lbs)
1 large onion, cut into quarters
1 tsp salt
1 tsp black pepper

### Barbecue Sauce
2 tsp olive oil
1 Tbsp minced garlic
¾ cup ketchup
¾ cup chili sauce
¼ cup cider vinegar
2 Tbsp Worcestershire sauce
½ tsp cayenne pepper
1 tsp dry mustard
¼ cup brown sugar
¼ cup orange juice
2 tsp grated orange rind

## Preparation
1. Place ribs, onion, salt and pepper in a large pot. Cover with water and bring to a boil, reduce heat, cover and simmer for one hour or until the meat is tender.
2. *Prepare sauce:* Heat the oil in a saucepan and sauté crushed garlic until fragrant. Add remaining ingredients; bring to a boil and cook for 14-18 minutes, stirring often to prevent sticking, until the sauce thickens. Remove from heat and let it cool.
3. Place boiled ribs in a shallow pan. Brush half of the sauce on both sides. Cover and refrigerate overnight.
4. Heat outdoor grill or broiler. Grill ribs 5 inches from heat source for 12-15 minutes, basting with the remaining sauce a few times, and turning ribs over occasionally to prevent burning until they have reached the right charred look.
5. Cut rack into individual ribs.

Makes 3-4 servings

## Tips
- *If you don't have a pot large enough to hold a whole rack, cut it into two or three pieces to fit it into the pot that you are using.*

# Veal Sticks

*This dish is my husband's very favorite dish. It reminds him of his youth when his mother used to make them. This was my mother-in-law's recipe.*

## Ingredients
1 lb veal tenderloin cut into 1-inch cubes
2/3 tsp salt
¼ tsp black pepper
2 eggs
½ cups flour
¾ cup seasoned bread crumbs
1/3 cup vegetable oil for frying

## Preparation
1. Season veal cubes with salt and pepper.
2. Skewer the veal on 5-6-inch long wooden skewers.
3. Put bread crumbs in a shallow dish, in a second dish put the flour, and in a third dish beat the eggs with one tablespoon of water and set aside.
4. Dredge skewered veal with flour, then dip in the egg-wash. Coat with the bread crumbs and place them on a tray. Let dry on a tray for 20-30 minutes. (This will help the bread crumb coating to adhere well to the veal).
5. In a large skillet, heat the oil on medium high heat and fry the veal sticks turning them to brown on all sides. Drain on a paper towel.
6. Serve with mashed potatoes (page 172) or butternut squash risotto (page 184).

Makes 2-3 servings

# Wiener Schnitzel

*Wiener Schnitzel also known as "Viennese cutlet" is the most popular dish in Austria. This dish is easy and very fast to prepare any night of the week.*

## Ingredients
4 veal cutlets (4 oz each)
Salt and pepper to taste
1 cup bread crumbs
½ cup flour
2 eggs
1 Tbsp water
4 Tbsp butter
¼ cup vegetable oil

## Preparation
1. Put bread crumbs in a shallow dish, in a second dish put the flour, and in a third dish beat the eggs with one tablespoon of water and set aside.
2. Place the cutlets between two sheets of waxed paper and pound them thin to ¼-inch thickness then season them with salt and pepper.
3. Working with one cutlet at a time dredge the cutlet in flour, shaking off the excess flour; dip it in egg and let the excess egg drip off of it; then coat with the bread crumbs. Lay them on a wire rack to dry for 20-30 minutes. (This will help the bread crumb coating to adhere well to the veal).
4. In a 10-12 inch skillet, heat the oil and butter over medium-high heat. Lay cutlets in the hot oil without overlapping them (probably two at a time) and cook 1-1½ minute per side until the crust turns golden brown. Drain on paper towels.
5. Serve immediately with lemon wedges and your favorite side dishes.

Makes 4 servings

# Poultry

## Grilled Chicken Kebab

*This dish is known as "Shish Tawouk" in the Middle Eastern countries. Grilling on outdoor grills gives the tastiest results. Great for summertime barbequing. To ensure best results, try to cube each piece of chicken the same size so it cooks evenly.*

### Ingredients
2 lbs breast of chicken, cut into cubes
¾ cup mayonnaise
2 Tbsp cream
1 Tbsp white vinegar
2 Tbsp lemon juice
3-4 cloves garlic, crushed
2 Tbsp grated onion
1 Tbsp mustard
1 Tbsp tomato paste
1½ tsp salt
½ tsp black pepper

### Preparation
1. Mix all the ingredients in a bowl, except the chicken. Add the chicken, cover the bowl and let the chicken marinate overnight.
2. Skewer the chicken on either bamboo or metal skewers; if bamboo skewers, soak them in water for at least half an hour so they don't burn while grilling.
3. Preheat the grill or broiler. Grill the chicken 15-20 minutes until cooked, turning the skewers to get even cooking.
4. Serve with Rice pilaf (page 178) or Bulgur pilaf (page 177) and lemon wedges.

Makes 4-6 servings

### Tips
- *The tomato paste helps the chicken brown nicely and the white vinegar and grated onion tenderize the meat.*
- *For variety, you can add Italian sausage sliced ¾-inch thick and slightly browned, and mushrooms simmered one minute in salted boiled water. When skewering, alternate chicken pieces with sausage and mushrooms. Grill as above.*

# Chicken Tikka

*This is one of the most popular Indian dishes. A very tasty dish that is easy to prepare. The chicken takes its color from the spices, mostly from turmeric.*

## Ingredients

1½ lb boneless and skinless chicken, cubed
1 tsp grated fresh ginger
1 Tbsp grated onion
1 tsp crushed garlic
1 tsp chili powder
¼ tsp ground turmeric
1½ tsp salt
½ tsp black pepper
2/3 cup plain yogurt
¼ cup lemon juice
1 Tbsp white vinegar
1½ Tbsp vegetable oil
1 Tbsp chopped fresh cilantro

## Preparation

1. Mix all the ingredients in a bowl, except chicken. Add the chicken, mix, cover the bowl and let the chicken marinate at least two hours. You can also marinate it overnight.
2. Skewer the chicken on either bamboo or metal skewers; if bamboo skewers, soak them in water for at least half an hour so they don't burn while grilling.
3. Preheat the grill or broiler. Grill the chicken 15-20 minutes until cooked, turning the skewers to cook evenly.
4. Serve with Basmati rice (page 179) lime wedges and fresh cilantro.

Makes 3-4 servings

## Tips

- *The grated onion and vinegar keep the meat moist and tender.*

# B'steeya

*B'steeya is a North African dish and traditionally it is prepared with pigeon. In Morocco, we had this dish prepared with chicken and it was excellent.*

## Ingredients
½ cup slivered almonds
½ cup pistachio nuts
½ cup cashew nuts
2 Tbsp sugar
½ tsp cinnamon for the nuts
4 cups chopped cooked breast of chicken
¼ cup butter, melted
12 sheets of Filo dough
2 Tbsp butter
2 large onions, chopped
2 Tbsp minced fresh ginger
½ tsp cinnamon for the chicken
4 eggs, slightly beaten
½ tsp black pepper
½ salt

## Preparation
1. In a frying pan, with one teaspoon butter, sauté the almond, cashew, and pistachio nuts for 2 minutes. Add 2 tablespoons sugar and ½ teaspoon cinnamon and continue sautéing until sugar melts, the cinnamon becomes fragrant, and the nuts take a light golden color. Set aside to cool.
2. Melt the remaining butter in a saucepan and sauté the onions; add ginger and ½ teaspoon cinnamon and sauté until onions are soft. Add the cooked chicken, mix with the onions then add the slightly beaten eggs, salt and pepper. Cook over gentle heat, stirring until the eggs are just cooked and creamy. Adjust seasoning. Set aside to cool.
3. Unwrap the filo dough, take out 12 sheets, wrap the rest and save for another use. Cut the sheets in half. Stack them up and cover with plastic wrap to keep them from drying out while assembling B'steeyas.
4. Using a medium size deep dish (I use a large custard dish) or a 4-inch loose bottom tart pan, lay a sheet of filo dough on the bottom of the dish; overhanging the excess dough. Brush on melted butter, and top with another layer of dough and butter it again. Sprinkle one tablespoon of the prepared nuts, and repeat with two more half sheets. Place ½ cup of chicken in the center; then sprinkle with another tablespoon of nuts.
5. Fold the overhang pastry over the top of the nuts, buttering the layers. Flip it out of the custard dish. Butter the top and arrange on a baking dish.
6. Preheat the oven to 375°F before baking B'steeyas. Bake 30 minutes or until golden brown and crisp. Serve sprinkled with powdered sugar and cinnamon.

Makes 6 servings

## Tips
- *To save time, store bought roasted chicken works well. Skin and bones removed, the diced chicken meat amounts to 4 cups.*

# Roast Chicken with Herb Butter

*A crisp-skinned juicy tender chicken flavored with herbs. Brine the night before, and the next day it will just take an hour of preparation from start to finish.*

## Ingredients
1 whole chicken (3-4 lbs)
½ cup salt for the brine
1 clove slightly crushed garlic (optional)
8 cups water
1 stick butter
1 Tbsp fresh chopped tarragon
1 Tbsp fresh chopped oregano
1 tsp salt
1 tsp black pepper
1 lemon
½ cup of chicken broth, or white wine
1 bunch watercress
    or parsley for garnish

## Preparation
1. Before roasting chicken, preheat oven to 450°F.
2. Trim off excess fat from the chicken. In a deep container, dissolve ½ cup of salt with 8 cups of water, drop in garlic and cover the chicken in the brine for 8 hours or overnight in the refrigerator. Next day, rinse and pat dry with paper towel.
3. Using a fork, mash half of the butter with chopped tarragon, oregano, salt and pepper.
4. Loosen the chicken skin wherever possible and spread some of the butter between the skin and the chicken meat, inside the cavity, and on top of the chicken breast. Place half the lemon inside the cavity.
5. Melt the remaining butter in the roasting pan; add the broth and the juice from the other half of lemon. Place the chicken on a rack in the roasting pan, breast down. Roast the chicken at 450°F oven for 20 minutes. Turn the chicken breast side up and baste with the melted butter and the drippings in the pan. Keep basting for the next 8-10 minutes, until the skin starts browning. Turn the oven temperature down to 350°F and continue roasting and basting until the thermometer inserted into the thickest part of the thigh reads 165° to 170°F. Total roasting time will take approximately 60-75 minutes.
6. Remove chicken from the oven onto a carving board; let it rest for 10 minutes. Bring the pan juices to a low boil, scraping up the brown bits, and cook until the sauce is reduced, about 2 minutes. De-fat the sauce.
7. Carve the chicken and arrange on a large platter. Pour the sauce over it and garnish the plate with watercress or parsley. Serve with roasted potatoes (page 174).

Makes 4-5 servings

## Tips
- *You may use dry herbs instead of fresh; just reduce the amount to 1 tsp each.*
- *You may choose to roast the potatoes with the chicken.*

# Mother's Fried Chicken

*Mother always served this dish with rice pilaf cooked with chicken broth and cooked spinach on the side.*

## Ingredients

3 lbs chicken, thighs, drumsticks, and breast
1 clove garlic cut in half
1 medium onion, quartered
1 carrot cut in half
2 tsp salt
2 eggs, well beaten with 1 Tbsp water
1 cup flour
Vegetable oil for frying
2 Tbsp flour for the gravy
1 Tbsp tomato paste for the gravy

## Preparation

1. In a 4 quart saucepan, cover the chicken pieces with water; add salt, onion, garlic and carrot. Bring to a boil and skim the foam from the top. Reduce the heat and simmer for 35-45 minutes until chicken is fork tender.
2. Remove chicken pieces from the broth and drain in a colander. Let them cool completely. Reserve the broth for the gravy.
3. Beat the eggs with one tablespoon of water; add a little salt and black pepper.
4. Heat the oil in a frying pan to moderately hot; dip chicken pieces in the egg then in flour. Shake off excess flour and fry until they turn golden brown. (Do not overcrowd the pan). Drain on paper towels.
5. To make the gravy, discard the oil from the frying pan except for 2 tablespoons. Add 2 tablespoons flour and tomato paste and cook for one minute. Gradually add reserved chicken broth, approximately 1 cup, stirring constantly until you have reached the desired consistency for the gravy. Adjust seasoning. Strain to get rid of lumps.
6. Serve gravy with the chicken and with rice pilaf.

Makes 4-6 servings

## Tips

- *Chicken breast usually turns out on the dry side. I use chicken tenders and poach them separately because they cook much faster than the drumsticks and thighs.*

# Electric Skillet Roast Chicken

*A simple, delicious, quick meal for a week night. I learned this from my mother. She made this dish with whole chicken as well as cut up chicken,*
*If you do not have an electric skillet, just use a skillet with a fitted cover.*

## Ingredients
1½ lb chicken breasts (3-4 breasts) boneless and skinless
1 tsp salt
¼ tsp pepper
3 Tbsp butter
2 Russet potatoes
1 cup vegetable oil

## Preparation
1. With ½ tsp of salt, sprinkle salt and pepper over the breasts.
2. Melt butter in electric skillet on medium-high heat and sauté chicken breasts turning them once until both sides are browned.
3. Reduce the heat and cover the pan. Let the chicken roast in its own juices.
4. Meanwhile peel the potatoes and cut them into 1-inch cubes. Salt the potatoes with the remaining ½ teaspoon salt.
5. In a 2-quart saucepan heat vegetable oil and fry the potatoes, in two or three batches, until they start browning. Remove from the pan and put them in the skillet with the chicken to continue roasting with the chicken juices.
6. When the chicken is cooked turn off the heat. Serve with cooked vegetables and/or salad.

Makes 3-4 servings

## Tips
- *If you do not have an electric skillet, you can use a covered saucepan but watch carefully so you do not dry out the chicken.*

# Chicken Lettuce Wrap

*A quick and healthy meal. Ideal for the diet conscious.*

## Ingredients
1 large head butter lettuce
1 lb ground breast of chicken
1 cup finely chopped shiitake mushrooms
2 Tbsp vegetable oil
2 cloves crushed garlic
1 tsp grated ginger
¼ cup diced red pepper
1 jalapeño pepper, seeded and finely chopped
3-4 scallions, chopped
3-4 Tbsp Oyster sauce

## Preparation
1. Separate lettuce leaves from the core, wash and pat dry with paper towel. Set aside.
2. In a large frying pan or wok, heat the oil. Add the chicken and stir fry for a few minutes until the chicken is almost cooked. Add the chopped mushroom, cook a few minutes longer; add the garlic and ginger, diced peppers, and chopped scallions. Continue cooking a few minutes longer, until the mixture has absorbed the juices.
3. Add oyster sauce and stir to coat the mixture.
4. Transfer chicken to serving dish and serve with the lettuce leaves.
5. To eat, pile tablespoonfuls into the lettuce leaves, and wrap the sides over filling. Hold in your hands and eat like you would eat a burrito.

Makes 3 servings

## Tips
- *Oyster sauce is a Chinese sauce and is found in most grocery stores on the shelves with other Chinese ingredients.*
- *You may use any kind of green leaf lettuce leaves that you like.*

# Chicken Parmesan

*This is a dish that appeals to both children and adults. It can be prepared ahead of of time and baked before serving. You cannot go wrong with such a and delicious meal.*

## Ingredients
1 lb breast of chicken, boned and skinned
1 tsp salt
½ tsp pepper
1½ cup bread crumbs
1/3 cup Parmesan cheese
2 eggs, slightly beaten
2 Tbsp butter
2 Tbsp olive oil
1 lb Mozzarella cheese, sliced
3 cups marinara sauce (page 204)
1/3 cup Parmesan cheese, for topping

## Preparation
1. Split chicken breasts in half, place between 2 sheets of wax paper and pound them thin to ¼ inch thickness. Season with salt and pepper
2. Mix bread crumbs and 1/3 cup Parmesan cheese in a shallow dish. Working with one piece at a time, dip them in beaten eggs, let excess egg drip off; coat with bread crumb mixture. Let dry on a wire rack. (This will help the bread coating to adhere well to the chicken).
3. Prepare marinara sauce (page 204) or use store bought Marinara Sauce.
4. In a 10-12 inch skillet, heat butter and olive oil. Fry chicken pieces, in hot oil without overlapping, a few pieces at a time. Cook 1-1½ minute per side until the crust turns golden brown. If needed add more butter and olive oil.
5. Spoon a few tablespoons of marinara sauce on the bottom of a shallow baking dish. Layer the fried chicken pieces in a large shallow baking dish, overlapping chicken and cheese if necessary. Top with marinara sauce. Sprinkle with the remaining 1/3 cup Parmesan cheese.
6. Bake for 20-30 minutes until cheese melts and the sauce starts bubbling.
7. For a true Italian flavor, serve with herbed pasta and your choice of cooked vegetables.

Makes 3-4 servings

## Tips
- *The purpose of the combination of butter and olive oil is: oil endures higher temperatures while butter burns. With the combination we get the butter flavor without the burned butter flavor.*
- *If you choose not to fry, but bake the chicken after it is breaded, you can do so in a 350° preheated oven for 30 minutes then follow steps 5-7.*

# Parmesan Crusted Oven Baked Chicken Tenders

*These chicken tenders are also good for appetizers. Kids will never refuse these tender chicken pieces for lunch, dinner or even a snack.*

## Ingredients
1 lb. chicken tenders
½ cup buttermilk
1 cup Italian seasoned bread crumbs
3 Tbsp Parmesan cheese
Salt and pepper to taste
2 tbsp vegetable oil or butter

## Preparation
1. Preheat oven to 375°F before baking.
2. Salt and pepper chicken tenders. Cover them with the buttermilk and let them marinate for an hour.
3. In a plastic bag mix bread crumbs and parmesan cheese.
4. Take the tenders out of the marinade and drop them in a plastic bag with bread crumbs. Shake the bag until tenders are coated with the crumbs.
5. Line a pan with aluminum foil and spray it with oil. Arrange tenders on the tray. Brush with vegetable oil or dot with butter.
6. Bake for 20-25 minutes, or until browned. Serve with mashed potatoes (page 172) or rice pilaf (page 178) and steamed vegetables.

Makes 2-3 servings

## Tips
- *If you do not have buttermilk handy around the house, mix ½ cup of milk and 1½ teaspoon of vinegar or lemon juice and let it sit for 5 minutes, then marinate the chicken.*

# Curried Chicken and Wild Rice Casserole
*This one dish meal, easy to assemble, can be prepared ahead of time and baked before serving.*

## Ingredients
1 pkg Uncle Ben's wild rice
1 whole chicken fryer
1 large onion, quartered
1 Tbsp curry powder
1 tsp salt
½ tsp pepper
1 can cream of mushroom soup
½ cup sour cream
1 cup frozen peas and/or corn

## Preparation
1. Preheat oven to 350°F before baking the casserole.
2. In a large Dutch oven, place the chicken and cover with water. Add onion, curry powder, salt and pepper. Bring to a boil and cook until the chicken is done. Remove chicken and cool. Strain the broth and save to use for preparing the rice.
3. Remove the skin off the chicken and shred the meat into bite size pieces for the casserole.
4. Cook rice according to package direction by using the reserved broth; if you do not have enough broth, add water to get to the right amount of liquid.
5. Combine chicken, cooked rice, mushroom soup and sour cream and peas. Adjust seasoning. Pour mixture into a casserole and bake for 25-35 minutes until hot and bubbly.

Makes 4 servings

## Tips
- *You may prepare the casserole ahead of time and refrigerate, in which case the cooking time will be 5-10 minutes longer.*

# Cashew Chicken Casserole

*Broccoli, chicken and rice, what a great combination! Cashew nuts add extra flavor and crunch to this dish. This is a crowd pleasing solution for a busy housewife. Extra delicious! Advanced preparation makes it extra easy at dinner time.*

## Ingredients
1 (6 0z box) Long Grain and Wild Rice
3 cups par-boiled broccoli florets
1 (14¾ oz can) whole corn drained
3 cups cooked chicken, cubed
1 can cream of mushroom soup
1 cup sour cream
2 cups shredded cheddar cheese
½ tsp red pepper flakes
¼ tsp pepper to taste
Salt to taste
1 cup crushed Ritz crackers
3 Tbsp butter
½ cup cashew pieces

## Preparation:
1. Preheat oven to 375°F before baking.
2. Cook rice according to package direction.
3. Combine rice, broccoli, corn, chicken, soup, sour cream, cheese, red pepper, black pepper and salt to taste. If needed adjust seasoning.
4. Pour mixture into a greased 9x13-inch baking dish.
5. Melt butter in a pan, add crushed crackers and stir until coated with butter.
6. Sprinkle crumbs and cashews on top and bake for 30 minutes.

Makes 4-6 servings

## Tips
- *Double or triple the recipe for a bigger group.*
- *For convenience, 10 oz package frozen broccoli can be substituted for the fresh broccoli.*
- *You may prepare this casserole, up to step 5 days ahead of time, cover and refrigerate. Before baking, top with crumbs and cashews.*
- *For Southwestern taste, add a can of chopped Ortega chilies, and instead of Ritz cracker crumbs, top with crushed baked tortilla chips. For extra zip, serve with tomato salsa.*
- *For convenience, use store bought cooked rotisserie chicken and shred it.*

# Mexican Chicken Casserole

*It's Fiesta time! This casserole is a nice week night meal that is quick to prepare. This recipe is simple and pleases everyone in the family. Also it is a nice casserole to take to pot luck dinners.*

## Ingredients
3 Tbsp olive oil
1 onion, diced
2 cloves garlic, crushed
½ tsp red pepper flakes
1 can cream of mushroom soup
1 small can chopped Ortega chili
1 (14¾ oz can) whole corn drained
1 (12 oz) jar Salsa Verde
2 cups chunky salsa, medium hot
12 corn tortillas
1 (16 oz) can refried beans
3 cups cooked chicken cubed (3 breasts)
½ cup sliced black olives
1 cup sour cream
3 cups shredded cheddar/or Jack cheese
½ cup chopped fresh cilantro
Extra Salsa and Guacamole on the side

## Preparation:
1. Preheat oven to 350°F before baking.
2. In a saucepan, heat the oil and sauté onion and garlic, add red pepper flakes, cream of mushroom soup, Ortega chilies and corn. Remove from heat and stir in sour cream.
3. Spray a 9 x13-inch baking dish with oil, spread two tablespoons of salsa on the bottom and arrange one layer of corn tortillas.
4. Spread tortillas with refried beans, spoon half of the creamy corn mixture over it. Sprinkle half of the shredded chicken over it, sprinkle with 1/3 of olives, and one cup of cheese, and top with a mixture of salsa Verde and tomato salsa. Repeat the same with another layer. Lay top layer of tortillas, using the remaining salsa, and the rest of the cheese over the top.
5. Sprinkle top with the remaining olives and cilantro. Bake covered for 20 minutes until heated through. Remove cover and bake uncovered for another 5 minutes, until the top cheese starts bubbling.
6. Serve with extra salsa and guacamole.

Makes 6-8 servings

## Tips
- *When pressed for time, I usually buy a rotisserie barbecued chicken from the store and shred it.*

# Chicken Enchiladas

*If you make the effort to make these enchiladas at home, you will never like the enchiladas served in any Mexican restaurant again. These are the best! You might want to make the sauce the day before and put the casserole together the next day. I use store bought cooked rotisserie chicken because it tastes better.*

## Ingredients
4 cups shredded cooked breast of chicken
¼ cup chopped fresh cilantro
4 cups shredded mixed cheese
12-14 (6-inch) white corn tortillas
Salsa, guacamole, shredded lettuce, and sour cream to serve

<u>Sauce</u>
1 lb tomatoes
3 Tbsp olive oil
1 large onion, chopped
2 red bell peppers, coarsely chopped
3 cloves garlic, crushed
1 green bell pepper, coarsely chopped
1 or 2 jalapeño peppers, finely chopped
¾ cup chicken broth
2 Tbsp masa harina or flour
8 oz cream cheese, cut into cubes
1 tsp cumin
1 tsp paprika
1 tsp ground coriander
½ tsp cardamom
1 tsp salt

## Preparation
1. Fill a medium saucepan with water, bring to a boil. Fill a large bowl with ice water, set aside. Cut an 'X' in tomato bottoms and drop in boiling water one at a time. Simmer until the skin starts curling. Transfer to ice bath immediately to cool. Peel tomatoes and discard skin. Coarsely chop and set aside.
2. *Prepare sauce:* In a large saucepan, heat the oil and sauté onion for few minutes. Add chopped peppers and garlic and continue sautéing until peppers are soft.
3. Dissolve masa harina in chicken broth, and add to the sautéed peppers, along with the chopped tomatoes. Add cream cheese and spices. Cook the mixture until cream cheese is melted. Adjust seasoning. Cool slightly, transfer to food processor in batches and blend until smooth. (If you wish, at this point refrigerate the sauce to use the next day).
4. Marinate the shredded chicken with 1/3 of the prepared sauce and the chopped cilantro for at least half an hour to let the flavors blend.
5. Place tortillas for a few seconds into hot oil to soften (or spray with vegetable oil and put in preheated oven for 2-3 minutes). Prepare a 9x13-inch baking dish by spreading ½ cup of sauce in the bottom.
6. Spread 3 tablespoons of marinated chicken along the diameter of the tortillas, top with 2 tablespoons of shredded cheese, roll up tortillas and place snugly seam side down in the prepared baking dish. Top with remaining enchilada sauce and remaining grated cheese.
7. Bake in 400°F preheated oven until enchiladas are heated through and the cheese is melted, about 30-35 minutes. Serve with extra sauce, sour cream, shredded lettuce, guacamole and salsa.

Makes 6-7 servings

# Chicken Stir-fry with Snap Peas and Cashews
*A quick and healthy dish to prepare any night of the week.*

## Ingredients
½ lb breast of chicken, skinned and boned
2 Tbsp cornstarch
2 Tbsp water
2 Tbsp vegetable oil
2 green onions cut into 1" long pieces
1 cup snap peas
¼ cup chicken broth or water
1 Tbsp oyster sauce
Pinch of sugar
1 tsp soy sauce
½ cup cashew nuts, roasted

*Marinade*
2 tsp soy sauce
2 tsp dry sherry wine
1 clove crushed garlic
1 tsp crushed ginger
Dash of black pepper

## Preparation
1. Prepare marinade by mixing all the ingredients together and set aside.
2. Cut chicken into ¾-inch long and about ¼-inch thick. Marinate the chicken for 10-15 minutes.
3. Remove chicken from marinade and dust with 1 tablespoon of cornstarch. Set aside.
4. Mix the other 1 tablespoon cornstarch with 2 tablespoons of water and set aside.
5. Heat 2 tablespoons oil in a wok or a deep skillet over high heat. Add chicken and stir-fry for 2 minutes. Add the green onions and snap peas continue stir frying for 30 seconds.
6. Add chicken broth, oyster sauce, sugar and soy sauce. Stir in cornstarch-water solution. Heat until the sauce thickens and glazes the chicken.
7. Add cashew nuts and mix well. Serve immediately with steamed rice

Makes 2 servings

## Tips
- *If you like this dish spicy, add a few dried red chili peppers to the oil along with the ginger and garlic.*
- *Consider this stir-fry recipe a blueprint for other stir-fried dishes. Just substitute beef for chicken and use your favorite vegetables in any combination. You can be very creative.*

# Stir Fried Chicken and Vegetables
*If you have all the ingredients handy this dish is very quick to prepare. Serve with steamed rice.*

## Ingredients
½ lb breast of chicken, boneless and skinless
1 Tbsp cornstarch
1 Tbsp cornstarch mixed with 2 Tbsp water
4 Tbsp vegetable oil
1 tsp ginger, crushed
1 tsp garlic, crushed
1 cup broccoli florets
1 cup snap peas
¼ cup carrots, julienne cut
½ cup sliced bell pepper
1 Tbsp oyster sauce
1 tsp soy sauce
¼ cup chicken broth
Pinch of sugar
1 cup bean sprouts

<u>Marinade</u>
¼ tsp five-spice powder
1 tsp cider vinegar
2 Tbsp soy sauce
2 Tbsp dry sherry wine
1 tsp sugar
1 clove garlic, crushed
1 Tbsp ginger, crushed

## Preparation
1. Prepare marinade by mixing all the ingredients together and set aside.
2. Cut chicken into pieces ¾-inch long and about ¼-inch thick. Marinate the chicken for 10-15 minutes.
3. Remove chicken from marinade and lightly coat with cornstarch. Set aside.
4. Mix 1 tablespoon of cornstarch with 2 tablespoons of water and set aside.
5. Heat 2 tablespoons oil in a wok or a deep skillet over high heat. Use ½ teaspoon of crushed ginger and ½ teaspoon of garlic to flavor the oil. Add chicken to it and stir-fry for 2-3 minutes. Remove chicken from the wok
6. In the same wok add the remaining oil, ginger and garlic. Stir-fry broccoli, snap peas, carrots and bell peppers for 30 seconds, seasoning with 1 teaspoon of sugar. Return cooked chicken to the wok.
7. Add chicken broth, oyster sauce, and soy sauce. Stir in cornstarch-water solution. Heat until the sauce thickens and starts bubbling. Add bean sprouts and stir fry for 30 seconds.
8. Serve immediately with steamed rice

Makes 2 servings

## Tips
- *If you like this dish spicy, add a few dried red chili peppers to the oil along with the ginger and garlic.*

# Pasta

## Lasagna with Spinach and Artichoke

*Totally meatless lasagna with three kinds of cheese paired with spinach and artichokes is delicious. This dish can be assembled in advance and refrigerated in which case you might want to adjust the cooking time. It will take 15 minutes longer to cook.*

### Ingredients
3 pkgs frozen creamed spinach
1 (15 oz) can artichoke hearts, chopped
2 cups ricotta cheese
¾ cup Parmesan cheese
2 eggs
¼ cup chopped fresh basil leaves
1 pkg no-boil lasagna noodles
4 cups shredded mozzarella cheese

### Preparation
1. Preheat oven to 400°F before baking.
2. Microwave the creamed spinach according to package directions, and then mix in chopped artichokes and chopped basil.
3. In a mixing bowl, mix ricotta cheese, 2 eggs, and Parmesan cheese. Set aside.
4. To assemble lasagna: Cover the bottom of a 9x13-inch baking dish with a ladle-full of the spinach.
5. Arrange 4 no-boil lasagna noodles to cover the bottom of the pan, breaking noodles if necessary.
6. Spread one cup of ricotta mixture on top of noodles. Over ricotta, spread one cup of prepared spinach-artichoke mixture. Sprinkle with 1 cup of shredded mozzarella cheese.
7. Repeat steps 5 and 6 two more times. On the last layer of noodles, spread the remainder of ricotta mixture, spinach-artichoke mixture, and sprinkle the rest of mozzarella cheese.
8. Bake covered for 30 minutes, until cheese is melted. Uncover and bake another 25 minutes until cheese starts browning. Cool 15 minutes before serving.

Makes 8 servings

### Tips
- *Freeze leftovers for another meal.*

# Lasagna with Meat Sauce

*This lasagna features tomato flavored meat sauce combined with three cheeses. This is a dish you can make a day in advance and refrigerate. It just takes extra 15 minutes baking time until it gets bubbly.*

## Ingredients
1 pkg no-boil lasagna noodles
2 cups ricotta cheese
2 eggs
¾ cup Parmesan cheese
4 cups shredded mozzarella cheese

<u>Meat Sauce</u>
1 lb ground beef
3 Tbsp olive oil
1 onion chopped
1 carrot chopped
1 celery stalk chopped
3 cloves garlic chopped fine
2 Tbsp fresh basil chopped
1 Tbsp fresh parsley chopped
1½ tsp salt
2 tsp dried oregano
¼ tsp black pepper
1 lb ground beef
2 (14 ½ oz) can chopped tomatoes
1 (8 oz) can tomato sauce

## Preparation
1. Preheat oven to 375°F before baking.
2. <u>Prepare Meat Sauce:</u> Sauté onion, carrots, celery, and garlic in the olive oil until the onions are transparent. Add chopped basil and parsley and cook a few minutes longer.
3. Add ground beef and brown it until no longer pink, about 15 minutes.
4. Stir in tomato sauce and crushed tomatoes, oregano, pepper and salt. Simmer for 20 minutes.
5. In a mixing bowl, mix ricotta cheese, 2 eggs, and Parmesan cheese. Set aside.
6. <u>Assemble lasagna:</u> Cover the bottom of a 9 x13-inch pan with a ladle full of the prepared tomato-beef sauce.
7. Arrange 4 no-boil lasagna noodles to cover the bottom of the pan, breaking noodles if necessary.
8. Spread 1 cup of ricotta mixture over noodles. Over the ricotta, spread one cup of prepared tomato-beef sauce. Sprinkle with 1 cup of shredded mozzarella cheese.
9. Repeat steps 7 and 8 two more times. On the last layer of noodles, spread the remainder of ricotta mixture, tomato-beef mixture, and sprinkle the rest of mozzarella cheese.
10. Bake covered for 50-60 minutes, until cheese is melted. Uncover and bake another 5 minutes. Cool 15 minutes before serving.

Makes 8 servings

## Tips
- *Freeze leftovers for another meal.*

# Creamy Baked Cheese Pasta

*This pasta dish is creamy, rich, and silky smooth. Large shell or elbow pasta will hold more of the cheesy sauce in each bite. Undercooking the pasta is the secret in preparing this dish. Keep in mind the pasta will cook further when you are baking the casserole.*

## Ingredients
¾ lb shell pasta or large elbow macaroni
1 Tbsp salt
<u>Cheese Sauce</u>
2 Tbsp butter
1 small onion, chopped
2 Tbsp flour
2 cloves garlic, crushed
1 tsp prepared mustard
3 cups whole milk
Salt to taste
½ tsp black pepper
2 cup grated Fontina cheese
1 cup grated Parmesan cheese
1½ cup grated Pecorino Romano or Gruyere cheese

## Preparation
1. Preheat oven to 500°F before baking.
2. Bring four quarts of water to boil in a large pot. Stir in 1 tablespoon salt and pasta and bring to a boil, stirring occasionally to keep pasta from sticking to each other. Cook the pasta al dente, about 7-8 minutes.
3. Drain the pasta reserving 1 cup of pasta cooking liquid. Return pasta to the pot and cover the pot to keep it warm.
4. <u>Prepare cheese sauce</u>: Melt the butter in another saucepan, and cook the onion until softened. Add the flour and cook, stirring constantly for a minute. Add the garlic and mustard and stir for another 30 seconds. Slowly whisk in the milk. Bring the mixture to a boil and simmer whisking until slightly thickened. Season the sauce with salt and pepper. Add the grated Fontina cheese, half of the Parmesan cheese and the Pecorino Romano. If the sauce is too thick, add a few tablespoons of the reserved liquid.
5. Pour the cheese sauce over the pasta, mix and pour into a 9 x13-inch baking dish and sprinkle the remaining ½ cup Parmesan.
6. Bake in the middle rack for 15-20 minutes, until the top browns. Serve immediately.

## Tips
- *If you prefer the flavor of other cheeses, by all means, substitute whatever cheese you like. You may use cheddar cheese instead of Fontina and Gruyere. I think children like that better.*
- *Serve as a side dish anytime with any meat or chicken dish.*
- *To prevent cheese from sticking to a grater, spray the grater with cooking oil before grating.*

# Shrimp Scampi with Linguini Pasta
*This is a quick and delicious meal to prepare on a busy day.*

## Ingredients
8 oz linguini pasta
1 lb large shrimps, peeled and deveined
3 Tbsp butter
2 Tbsp Extra-virgin olive oil
3 cloves garlic, minced
¾ tsp salt
½ tsp black pepper
¼ tsp red pepper flakes
1 Tbsp lime juice
1/3 cup chopped parsley
1 lime sliced into thin rounds
Parmesan cheese on the side

## Preparation
1. Cook linguini according to package direction, approximately 9-10 minutes.
2. In a large skillet, heat the butter and olive oil over medium-high heat. Add the garlic and sauté for one minute. Add the shrimp, salt, black pepper, and continue sautéing until shrimp turns pink, about 4-5 minutes.
3. Remove skillet from heat and add lime juice, red pepper flakes, and parsley. Toss lightly to combine.
4. When pasta is ready, drain and add to the shrimp along with round lime slices, and toss. Serve with parmesan cheese on the side.

Makes 2-3 servings

# Broccoli and Bow Tie Pasta

*This simple but delicious pasta dish is sure to please the family. Chop the veggies and blanch them ahead of time and you can prepare the dish later in a snap.*

## Ingredients
7-8 cups broccoli florets, blanched
1 (8oz) pkg bow tie pasta
4 quarts boiling water
2 tsp salt
2 Tbsp Extra-virgin olive oil
2 Tbsp butter
2 cloves crushed garlic
1 Tbsp lemon juice
½ tsp. pepper
¼ tsp red pepper flakes
Salt to taste
¾ cup toasted pine nuts
1 cup Parmesan cheese

## Preparation
1. In a pot of boiling water, cook the broccoli for 3 minutes. Remove from the water and set aside.
2. In the same pot of water add the pasta and cook according to package direction.
3. In a large skillet heat the butter and olive oil, add the garlic, and blanched broccoli and sauté for 2-3 minutes. Add lemon juice, salt and pepper to taste.
4. Toss pasta with the broccoli, add pine nuts, and pour into a serving dish. Sprinkle top with Parmesan cheese.

Makes 4-6 servings

## Tips
- *To toast pine nuts, put them in a skillet and stir until golden brown over medium-high heat.*

# Zucchini Pasta

*This recipe was given to me by my Italian friend, Michelle Morro. She says "For the Italians, the more garlic and black pepper, the tastier the dish." I have slightly modified the recipe to please my family. Trust me, you will make this dish again and again. It is delicious!*

## Ingredients
1 lb thin spaghetti
2 lb small zucchini,
    diced to ½-inch squares
2 large onions sliced (optional)
½ stick butter
¼ cup olive oil
4 cloves garlic, minced
2 eggs
2 Tbsp cream
¾ cup Parmesan cheese, grated
½ tsp black pepper
Salt to taste
Extra Parmesan cheese for serving

## Preparation
1. Scrub zucchini, leaving the rind on and cut up into ½ inch cubes or ½ inch slices.
2. Heat butter and oil in a large frying pan, add onions and cook until tender. With a slotted spoon, transfer cooked onions into a bowl.
3. In the same frying pan add ½ of the minced garlic and half of the diced zucchini and sauté over high heat until the zucchini starts to brown. With a slotted spoon, move cooked zucchini into the bowl.
4. There should be some oil left in the same pan. If not, add 2 tablespoons more olive oil and sauté the rest of the garlic and zucchini until they start browning.
5. Cook thin spaghetti according to package direction.
6. While pasta is cooking, beat the eggs and cream with a fork and add the Parmesan cheese.
7. Drain pasta and while it is hot, pour the egg mixture over it and stir. The hot pasta will cook the eggs.
8. Pour the cooked zucchini-onion mixture and all the leftover olive oil over pasta. Toss lightly. If needed add some salt and more pepper. To serve, sprinkle with more Parmesan cheese.

Makes 4-6 servings

## Tips
- *When sautéing the zucchini, try not to put too much zucchini in the pan; if you do, the zucchini will not brown. I sauté them in two batches in a large frying pan and they turn out perfect.*

# Spaghetti with Meatballs

*This kids' favorite dish has as much grown-up appeal. For a quicker preparation, make these meatballs ahead of time and freeze them. Before using, thaw, combine with sauce and heat through. Grating Parmesan cheese over the entire dish is always a good idea.*

## Ingredients
Meatball recipe (page 114))
Spaghetti sauce recipe on (page)
2 Tbsp finely chopped parsley
    for garnish
Parmesan cheese for sprinkling on top
1 pkg thin spaghetti noodles

## Preparation
1. Place meatballs in a saucepan and cover with the spaghetti sauce. Simmer for 20-25 minutes, stirring gently and occasionally being careful not to disturb the meatballs.
2. Prepare spaghetti according to package directions.
3. Serve the meatballs and sauce over spaghetti. Sprinkle with chopped parsley. Serve with Parmesan cheese on top or on the side.

## Tips
- *The sauce adheres better to pasta if you do not use oil in the boiling water. If you get distracted and pasta sticks to each other, just run hot water over them and they will separate.*
- *I usually make extra meatballs for sandwiches for the next day (page 190).*

# Potato Kibbeh

This dish is another variety of the Middle Eastern traditional dish Kibbeh made with potatoes during lent.

## Ingredients

5 medium size russet potatoes (about 3 lbs)
1 tsp salt

*Filling*
4 Tbsp olive oil
2 large onions, diced
1½ tsp cumin
½ tsp red pepper flakes
¾ tsp salt
1/3 tsp black pepper

*Kibbeh Outer Layer*
1 cup small cracked wheat (bulghur #1)
1 small onion grated
2 tsp pepper paste
1 tsp paprika
2 tsp cumin
1 tsp salt
¼ tsp black pepper
1 Tbsp flour (optional)
¼ cup olive oil for baking kibbeh

## Preparation

1. Scrub the potatoes and cover with water 1-inch above the potatoes. Add 1 teaspoon salt and boil for 20-30 minutes until fork tender. Let them cool and peel.
2. *Preparing filling:* Dice 2 potatoes into ½-inch cubes and set aside.
3. In a skillet heat 4 tablespoons of olive oil, sauté the onions until they start browning and add cubed potatoes. Add the spices, mix well; adjust seasoning with salt and pepper. Set aside to cool.
4. *Preparing outer layer:* Mash the other three cooked potatoes and set aside.
5. Measure 1 cup of cracked wheat into a strainer and rinse with cold water. Place it in a mixing bowl and let it stand for 15 minutes to absorb the moisture.
6. Add the mashed potatoes, grated onion, pepper paste, paprika, cumin, salt and black pepper and knead by hand, occasionally wetting your hands with cold water to prevent sticking, until mixture holds together like dough. If the mixture is too soft add a little flour to make a firm paste.
7. **Assembling**: Grease a 9 x 13-inch pan and press half of the mixture on the bottom of the pan flattening it with your hands about ½-inch thick. Spread the filling over it and cover the filling with the remaining mixture. Press down and smooth the surface then score into diamond shapes. Drizzle the ¼ cup olive oil over the top and bake in a preheated oven at 375°F for 45-50 minutes until golden brown. Serve warm or cold with a salad.
8. Alternatively if you wish to make fried stuffed patties, take a walnut size piece of the paste in your hands and working with one piece at a time, make an indentation in the center with your index finger, and turning it around in the palm of your hand make a round pocket with thin outer layer. Fill in a teaspoon of filling, and close the opening by gradually squeezing the opening and reducing it until it closes. Dip fingers in water as needed.
9. In a medium size deep pan fill up to about 1-inch with vegetable oil. Heat the oil and deep fry the patties until golden brown. Remove from oil and drain on paper towels. Serve warm or cold.

Makes 6-8 servings

# Mashed Potatoes

*The easiest side dish to make is mashed potatoes. In recent years, the addition of different ingredients, like spinach, bacon, garlic etc. has made mashed potatoes one of the most popular accompaniments to any meat dish. If you like creamier mashed potatoes, use a food mill or ricer but never a food processor, which will turn it gummy. We like our mashed potatoes lumpy.*

## Ingredients
3 lbs Idaho/russet potatoes
    or Yukon potatoes
2 cloves crushed garlic (optional)
4 Tbsp butter
1½ cup milk + more if needed
1 cup shredded Jarlsberg
    cheese (optional)
Salt to taste
¼ tsp black pepper

## Preparation
1. Peel and cube the potatoes 1x1x2-inch pieces.
2. In a large saucepan over medium high heat, cook potatoes covered in enough salted water for 18 minutes or until tender. Drain.
3. Mash the garlic and in a small skillet cook with the butter for 2 minutes. Add the milk, mix and heat.
4. Using a hand masher or potato ricer, mash potatoes until smooth.
5. Stir in hot milk with garlic, cheese, salt, and black pepper. Adjust seasoning. If needed add more milk to get the needed consistency.
6. Keep mashed potatoes warm, in a bowl, placed on simmering water until serving time.

Makes 6-8 servings

## Tips
- *You may prepare mashed potatoes an hour in advance of serving and keep warm in a bowl over simmering water. You might need to add more milk before serving.*
- *Without garlic and cheese, it is your plain standard mashed potatoes.*
- *You may wish to add any of the following to plain mashed potatoes:*
    *Spinach*
    *Corn*
    *Bacon bits*
    *Chopped jalapeno*
    *Grated Parmesan cheese*

# Twice Baked Potatoes

*These potatoes are a hit every time I serve them. Makes a great side dish for any meat dish. You may prepare them a week in advance and freeze them or prepare one day in advance before baking.*

## Ingredients
4 large russet potatoes
4 Tbsp butter
½ cup thinly sliced scallions
½ cup milk
½ cup sour cream
1 tsp salt
½ tsp white pepper
1 cup shredded cheddar cheese
Paprika

## Preparation
1. Preheat oven to 400°F before baking.
2. Pierce the potatoes in a couple of spots with a fork and place them directly on the rack in a preheated oven. Bake for 1 hour or until potatoes are tender. Remove from the oven and let cool slightly.
3. Cut potatoes in half lengthwise; carefully scoop out pulp leaving a thin shell.
4. Mash the potato pulp along with milk, sour cream and 4 tablespoons of butter. Add salt and pepper and stir in scallions. Fold in half of the cheddar cheese reserving the other half for topping.
5. Refill potato shells with the mashed potatoes, sprinkle the remaining cheese over the top, and then sprinkle with paprika. (At this point you may want to wrap them individually and freeze them until ready to use, or if you wish to serve the same day, cover with plastic wrap and refrigerate).
6. When ready to bake, remove wrapping, place stuffed potatoes on a baking sheet and bake until heated through, about 20-30 minutes. (If potatoes were frozen or refrigerated, allow extra time for reheating.

Makes 8 servings

## Tips
- *For variety and color, you may use bacon, peas, spinach or broccoli instead of the scallions.*

# Lemon Roasted Potatoes
*These potatoes are good with any roast dish; meat or chicken.*

## Ingredients
1½ lb small golden potatoes
2 Tbsp Extra-virgin olive oil
1 tsp salt
¼ tsp black pepper
1 tsp chopped fresh rosemary
   or oregano
3 Tbsp lemon juice
1 tsp lemon zest
2 tsp crushed garlic

## Preparation
1. Preheat oven to 350°F before baking.
2. Wash and dry potatoes, leaving the skin on. Cut the larger ones in half.
3. In a frying pan, heat the olive oil and sauté potatoes until they start browning. Remove to a baking pan. Bake for 45 minutes.
4. Mix the garlic, lemon juice, with salt and pepper and rosemary. When the potatoes are tender, drizzle over the roasted potatoes and continue roasting for another 5-10 minutes.
5. Serve with any chicken or meat dish.

Makes 6 servings

## Tips
- *For variation:* Instead of rosemary use oregano or roast potatoes with Indian spices.
  Follow steps 1, 2, and 3. In a small frying pan, heat 1 tablespoon oil, add 1 tsp mustard seeds and sauté until they start popping. Stir in:
    1 tsp minced ginger,
    1 tsp minced garlic
    ½ jalapeño, seeded and minced
    ½ tsp turmeric
    ½ tsp garam masala
  Cook one minute stirring constantly. Add spice mixture to potatoes, tossing to coat, and continue roasting for another 5-10 minutes. Before serving, sprinkle with ¼ cup chopped cilantro and ¼ cup chopped mint.

# Crispy Oven Fried Potato Wedges

*An alternative to French Fries, these oven fried potatoes are good accompaniment to a lot of dishes. You have the choice of adding any spice you like to give that extra zing to it.*

## Ingredients
4 medium size baking potatoes
3 Tbsp olive oil
½ tsp salt
¼ tsp black pepper
¼ tsp paprika
½ tsp dried thyme (optional)
½ tsp dried basil (optional)
½ tsp dried oregano leaves (optional)
¼ cup grated Parmesan cheese

## Preparation
1. Preheat oven 425°F before baking.
2. Scrub unpeeled potatoes well, cut each potato in half lengthwise, then each half into four wedges.
3. Combine olive oil and seasoning in a bowl. Coat each wedge in the seasoned oil.
4. Arrange potatoes in single layer in a greased shallow baking pan.
5. Bake uncovered for 15 minutes, then sprinkle with Parmesan cheese and continue baking for another 15-20 minutes or until potatoes are tender and browned, turning them once.

Makes 4 servings

## Tips
- *If you like garlic, add a clove of crushed garlic to the oil before coating the potatoes with oil.*
- *For variety you may use sweet potatoes, yams, or red potatoes.*
- *Yams and sweet potatoes will cook faster than russet or red potatoes. I suggest you sprinkle with the Parmesan cheese from the start.*

# Bulgur Pilaf with Onions, Peppers and Tomatoes

*Cracked wheat pilaf with onions, peppers and tomatoes is a fiber-rich dish that could be used as an alternative to any rice dish.*

## Ingredients
¼ cup olive oil
1 onion cut in half and sliced
1 bell pepper sliced thin
1 cup chopped fresh tomatoes
1 cup coarse bulgur #4 (cracked wheat)
1¾ cup water or chicken broth
1 tsp salt
¼ tsp black pepper

## Preparation
1. In a medium pan, sauté onion in olive oil, add peppers and sauté some more, then add tomatoes.
2. Add bulgur, water, salt and pepper. Bring the liquid to a boil. Reduce heat to low. Cook about 20 minutes or until all the liquid is absorbed. Let it rest for 5 minutes.
3. Fluff the pilaf with a fork and transfer to serving platter.

Makes 3-4 servings

## Tips
- *If you like the pilaf slightly spicy, add a small jalapeno pepper with the bell pepper.*

# Bulgur Pilaf with Vermicelli Noodles

*Cracked wheat pilaf with vermicelli noodles makes an excellent accompaniment to shish kebab, steak, or poultry dishes. It is an alternative to rice pilaf. Our grandchildren prefer bulgur pilaf over rice pilaf.*

## Ingredients
½ stick butter
½ cup vermicelli broken into small pieces
2 cups large bulgur #4
4 cups water or chicken broth
1½ tsp salt
1 (15.5 oz )can Garbanzo beans, (optional) drained and rinsed
½ cup bread cubes
2-3 tbsp olive oil

## Preparation
1. Heat the butter in a saucepan. Sauté vermicelli until lightly browned - keep stirring to avoid scorching.
2. Add the bulgur and sauté a few seconds longer.
3. Add the water or broth and the salt. Bring to boil.
4. Add garbanzo beans. Cover and reduce heat. Let it simmer for approximately 20 minutes or until the liquid is absorbed. Remove from heat. Let it rest 5 minutes before serving.
5. In a small skillet over medium-high heat, heat the olive oil and fry the bread cubes until they turn golden brown.
6. Garnish with fried bread cubes.

Makes 6-8 servings

## Tips
- *Instead of 4 cups water or chicken broth, you may use 2 cups water with 2 cups chicken broth or beef broth, or 2 cups tomato juice depending on what main course you serve it with.*

# Rice Pilaf with Vermicelli Noodles

*Sautéing the noodles in butter gives a nutty taste. The flavor of toasted almonds or pine nuts and browned noodles are a perfect combination in this pilaf.*

## Ingredients
4 Tbsp butter
½ cup vermicelli noodles,
  broken into 1½-inch pieces
1 cup long grain rice
2¼ cups water or chicken broth
1 tsp salt
½ cup toasted slivered almonds
  or pine nuts

## Preparation
1. Melt butter in a heavy saucepan over medium heat. Sauté vermicelli until lightly browned - keep stirring to avoid scorching.
2. Add the rice and sauté a few seconds longer making sure rice, vermicelli and butter are all combined.
3. Add the water or broth and the salt. Bring to a boil. Cover and reduce heat to low. Let it simmer for approximately 20-25 minutes or until the liquid is absorbed. Remove from heat. Let it stand 5-10 minutes. Fluff it and transfer to a serving dish and sprinkle the top with toasted nuts.

Makes 3-4 servings

## Tips
- *This rice can be prepared without the vermicelli noodles. It tastes just as good.*
- *If using chicken broth, taste for salt before adding salt.*
- *You may use less broth and use water for the difference.*
- *If you are not serving the rice immediately, to keep it moist, remove the lid, lay a kitchen towel over the top and replace the lid. Stir before serving.*

# Plain Basmati Rice Pilaf

*Basmati rice is known as the prince of rice. It has long grains and a distinct aroma and a nutty taste. Always make sure you have a tight-fitting lid for your rice pan.*

## Ingredients
1 cup basmati rice
3 Tbsp butter
2 cups water or chicken broth
¾ tsp salt

## Preparation
1. Soak the rice in cold water for 20-30 minutes.
2. In a medium saucepan with a tight fitting lid, over medium heat melt the butter. Drain the rice, add to the butter and cook for 2 minutes stirring to coat the rice grains in butter.
3. Add 2 cups of water or chicken broth and salt and bring to a boil, reduce heat, cover and simmer very gently for 12 minutes without stirring or opening the lid.
4. Remove from heat, do not open the lid, and let it stand for 10 minutes.
5. Before serving, gently fluff up the rice with a fork.

Makes 4 servings

Tips
- *Basmati rice is available in most grocery stores.*
- *The aim in cooking basmati rice is that the rice grains stay separated, be cooked and retain a slight bite.*

# Tri-color Basmati Rice

*Basmati rice is the natural choice for Indian dishes. It has a nutty flavor, and cooked with colored vegetables, it is not only attractive but delicious as well. Serve with chicken or fish dishes, and any Indian food preparation.*

## Ingredients
1 cup basmati rice
2 Tbsp butter or vegetable oil
1 onion, finely chopped
1 large carrot, finely chopped
½ cup frozen peas, thawed
½ cup frozen corn, thawed
Salt and peer to taste
½ cup cashew nuts, toasted
2 cups water or chicken broth

## Preparation
1. Wash the rice, and then soak in cold water for a couple of hours.
2. Heat oil, add onion and sauté until onions are soft; add carrots and cook for 3-4 minutes.
3. Drain basmati rice and add to the onion and carrot mixture. Stir until well mixed. Add the peas, corn and 2 cups of water or broth. Add salt and pepper and bring to a boil.
4. Reduce heat and continue simmering for 15-20 minutes or until all the liquid is absorbed. Let the rice stand covered for 10 minutes.
5. Add cashew nuts, fluff up the rice with a fork and transfer to serving dish.

Makes 4-6 servings

## Tips
- *If you wish to give an authentic Indian flavor to this rice, add a pinch of cardamom and half a teaspoon of cumin to the water before bringing to a boil.*

# Lentils with Rice (Moudardara)

*This is a very popular dish in the Arab countries, not only because of its nutritional value, but because it can be cooked ahead of time and can be eaten at room temperature. Caramelized onions give a unique taste to the dish. In Middle Eastern countries, this dish is also known as Moudardara.*

## Ingredients
1 cup brown lentils
4 cups water
1¼ cups long grain rice
½ cup olive oil
2 large onions, sliced thin
1 tsp salt

## Preparation
1. In a 4 quart saucepan, cover the lentils with water and bring to a boil. Reduce heat and simmer uncovered until lentils are just tender, 20-25 minutes. Drain lentils and reserve the liquid for the pilaf.
2. Return drained lentils to the pan they were cooked in and add rinsed rice. Measure the drained liquid and add more water to make 2½ cups of liquid. Pour over the rice. Add salt and bring the mixture to a boil, reduce heat and let it simmer until the rice is cooked and all the liquid is absorbed. Approximately 20 minutes.
3. In a frying pan, heat the olive oil and sauté the sliced onions until they are caramelized. Save some of the caramelized onion for garnishing the plate and mix the rest of the onions with the frying oil over the pilaf. Mix and transfer to serving plate. Garnish with the reserved caramelized onions.

Makes 6-8 servings

## Tips
- *This dish can be served warm or at room temperature.*
- *Could be served as a vegetarian main dish with a salad, or alongside a meat dish.*

# Lentils with Cracked Wheat

*During Lent, lentil dishes are very popular. Lentils combined with cracked wheat make a flavorful pilaf.
Caramelized onions give a unique taste to this dish.
In Middle Eastern countries, this dish is also known as Moudardara.*

## Ingredients
1 cup brown lentils, rinsed
5 cups water
2 cup cracked wheat (#4)
1 large onion, sliced thin
1/3 cup olive oil
Salt and pepper to taste

## Preparation
1. In a 4-5 quart saucepan, cover the lentils with water and bring to a boil. Reduce the heat and simmer uncovered until lentils are just tender, 20-25 minutes. Drain lentils and reserve the liquid for the pilaf.
2. Add drained lentils to the pan and then add cracked wheat. Measure the drained liquid and add more water and/or chicken broth to make 4 cups of liquid. Pour over cracked wheat. Add salt and pepper and bring the mixture to a boil, reduce heat and let it simmer until the wheat is cooked and all the liquid is absorbed. Approximately 20 minutes.
3. In a frying pan, heat the olive oil and sauté the sliced onions until they are caramelized. Pour the onions with the frying oil over the pilaf. Mix and serve.

Makes 6-8 servings

## Tips
- *This dish can be served hot or at room temperature.*
- *Could be served as a vegetarian main dish with a salad, or alongside a meat dish.*

# Mushroom Risotto

*Arborio rice is short-grain rice that has high starch content, which gives this dish a creamy texture. Italian chefs insist cold broth should be added while cooking risotto, because the rice will have a better chance of absorbing more of the broth flavor; while American chefs say the liquid added should be hot, it helps to cook the rice faster. Well, you try it both ways and decide which way you like it better. You can add almost anything to a risotto: cooked vegetables, meat, fish, shellfish, herbs, etc.*

## Ingredients

3 small shallots, finely chopped
2 small cloves garlic, finely chopped
6 Tbsp Extra-virgin olive oil
¾ cup dry white wine
1½ cups Arborio risotto rice, washed
4½ cups chicken broth
8 oz Shitake mushrooms, sliced
½ tsp salt
¼ tsp black pepper
½ tsp red pepper flakes
¾ cup Parmesan cheese
2 Tbsp butter
Salt and pepper to taste

## Preparation

1. In a medium saucepan, heat 3 tablespoons olive oil over medium heat. Sauté the shallots and garlic until tender. Add the rice; stir until well coated with the oil, about 2 minutes. Add the wine, stirring until it is absorbed.
2. Slowly add the chicken broth, ladle by ladle, stirring occasionally until it is all absorbed. Continue adding more broth, one ladle at a time, and cook until the rice is tender but still has a bite (al dente). At this point, the liquid in the risotto should have a creamy consistency.
3. Meanwhile, as the risotto is almost ready, sauté the mushrooms in the remaining 3 tablespoons of olive oil with a little salt, pepper and red pepper flakes.
4. Add the sautéed mushrooms to the rice mixture and stir to incorporate into the risotto.
5. Remove the pan from the heat. Stir in Parmesan cheese and butter; season with salt and pepper. Serve immediately.

Makes 4-6 servings

## Tips

- *This is an excellent side dish with chicken or beef, or as a first course.*

# Butternut Squash Risotto

*Arborio rice is short-grain rice that has high starch content, which gives this dish a creamy texture.*

## Ingredients
2 lb butternut squash
5 Tbsp Extra-virgin olive oil
¾ tsp salt
½ tsp black pepper
2 small shallots, diced
1½ cup Arborio risotto rice, washed
½ cup dry white wine
1 tsp saffron, crushed
6 cups chicken broth
1 cup Parmesan cheese
2 Tbsp butter

## Preparation
1. Preheat oven to 400°F. Peel the butternut squash, remove the seeds, and cut it into ¾ inch cubes. Place the squash on a sheet pan and toss it with 2 tablespoons olive oil, 1 teaspoon salt, and ½ teaspoon pepper. Roast for 25-30 minutes, turning them once, until very tender. Set aside.
2. In a medium saucepan, heat the remaining 3 tablespoons olive oil over medium heat. Sauté the shallots until tender. Add the rice; stir until well coated with the oil, about 2 minutes. Add the wine, stirring until it is absorbed.
3. Slowly add the chicken broth, ladle by ladle, and the saffron, stirring occasionally until it is all absorbed. Continue adding more broth, one ladle at a time and cook until the rice is tender but still has a bite (al dente). At this point the liquid in the risotto should have a creamy consistency.
4. Add the cooked squash, and stir to incorporate into the risotto.
5. Remove the pan from the heat. Stir in Parmesan cheese and butter; season with salt and pepper. Serve immediately.

Makes 4-6 servings

## Tips
- *This is an excellent side dish with chicken, veal or beef, or as a first course.*

# Lobster Risotto

*Arborio rice is short-grain rice that has high starch content, which gives this dish a creamy texture. Italian chefs insist cold broth should be added while cooking risotto, because the rice will have a better chance of absorbing more of the broth. This recipe was adapted from a culinary demonstration on Silversea's Silver Wind cruiseship*

## Ingredients

- 8-9 oz lobster tails, shelled and cut into bite size pieces.(Save the shell for the stock)
- 5 Tbsp Extra-virgin olive oil
- ½ cup finely chopped shallot
- ½ tsp finely chopped garlic
- ¾ cup dry white wine
- 1½ cups Arborio risotto rice, washed
- 6 cup lobster stock
- ½ tsp salt
- ¼ tsp black pepper
- ¼ cup Cognac
- ¾ cup Parmesan cheese
- 2 Tbsp butter
- Salt and pepper to taste

## Preparation

1. Take out lobster meat out of the shells, chop and set aside. Prepare lobster stock by following the instructions below. Set aside
2. In a medium saucepan, heat 3 tablespoons of olive oil over medium heat. Sauté the shallots and garlic until tender. Add the rice; stir until well coated with the oil, about 2 minutes. Add the wine, stirring until it is absorbed.
3. Slowly add the lobster stock, ladle by ladle, stirring occasionally until it is all absorbed. Continue adding more, one ladle at a time and cook until the rice is tender but still has a bite (al dente). At this point the liquid in the risotto should have a creamy consistency.
4. Meanwhile as the risotto is almost ready, sauté the lobster pieces in the remaining 2 tablespoons olive oil, add salt and pepper and ¼ cup cognac.
5. Add the sautéed lobster and stir to incorporate into the risotto.
6. Remove the pan from the heat. Stir in Parmesan cheese and butter; adjust seasoning. Serve immediately.

Makes 4-6 servings

## Tips

- *This is an excellent dish as a first course.*
- <u>*Lobster stock*</u>*: In a large saucepan heat 2 tablespoons olive oil and sauté 1 chopped onion until softened. Add lobster shells and sauté for 2 minutes longer. Pour 4 cups of water and season with ½ teaspoon salt and ¼ teaspoon pepper. Bring to a boil. Reduce heat and simmer, partially covered, for 20 minutes. Strain, measure the stock and add more water to make 6 cups and use to make the risotto.*

# Broccoli, Cheese and Rice Casserole

*I do not know the origin of this recipe, but ever since my sister-in-law, Kathy Adrian, introduced the family to this dish, she can never go to a family party without being asked to bring everyone's favorite broccoli rice casserole. Who said kids don't like broccoli? Try this recipe.*

## Ingredients
1 small onion, chopped
¼ cup butter
1 (10 oz pkg) chopped broccoli,
    cooked and drained
½ cup Cheese Whiz
1 can (10 ¾ oz) cream of chicken soup
½ cup water
1 cup Minute Rice
¼ cup milk

## Preparation
1. Preheat oven to 350F° before baking.
2. In a 4 quart saucepan, sauté onion in butter until transparent.
3. Add the remaining ingredients and mix until well combined.
4. Transfer to a greased baking dish and bake uncovered for one hour.

Makes 4-6 servings

## Tips
- *This casserole can be prepared ahead of time, add the rice just before baking*
- *You can use Minute Brown Rice instead of white rice. It tastes just as good.*

# Snacks and Sandwiches

## Eggplant Parmesan Panini

*Paninis are Italian-style press grilled sandwiches. Usually made with a combination of meat and cheese, or vegetables and cheese. Having a panini press makes serving hot sandwiches a cinch.*

### Ingredients
1 Ciabata or panini roll
3 Tbsp Marinara sauce (page 204)
3-4 slices fried eggplant (page 214))
2 slices fresh mozzarella cheese
1 Tbsp Parmesan cheese
Salad greens on the side

### Preparation
1. Heat a panini press.
2. Split the roll in half horizontally.
3. Spread the marinara sauce on both sides of the bread.
4. Layer it with eggplant slices. Top with mozzarella cheese and sprinkle with parmesan cheese.
5. Put the sandwich in the panini press for 3-4 minutes, until the bread starts browning and gets crispy.
6. Cut the panini in half and place on a plate. Garnish the plate with some salad greens.

Makes one panini

### Tips
- *If a panini press is not available, heat a skillet over the stove. Place the sandwich in the skillet and place another pot filled with water on top of the sandwich to press it down. After a few minutes, turn the sandwich over and brown the other side the same way.*

# Nutella and Banana Panini
*This is a sweet Panini that delights kids as well as adults. Yummy!*
*Nutella is hazelnut flavored soft chocolate spread, sold in jars, and is available in most grocery stores.*

## Ingredients
2 slices of brioche bread
   or buttermilk bread
2 Tbsp Nutella
1 small banana, sliced
1 tsp soft butter

## Preparation
1. Spread Nutella on one slice of bread.
2. Slice the banana into ¼-inch thin slices and arrange them over the Nutella. Top with the other slice of bread.
3. Spread the butter on both sides of the sandwich and place in the Panini press. Grill until the bread gets a golden color and the Nutella is melted.

Makes 1 serving

## Tips
- *For variation, you can substitute peanut butter for the Nutella. Makes a nice breakfast treat.*
- *If you do not have a panini press, try grilling it in a heated frying pan over the stove top; flip over when one side is browned and brown the other side.*

# Lobster Roll

*When we travel to Maine or Boston this is my favorite sandwich to have. It is the easiest sandwich to make at home and a nice luncheon treat for yourself.*

## Ingredients
1¼ lb lobster meat cooked and cubed
½ cup mayonnaise
2 tsp lemon juice
1/8 tsp black pepper
1 tsp chopped chives
¼ cup chopped celery
2 Tbsp butter melted
4 hot dog buns
Dash of paprika
Chopped lettuce for garnish
Potato Chips on the side

## Preparation
1. In a medium bowl, combine mayonnaise, lemon juice, black pepper and chives. Mix well.
2. Fold in chopped celery and mix.
3. Fold in lobster meat and toss lightly.
4. Brush the hot dog buns with melted butter and grill under a preheated broiler for a minute to heat them through.
5. Scoop a generous portion of the salad on the bun. Sprinkle with paprika and chopped lettuce. Serve with potato chips.

Makes 4 servings

## Tips
- *If using frozen lobster tails first thaw them out. Bring a pot of water to a boil and add 1 teaspoon of salt. Drop the lobster tails in the boiling water and cook for 10-12 minutes until the tails have turned bright red and have curled.*
- *You can buy and cook the lobster a day in advance, remove the meat from the shell and refrigerate it ready to be used the next day or you can buy already cooked lobster from a seafood store.*
- *Hot dog buns are the recommended buns for this sandwich because they do not take away from the lobster flavor.*

# Meatball Marinara Sub

*A sandwich made with leftover meatballs coupled with a fresh green salad is the perfect meal for a busy day.*

## Ingredients
2 8-inch French rolls
4 Tbsp marinara sauce (page 204)
8-10 meatballs (page 114))
4 slices mozzarella cheese
1 cup shredded lettuce
¼ red bell pepper, sliced thin
Vinegar and oil
Sliced pickled peperoncini

## Preparation
1. Preheat the oven to broiler.
2. Drizzle the shredded lettuce and sliced peppers with vinegar and oil.
3. Split the rolls in half horizontally but not completely through on long side.
4. Arrange meatballs onto bottom halves of the rolls. Spoon a generous amount of marinara sauce over the meatballs. Arrange the mozzarella cheese on top and put under the broiler to melt the cheese.
5. Top with the shredded lettuce, bell pepper and lettuce mixture and sliced peperoncini. Serve immediately with extra marinara sauce for dipping.

Makes 2 sandwiches

## Tips
- *When you make spaghetti and meatballs, make extra meatballs for sandwiches for the next day.*

# Smoked Salmon Bagel Sandwich
*A classic smoked salmon and cream cheese on bagel sandwich, flavor enhanced with the spicy sprouts or watercress.*

## Ingredients
1 egg bagel split in half
2 Tbsp cream cheese
1 tsp chopped red onion
1 tsp capers
3 oz. sliced smoked salmon
1 hardboiled egg sliced
¼ cup spicy sprouts or
  few sprigs of watercress

## Preparation
1. Lightly toast the bagel. On the bottom half spread the cream cheese, sprinkle with chopped onions and capers. Top with sliced smoked salmon.
2. Slice the hardboiled egg in thin slices and lay over the smoked salmon. Top with the sprouts or watercress.

Makes 1 serving

## Tips
- *If using capers pickled in salted brine, rinse them before using, to wash out some of the salt.*

# Egg Salad Sandwich

*Sometimes the simplest and tastiest sandwich is the most satisfying. It can't get much simpler and healthier than this. The spicy sprouts or watercress give a little zing to the sandwich.*

## Ingredients
3 hardboiled eggs
1 tsp chopped chives
½ tsp chopped fresh oregano (optional)
2½ Tbsp mayonnaise
Salt and pepper to taste
4 slices multi-grain bread
¼ cup spicy sprouts or few
   sprigs of watercress (optional)
Sliced cucumbers
Cherry tomatoes

## Preparation
1. In a medium bowl, chop the hardboiled eggs and mix in chopped chives and fresh oregano. Mix in the mayonnaise and adjust the seasoning with salt and pepper.
2. Slightly toast the bread and divide the egg salad on 2 slices of the toasted bread and spread around. Top with spicy sprouts or watercress. Top with the other two slices of bread.
3. Serve with sliced cucumbers and cherry tomatoes.

Makes 2 servings

## Tips
- *Top these sandwiches with smoked salmon or crispy bacon, they make a wonderful luncheon treat.*
- *<u>Perfect hard boiled eggs:</u> Place the eggs in a saucepan and cover with cold water one inch above the eggs. (To prevent cracking, add half a teaspoon salt to the water). Bring the water to a boil, lower the heat and simmer for 6 minutes. Turn off the heat and let the eggs stay in the hot water for 5 minutes. Drain the water and fill up the saucepan with cold water. Let the eggs cool in cold water.*

# Meatloaf Ciabata

*When preparing a big meal is not on the agenda, a meatloaf sandwich just hits the spot. A wonderful way to use leftover meatloaf. These sandwiches are also good for picnics.*

## Ingredients
1 6-inch Ciabata roll
1 Tbsp Mayonnaise
½-inch thick slices of leftover
 meatloaf (page 116)
Sliced mozzarella cheese
Lettuce leaves
Avocado
Sliced pickled peperoncini

## Preparation
1. Split the roll in half horizontally but not completely through one long side.
2. Arrange meatloaf slices onto bottom halves of the rolls top with mozzarella. (If you wish, put under the broiler to melt the cheese). Top with lettuce, sliced avocadoes, and sliced peperoncini.

Makes 1 serving

# Grilled Bratwurst Sandwich

*If you are not a fan of bratwurst, you may use knockwurst or any other kind of sausage. Heating sauerkraut in apple cider brings a little sweetness countering the tartness of the sauerkraut and it balances the flavors. A potato salad will be the perfect accompaniment.*

## Ingredients
4 Bratwursts, or any other sausages
8 slices of rye bread
2 Tbsp butter, room temperature
1 small can sauerkraut
½ cup apple juice
4 Dill pickles, quartered lengthwise
4 large slices tomatoes
4 slices Swiss cheese

## Preparation
1. Split the sausages in half lengthwise but do not cut through. Open flat and place on the grill over medium heat and cook 3-5 minutes per side or until cooked through.
2. Drain the sauerkraut, squeezing out all the salty brine. Add the apple juice and heat until warm.
3. Heat a large flat grill, or sauté pan. Butter one side of each slice of bread and place in the hot sauté pan buttered side down. Top with grilled sausage, warm sauerkraut, tomato and Swiss cheese. Top with the other slice of bread buttered side up. Grill the sandwich in a heated skillet until one side of the bread is browned, then flip over and grill the other side, or until the cheese is melted and the bread is golden brown. Cut sandwich in half and add pickles to the plate.
4. Serve on the side: mayonnaise, mustard, and Thousand Island dressing.

Makes 4 servings

## Tips
- *The thicker sliced rye bread works better for these sandwiches.*
- *If you have a panini press, that will work too.*

# Chicken Burger

*Burgers don't have to be the same all the time. By using a little imagination and flavors complementing each other, we can create super burgers. This is a delicious alternative to a beef hamburger. Chicken burgers have a tendency to fall apart easily on the grill, so it is best to pan sauté with a little butter or olive oil.*

## Ingredients

1 lb ground dark chicken meat
1 lb ground breast of chicken
1 onion, minced
2 cloves garlic, crushed
2 slices white bread, soaked in water
  and squeezed dry
1 egg
2 Tbsp chopped fresh oregano
3 Tbsp chopped fresh parsley
½ tsp cumin
¾ tsp red pepper flakes
½ tsp black pepper
1¼ tsp salt
2-3 Tbsp butter or olive oil for frying
Lettuce leaves, sliced tomatoes,
  sliced Jack cheese, sliced avocadoes,
  radishes, sprouts, pickles, mayonnaise
  and mustard.

## Preparation

1. In a medium size bowl combine: chicken, onion, garlic, bread, egg, oregano, parsley, cumin, chili powder, salt and pepper. If too soft, add some bread crumbs to give body to the mixture. Mix thoroughly until well blended. Form into 6 patties. Refrigerate at least half an hour to firm up the patties and to allow flavors to blend.
2. Melt butter in the skillet. Add patties (do not overcrowd the pan) and fry until browned on one side, 3-4 minutes, then turn them over and brown the other side. Serve with sesame hamburger buns and the toppings.
3. For toppings use; lettuce, sliced tomatoes, Swiss or Jack cheese, sliced avocado, radish sprouts or a combination of sprouts. Serve Dijon mustard, mayonnaise and dill pickles on the side.

Makes 6 patties

## Tips

- *You really want to serve the chicken well cooked, so I suggest making the patties not very thick to make sure they cook through in a short period of time.*
- *To make even sized patties; use a jar lid, lay a piece of plastic wrap over the lid, then take a piece of the ground chicken and press it in the lid to take the shape of the lid. Flip out the plastic wrap with the patty and place on a tray. All your patties will be the same size and thickness.*

# Falafel Sandwich

*Falafel sandwiches were our favorite sandwiches to eat where we grew up in Beirut, Lebanon. They have become quite popular in the Unites States, especially with vegetarians.*

## Ingredients
2 6-inch round pita breads
1 cup chopped lettuce
½ cup chopped tomatoes
8 falafel patties, fried (page 44)
2-3 Tbsp Tahini Sauce (page 207)

## Preparation
1. Open the pita breads half-way (If using larger size pita bread, cut them in half)
2. Sprinkle ½ cup chopped lettuce in each pita bread pocket, top with ¼ cup chopped tomatoes. Arrange fried falafel patties and drizzle with Tahini Sauce.
3. Serve immediately with extra Tahini Sauce on the side.

Makes 2 sandwiches

## Tips
- *Falafel sandwiches are good when served while the falafels are still hot.*
- *Place the uncooked falafel in a plastic bag and freeze it. It will keep good for several weeks. When using frozen falafel mixture, just add half a teaspoon of baking soda before frying.*

# Sauces and Marinades

## Basic Tomato Salsa

*Most people associate this Tomato Salsa with Mexican food. There are numerous recipes for it; this one has just the basic ingredients of tomato, onion, jalapeno and cilantro.
It goes well with a variety of dishes, especially with Mexican dishes.*

### Ingredients
3 cups diced ripe firm tomatoes
1 white onion, diced
    or 3-4 scallions, chopped
1 jalapeño pepper, chopped fine
½ cup chopped cilantro
½ tsp salt
2 Tbsp lime juice

### Preparation
1. Put diced tomatoes, onion, jalapeño pepper, and cilantro in a medium bowl. Drizzle with lime juice and add salt. Toss gently until well mixed.
2. Cover and refrigerate for an hour allowing the flavors to blend.

Makes 3 cups

### Tips
- *If you like your salsa spicy, add one more jalapeno pepper to the salsa.*
- *Always wear rubber gloves when chopping jalapeños; if not make sure you wash your hands well with warm water and soap when finished chopping.*
- *This salsa is good served as an appetizer with tortilla chips.*
- *Can be prepared several hours in advance; add salt and lime juice just before serving.*

# Mediterranean Salsa

*This particular salsa is good accompaniment for Greek dishes, especially for spicing up any grilled meat used in sandwiches.*

## Ingredients
½ cup diced cucumbers
1 firm tomato, seeded and diced
¼ cup diced green bell pepper
¼ cup diced red bell pepper
1 jalapeño pepper, seeded, diced fine
¼ cup diced red onion
2 Tbsp diced Kalamata olives
1½ tsp balsamic vinegar
1 Tbsp lemon juice
2 Tbsp Extra-virgin olive oil
½ tsp dried oregano
½ tsp dried thyme
1 clove crushed garlic
Salt and pepper to taste
¼ cup crumbled feta cheese

## Preparation
1. In a medium size bowl, combine all ingredients together except feta cheese. Mix and refrigerate.
2. Before using mix in feta cheese. Serve with any meat dish.

Makes 2 cups

## Tips
- *This sauce is particularly good when making sandwiches with leftover kebabs.*

# Chili Spiced Mango Sauce

*Don't let the long list of ingredients intimidate you. It is very easy to prepare.
A zingy sauce that is good with chicken and delicious with any strong flavored fish dish,
like swordfish. Also good with cheese quesadillas.*

## Ingredients
1 large ripe mango
1 Tbsp vegetable oil
1 red onion, very thinly sliced
3 cloves garlic, finely chopped
1 Tbsp grated fresh ginger
1 jalapeño pepper, finely chopped
1 Tbsp honey
¼ tsp cinnamon
Pinch of cloves
Pinch of nutmeg
¼ cup dark rum
¼ cup lemon juice
¼ cup chopped cilantro
Salt and pepper to taste

## Preparation
1. Peel the mango and dice into half inch pieces.
2. Heat the oil in a saucepan and add the sliced onion, garlic, ginger and jalapeño pepper. Cook for 3-4 minutes or until the onions are soft.
3. Add the mango, honey, cinnamon, cloves and nutmeg. Mix and heat through for 3-4 minutes. Add the rum and simmer to evaporate the alcohol. Add the lemon juice, cilantro, salt and pepper to taste. Remove from heat.

Makes 1½-2 cups

## Tips
- *Can be prepared earlier in the day and just heat it through before serving.*
- *To chop jalapeño peppers, wear rubber gloves, if not, make sure you wash your hands well with warm water and soap.*

# Whole Cranberry Sauce

*A Thanksgiving dinner is not complete without Cranberry Sauce.
This sauce is easy to prepare and much tastier than canned Cranberry Sauce.*

## Ingredients
1 cup sugar
½ cup water
½ cup orange juice
2 tsp orange zest
1 (12 oz) pkg fresh cranberries

## Preparation
1. Combine sugar, water, orange juice, and orange zest in a medium saucepan and bring to a boil over medium-high heat. Boil for a few minutes until sugar is completely dissolved.
2. Rinse the cranberries. Add to the syrup and return to boil. Reduce the heat to medium-low and simmer for 8-10 minutes until the skins burst and the liquid is clear. Skim the foam.
3. Cool completely to room temperature. Refrigerate until serving time.

Makes 2½ cups

## Tips
- *For variation you may add any one of the following ingredients: chopped nuts, chopped apple, lemon peel, rum, ginger, cinnamon, or nutmeg.*

# Three-Pepper Sauce

*This colorful sauce provides the finishing touch to any meat dish. The combination of red, yellow, and green peppers, combined with mushrooms also makes it as a good vegetable side dish or a flavorful addition to a pasta dish.*

## Ingredients
- 2 Tbsp olive oil
- 1 large onion, sliced into thin strips
- 1 clove crushed garlic
- 1 red bell pepper, sliced into thin strips
- 1 green bell pepper, sliced into thin strips
- 1 yellow bell pepper, sliced into thin strips
- 8 oz. crimini or white mushrooms, sliced
- 2 tsp minced basil leaves
- ½ tsp red chili pepper
- ½ cup red wine
- Salt and pepper to taste

## Preparation
1. Heat the oil in a frying pan, sauté the onions and garlic.
2. Add the peppers and sauté until they start wilting. Add the mushrooms. Keep sautéing until the mushrooms release their juices. Add the basil and red chili pepper.
3. Add the wine and simmer until liquid is reduced. Adjust seasoning.

Makes 3-4 cups

## Tips
- *This pepper sauce is good with any meat dish, chicken or fish.*

# Mushroom Sauce

*This simple mushroom sauce is good as a side dish or as a topping for any meat dish: chicken, beef, pork, or veal.*

## Ingredients
2 Tbsp butter
1 Tbsp olive oil
1 onion, chopped
2 cloves garlic, chopped
1 cup sliced fresh button mushroom
1 cup sliced fresh crimini mushrooms
2 tsp Worcestershire Sauce
1 tsp lemon juice
¼ tsp red pepper flakes
Salt and pepper to taste
2 Tbsp chopped parsley

## Preparation
1. In a skillet on medium heat, melt the butter and oil. Sauté onion for a few minutes, then add garlic and mushroom. Continue sautéing for a few minutes longer until mushrooms start getting softer. Add Worcestershire Sauce, lemon juice and red pepper flakes.
2. Remove from heat and adjust seasoning. Add chopped parsley and stir.

Makes 1½ cup

## Tips
- *The sauce can be prepared ahead of time. Just heat before serving and add chopped parsley.*
- *You may use any kind of fresh mushrooms in any combination.*

# Shitake Mushroom Sauce

*Good with meatloaf, turkey, chicken, or any grilled meat dish.*

## Ingredients
½ lb shitake mushrooms, chopped
3 Tbsp butter
2 Tbsp chopped shallots
2 tsp chopped garlic
1/3 cup dry white wine
3 cups chicken stock
1 cup whipping cream
¼ tsp cayenne pepper
½ tsp salt
½ tsp pepper

## Preparation
1. Sauté shallots, garlic and mushrooms in butter.
2. Deglaze pan with white wine, reduce to one tablespoon. Add chicken stock, and reduce by half. Add cream and reduce by half again. Remove from heat. Season with cayenne pepper, salt and pepper.

Makes 3 cups

## Tips
- *To thicken the sauce, use half of the cooked chopped mushrooms in a food processor and chop them finely, then add to the sauce.*

# Super Easy Marinara Sauce

*If you have fresh ripe tomatoes, by all means use them to make your tomato sauce, otherwise use canned crushed tomatoes. The sugar balances the flavors and cuts the acidity.*

## Ingredients
2 Tbsp olive oil
1 medium onion, chopped
2 cloves garlic, crushed
1 (28 oz) can crushed tomatoes
1 tsp salt
½ tsp black pepper
¼ tsp red pepper flakes
1 tsp sugar
2 tsp crushed oregano
2 Tbsp chopped fresh basil

## Preparation
1. Heat olive oil in a 4-5 quart saucepan over moderately-high heat.
2. Sauté chopped onion until softened and changing color. Add garlic and sauté for another minute.
3. Add crushed tomato, salt, peppers, sugar, and oregano. Simmer uncovered for approximately 30 minutes, stirring occasionally, until slightly thickened. Add chopped basil and cook a few minutes longer.
4. Use in any pasta dish that calls for Marinara Sauce.

Makes 4 cups

## Tips
- *The sauce can be refrigerated for up to two days before using. It keeps for a month in the freezer in an airtight container.*
- *For spicier Marinara Sauce, increase the red pepper flakes.*

# Pesto Sauce

*Nothing compares to aromatic and flavorful fresh-made basil pesto sauce. It is quick and easy to make in a blender or food processor and is freezer friendly. Use it on pizzas or pasta dishes. Using parsley keeps the sauce vibrant green since basil darkens on its own.*

## Ingredients

4 cups coarsely chopped fresh basil
1 cup chopped fresh parsley leaves
2 cloves chopped garlic
1 cup pine nuts
¾ cup extra virgin olive oil
1 cup grated Parmesan cheese
Salt and pepper to taste

## Preparation
1. In a food processor fitted with a metal blade or in a blender, puree all the ingredients.
2. Add salt and pepper to your taste.

Makes 2 cups

## Tips
- *Pesto can be refrigerated for a few weeks, or frozen for a longer period of time. Divide leftovers among the wells of an ice-cube tray. Once frozen, pop out the cubes and store in a freezer bag.*

# Cilantro Pesto with Peanuts
*This pesto is good with pasta or grilled vegetables.*

## Ingredients
½ cup roasted, unsalted peanuts
1 clove crushed garlic
2 cup loosely packed cilantro leaves
1 jalapeno pepper, seeded and deveined
2 Tbsp fresh lime juice
½ cup vegetable or peanut oil
½ tsp salt
½ tsp black pepper
¼ cup Parmesan cheese

## Preparation
1. In a food processor fitted with a metal plate, puree 2 tablespoons oil with the peanuts.
2. Add cilantro, garlic, jalapeno pepper, lime juice, salt and pepper. Puree.
3. Add the cheese, and gradually add the oil to your desired consistency. (If the sauce is too thick, add a little more oil.)
4. Serve over pasta or grilled vegetables.

Makes 1¼ cup

# Bolognese Sauce

*This simple Bolognese Sauce can be used over pasta or in Lasagna preparation.*

### Ingredients
¼ cup olive oil
1/3 cup finely diced carrots
1 medium onion, chopped
2 tsp crushed garlic
¾ lb ground beef
¾ cup white wine
1 (28 oz) can crushed tomatoes
1 tsp dried thyme
1½ tsp dried oregano
½ tsp sugar
1 tsp salt
½ tsp black pepper
¼ tsp red pepper flakes
2 cups water or chicken broth

### Preparation
1. Heat olive oil in a 4-5 quart saucepan over medium-high heat.
2. Sauté chopped onion and carrots until they get soft and start changing color. Add garlic and sauté for another minute.
3. Add ground beef and sauté stirring frequently and breaking up any large clumps. Cook until the meat is no longer pink.
4. Deglaze the pan with ¾ cup of white wine and cook until wine evaporates.
5. Add crushed tomatoes with its juice, thyme, oregano, sugar, salt, pepper, pepper flakes and water. Simmer uncovered for approximately 30 minutes, stirring occasionally, until slightly thickened. Remove from heat. Use as needed.

Makes 5-6 cups

### Tips
- *You can refrigerate the Bolognese Sauce for a week or freeze up to several months.*

# Spaghetti Sauce

*This basic Spaghetti Sauce could be used in any pasta dish that calls for Spaghetti sauce.*

1. To prepare Spaghetti Sauce follow the Bolognese Sauce measurements and instructions. Eliminate the meat and reduce the water to 1 cup.
2. If you wish to have a creamy sauce, transfer the sauce to a blender and puree (or puree with a hand held blender).
3. Use in any pasta dish that calls for Spaghetti Sauce.

Makes 4 cups

### Tips
- *You can refrigerate the Bolognese Sauce for a week or freeze up to several months.*

# Tahini Sauce
*This is a good sauce to serve with fish or fried eggplant.*

## Ingredients
2 Tbsp tahini (sesame paste)
4 Tbsp lemon juice
6 Tbsp water
Salt to taste
2 Tbsp chopped parsley

## Preparation
1. In a small bowl, measure tahini, lemon juice and water. Mix to a thin creamy consistency. Add salt to taste and parsley.

Makes 1 cup

# Tahini Sauce (Taratour)
*This is a good sauce to serve with falafel.*

## Ingredients
½ cup tahini (sesame paste)
2 cloves garlic, crushed
1/3 cup lemon juice
½ cup cold water
Salt to taste

## Preparation
1. In a food processor, combine, tahini, garlic, and lemon juice. Start processing while you add the water a little at a time, until desired creamy consistency is reached.
2. Add salt to taste. Serve with Falafel (page 44)

Makes 1¼ cup

# Mayonnaise

## Ingredients
2 egg yolks
¼ tsp salt
1 tsp dry mustard
1 tsp wine vinegar or lemon juice
1 cup vegetable oil or light olive oil

## Preparation
1. In a food processor combine egg yolks, salt, mustard and vinegar and process at lowest speed until well blended.
2. With the processor running at lowest speed, very slowly pour in the oil until mixture thickens and is completely emulsified. Taste mayonnaise and add a little more vinegar or lemon juice if necessary.

Makes 1¼ cup

# Lemon Herb Mayonnaise
*Lemon Herb mayonnaise is versatile and can be used in a variety of sandwiches.*

## Ingredients
¾ cup prepared mayonnaise
1 Tbsp lemon juice
1 Tbsp prepared horseradish
2½ tsp chopped fresh thyme

## Preparation
1. Mix all the ingredients together in a small bowl.

Makes 1 cup

## Tips
- *Good with Salmon patties on (page 108).*

# Mustard Mayonnaise
*Mustard mayonnaise can be used in practically all sandwiches.*

## Ingredients
¾ cup prepared mayonnaise
1 tsp lemon juice
1 Tbsp prepared Dijon mustard
1 tsp grainy mustard

## Preparation
1. Mix all the ingredients together in a small bowl.

Makes 1 cup

# Garlic Sauce

*If you like garlic, this garlic sauce is very good with grilled chicken. It can be used as a marinade for chicken dishes or served on the side.*

## Ingredients
3 cloves garlic, crushed
½ cup vegetable oil
¼ cup lemon juice
Salt to taste

## Preparation
1. In a food processor, combine garlic, oil, lemon juice and salt to taste. Process until sauce is creamy.
2. Serve with grilled or broiled chicken.

Makes ¾ cups sauce

# Steak Marinade

*This is a good marinade to use with any steak.*

## Ingredients
½ cup ketchup
1 tsp Worcestershire sauce
1 envelope Italian salad dressing mix
1½ tsp Dijon mustard
½ tsp black pepper
½ tsp red pepper flakes
¾ cup water
Salt to taste

## Preparation
1. Mix the above ingredients in a small bowl. Set aside.
2. If the steaks you are using are thicker than an inch, with a fork poke a few holes and place the steaks in a plastic bag.
3. Pour marinade over the steaks and refrigerate 6-8 hours. Turn the bag occasionally to marinate the steaks evenly.
4. Drain steaks and grill using the excess marinade for basting.

# Asian Steak Marinade
*This flavorful marinade is also good with beef tenderloin, chicken, or lamb chops*

## Ingredients
1 cup soy sauce
1 cup sake (Japanese rice wine)
½ cup sugar
1½ cup coarsely chopped cilantro
1 Tbsp crushed fresh ginger
4 cloves garlic, crushed
1 tsp crushed red pepper

## Preparation
1. In a food processor attached with a metal plate, puree the above ingredients.
2. If the steaks you are using are thicker than an inch, with a fork poke a few holes and place the steaks in a plastic bag.
3. Pour marinade over the steaks and refrigerate 4 hours or up to a day. Turn the bag around occasionally to marinate evenly.
4. Drain steaks and grill using the excess marinade for basting.

# Meat Marinades

*To give a different flavor to grilled meat, use any of these marinades.*
*Meat always benefits from infusion of flavors. It enhances the flavor and improves the texture.*

## Ginger Soy Marinade (For 1 lb meat)
1 Tbsp soy sauce
1 Tbsp olive oil
2 tsp lemon juice
1 clove garlic, crushed
1 tsp sesame oil
1 tsp sugar
    Mix all the ingredients together and marinate the meat.

## Sesame Marinade (For 1-2 lb meat)
¼ cup soy sauce
¼ cup lemon juice
2 Tbsp sesame oil
1-2 tsp Tabasco sauce
2 cloves garlic, crushed
    Mix all the ingredients together and marinate the meat.

## Tex-Mex Marinade (For 1-2 lb meat)
1 Tbsp ground cumin
2 tsp oregano
1 tsp chili powder
¼ cup lemon juice
2 Tbsp Worcestershire sauce
2 Tbsp vegetarian oil
2 cloves garlic, crushed
    Mix all the ingredients together and marinate the meat.

## Spicy Indian Marinade (For 1-2 lb meat)
¼ cup yogurt
1 tsp grated fresh ginger
1 tsp chili powder
1 tsp crushed garlic
½ tsp turmeric
2 tsp coriander
1 tsp ground cumin
2 tsp lemon juice
1 tsp salt
¼ cup vegetable oil
    Mix all the ingredients together and marinate the meat.

# Vegetables

## Artichokes with Fava Beans

*Fava beans also known as broad beans, are seasonal, best savored when fresh. They have a rich nutty flavor and a buttery creamy texture. They look like giant bumpy string beans. Shell the beans and discard the pods. You can eat the whole bean only when young and tender.*

### Ingredients
3 lbs fava beans
2 artichokes
4 Tbsp lemon juice
3 Tbsp Extra-virginolive oil
1 chopped onion
1 clove garlic, chopped
1 cup water
1 tsp salt
¼ tsp black pepper

### Preparation
1. Remove the beans from the fava bean pods.
2. Cut the stem off the artichokes and clean some of the tough leaves. Trim off the leaf tips. Cut the artichoke into quarters or sixths and remove the purple leaves and the fuzzy choke. Keep them in water and add 3 tablespoons of lemon juice to keep them from turning brown.
3. Sauté the chopped onions and garlic in the olive oil. Add the artichokes and beans and sauté a few minutes longer.
4. Cover with 1 cup water. Add the remaining 1 tablespoon lemon juice, salt and pepper. Bring to a boil. Simmer for 20-25 minutes until beans and artichokes are tender and the liquid is reduced. Remove from heat. Serve as a side dish warm, or at room temperature.

Makes 4 side dish servings

### Tips
- *Makes a nice vegetarian entrée.*

# Paella Vegetarian
*A treat for those who want a nice mix of vegetables and spices.*

## Ingredients
4 Tbsp Extra-virgin olive oil
1 cup chopped onion
2 cloves garlic, crushed
¾ cup chopped red pepper
¾ cup chopped yellow pepper
1 cup sliced carrots
1 small jar marinated artichoke hearts, drained
1 cup fresh string beans cup up
1 cup fresh asparagus cut up
¾ tsp saffron threads, crushed
2 bay leaves
8 peppercorns
¼ tsp crushed red pepper flakes
½ tsp paprika
2 tsp salt
¾ tsp black pepper
1 cup chopped tomatoes
½ cup dry white wine
2 cups Arborio Spanish rice
4 cups chicken broth
1 cup snap peas
1 cup frozen corn
¼ cup chopped parsley
Lemon wedges for garnish

## Preparation
1. Cut up all your vegetables and set aside.
2. Heat the olive oil in a paella pan or a large deep frying pan with a lid. Sauté chopped onion, peppers, and garlic until they are soft. Add carrots, artichoke hearts, string beans and asparagus and sauté for another minute.
3. Add the spices: peppercorns, bay leaves, saffron, pepper flakes, paprika, salt and pepper. Stir fry for a few minutes until the spices get aromatic.
4. Add the tomatoes and cook for 2-3 minutes until tomatoes release their juices. Add the wine and cook until the liquid is absorbed and the alcohol from the wine is evaporated.
5. Stir in the rice and add the broth and bring to a boil, reduce the heat, cover the pan and let it simmer until the rice has absorbed most of the water. Add the frozen corn and snap peas and continue cooking until all the liquid is absorbed. Fluff the rice with a fork, transfer to a shallow bowl. Sprinkle with chopped parsley and garnish with lemon wedges.
Serve with a nice green salad.

Makes 6-8 serving

## Tips
- *To prepare Paella for the vegetarians, use vegetable stock instead of chicken broth.*

# Fried Eggplant with Basil and Balsamic Vinegar

*A wonderful vegetable used in sandwiches also makes a pretty presentation for a variety of food on a buffet table.*

## Ingredients
2 large eggplants
3 eggs
3 Tbsp water
1/3 cup flour
Salt & pepper to taste
Oil for frying
Basil leaves
Balsamic Vinegar

## Preparation
1. Wash and peel the eggplants. Slice them into ½ rounds or lengthwise. Sprinkle with salt and arrange them in a colander to drain for 30 minutes.
2. Beat the eggs with water, add flour and season with salt and pepper.
3. Dry the eggplant with a paper towel and dip in the egg mixture.
4. Heat the oil and fry the eggplant slices until both sides are golden brown. Drain on paper towels.
5. Arrange the eggplant on a serving platter, drizzle with balsamic vinegar and sprinkle with basil leaves.

<u>Note</u>: *In the past, eggplant was salted to release its bitter juices and reduce bitterness. With modern agricultural growing techniques, they are usually not bitter. To salt an eggplant, cut according to your recipe instructions, place the eggplants in a colander and salt evenly. Half an hour later wipe off excess salt and pat eggplant dry and use.*

## Tips
- *For variety, you may use a different dressing made from:*
    *½ cup olive oil*
    *Juice of a lemon*
    *2 Tbsp chopped fresh cilantro or parsley*
    *Salt and freshly ground black pepper*
  *Put the ingredients in a bowl and whisk together then drizzle over eggplant.*
- *Another variety would be crumbled feta cheese sprinkled over eggplant then drizzled with the above dressing.*
- *Another possibility is to drizzle tahini sauce (page 207) over the eggplant.*

# Eggplant Imam Bayeldi

*There are many versions of this recipe from Greece to Iran. This dish is a Turkish specialty. The Greeks claim it was a Greek chef who created this dish for the Turkish Imam (priest) who at the time was living in Greece. When he overate this tasty dish he died.*
*The question remains whether he died from its good taste or from overeating.*

## Ingredients
12-14 Japanese eggplants
½ cup olive oil
½ yellow bell pepper, chopped
½ green bell pepper, chopped
½ red bell pepper, chopped
1 Jalapeno pepper chopped fine
4 large onions, chopped
4-5 large tomatoes, chopped
4 cloves garlic, chopped
1 Tbsp tomato paste
1 Tbsp red pepper paste
1 tsp red pepper
Salt and pepper to taste
12-14 cloves garlic sliced in half
½ cup chopped parsley

## Preparation
1. Remove stems from eggplants and peel off ½-inch strips of the skin lengthwise at intervals to give the eggplant a striped look.
2. Make a lengthwise cut in each eggplant.
3. In a large heavy skillet, heat 2 tablespoons of olive oil and sauté the onion, garlic, and peppers until the onions become transparent. Add tomato paste, pepper paste, pepper and chopped tomatoes. Add salt and pepper to taste. Cook a few minutes longer until tomatoes wilt and some of the liquid is evaporated.
4. In another large skillet, fry the eggplants turning them until they start browning. Set aside.
5. Using the same skillet, drain the remaining olive oil and arrange the eggplants in it with the cut side up.
6. Spoon the vegetable mixture into the slits, forcing in as much filling as possible. Spread the extra filling on top of the eggplants. Top each eggplant with a clove of garlic sliced in half.
7. Pour enough water to barely cover the eggplants. Bring the water to boil over high heat, a reduce the heat to moderately low, and simmer covered for 45 minutes or until the eggplants are tender. Add more water if necessary. Cool to room temperature.
8. To serve, remove eggplants carefully to a plate and pour the pan juices around them. Sprinkle chopped parsley before serving with pita bread. You may serve it hot, at room temperature or chilled.

Makes 12-14 servings

## Tips
- *This dish can be used either as an appetizer or as an entrée.*
- *It is an excellent vegetable dish for a buffet table.*

# Eggplant Parmesan

*If you are counting calories, bake or grill the eggplant instead of frying. Brush eggplant with olive oil and bake at 400° for 15-20 minutes until eggplant slices are soft, or grill.*

## Ingredients

2 medium eggplants, about 1½ lb
½ tsp salt
2 eggs
1 Tbsp milk
2/3 cup flour
Vegetable oil for frying
Salt and pepper to taste
8 oz Mozzarella cheese, sliced thin
1 cup shredded blend of four cheeses (Asiago, Romano, Provolone, & Fontina)
½ cup Parmesan cheese
3 cups of prepared marinara sauce (page 204)

## Preparation

1. Peel eggplant, then cut into rounds 1/3-inch thick. Sprinkle with salt and set in a colander for 20 minutes and let it drain. Blot with paper towel to dry.
2. Beat the eggs with 1 tablespoon of milk. Set aside. Heat the oil in a frying pan.
3. Place the flour in a shallow bowl. Flour each slice of eggplant, then dip in egg mixture and place in a single layer in the frying pan, fry until lightly browned. Remove from pan and drain on a paper towel.
4. Lightly oil a 2 quart gratin dish or an 9x11-inch baking dish. Spread ½ cup of marinara sauce on the bottom of the dish and make an overlapping layer of eggplant. Top with a layer of Mozzarella cheese. Make one more layer of marinara sauce, eggplant and cheese. Sprinkle the top with Parmesan cheese.
5. Bake in the middle of preheated oven 375°F for 30 minutes until hot and bubbly. Let the cheese set for five minutes. Cut into squares and serve.

Makes 4-5 servings

## Tips

- *I like using fresh mozzarella cheese, because of its smooth consistency.*
- *The blend of shredded cheese is sold prepackaged in the grocery store as "Quattro Formaggio".*
- *If you have prepared your casserole earlier in the day and refrigerated, baking time will be five to ten minutes longer.*

# Oven Fried Cauliflower

*Instead of frying cauliflower in oil, oven frying makes it much lighter.*

### Ingredients
1 head cauliflower
3 Tbsp olive oil
Garlic powder (optional)
Salt and pepper to taste

### Preparation
1. Preheat oven to 400°F before baking.
2. Break the cauliflower into florets and put them in a large plastic bag.
3. Sprinkle with salt and pepper and drizzle with the olive oil. Shake the bag to coat the the cauliflower with oil. Spread them on an oiled pan and bake 20-30 minutes until they start turning brown. Halfway through baking, turn them over to brown all sides.
4. Serve as a side dish.

Makes 4-5 serving

# Cheesy Cauliflower
*This cheesy cauliflower casserole is a great way to get the kids to eat cauliflower.*

## Ingredients
1 head cauliflower
2 Tbsp butter
4 Tbsp flour
1¼ cup warm milk
1 tsp Dijon mustard
½ cup grated cheddar cheese
¼ cup Parmesan cheese
2 Tbsp bread crumbs
3 Tbsp grated cheddar cheese
Garlic powder (optional)
Salt and pepper to taste

## Preparation
1. Preheat oven to 400°F before baking.
2. Break the cauliflower into florets and cook them until just tender. Drain. Place them in baking dish.
3. Melt the butter in a saucepan. Stir in flour and cook for 1-2 minutes.
4. Remove from the heat and whisk in the warm milk. Return to the heat and cook for 2 minutes stirring constantly until mixture thickens. Remove from heat, and add the cheeses and stir until the cheese is melted. Season with salt, pepper and garlic powder.
5. Spoon the cheese mixture over the cauliflower in the baking dish.
6. Mix together the bread crumbs and the extra 3 tablespoons of cheddar cheese and sprinkle over the sauce.
7. Bake in the preheated oven on the top shelf for 15 minutes, until it is heated through and the top starts browning. Serve as a side dish.

Makes 6 servings

## Tips
- *You can prepare this dish up to step 5 ahead of time. Right before serving, sprinkle bread crumbs mixture and bake.*

# Cauliflower and Garbanzo Bean Curry

*This is a spicy and hot vegetable dish. It could be used as a side dish or as a vegetarian entree served with basmati rice. Even if you do not like cauliflower, you will love this dish.*

## Ingredients
2 Tbsp vegetable oil
1 onion, diced
2 cloves crushed garlic
2 tsp grated fresh ginger (optional)
½ tsp turmeric
2 tsp curry powder
1 jalapeno pepper, finely chopped
2 Tbsp chopped red bell pepper
2 Tbsp chopped green bell pepper
1 head cauliflower, cut into florets
2 large tomatoes, chopped
1 (15 oz) can garbanzo bean, drained
1 (13.4 oz) can coconut cream
1 (10½ oz) can cream of mushroom soup
1 cup water
1¼ tsp salt
½ tsp black pepper
2 Tbsp lemon juice
2 Tbsp chopped fresh coriander

## Preparation
1. In a large saucepan heat 2 tablespoons vegetable oil and sauté onions until soft. Add garlic, ginger, jalapeno, bell peppers, turmeric and curry powder. Cook for another minute.
2. Add the cauliflower florets and stir well to coat with all the spices.
3. Add chopped tomatoes and cook for a minute to release its juices. Add coconut milk, mushroom soup and water bring to a boil over medium to high heat. Lower heat, add salt and pepper and adjust seasoning, cover and simmer for 10 minutes. Add the garbanzo beans and cook uncovered for another 10 minutes.
4. Add the lemon juice, and adjust seasoning one more time. Transfer to serving dish and sprinkle chopped coriander on top. Serve with basmati rice.

Makes 4-6 servings

## Tips
- *If you do not like this dish spicy hot, but like the curry flavoring, eliminate the jalapeno pepper.*

# Swiss Cheese - String Bean Casserole

*This is a great vegetable side dish to prepare for a large group. This casserole is our family's favorite vegetable side dish.*

## Ingredients

4 cups cooked fresh string beans, or (20 oz) frozen French cut string beans cooked
2 Tbsp butter
2 Tbsp flour
1 tsp sugar
1 tsp salt
½ tsp black pepper
2 Tbsp grated onion
1 cup sour cream
2 cups grated Swiss cheese
½ cup corn flakes crumbs or crumbs of Ritz or any other crackers
2 Tbsp butter melted

## Preparation

1. Preheat oven to 400°F before baking.
2. Cook the beans until tender. Drain and set aside.
3. In a large saucepan, melt butter. Stir in flour, sugar, salt, pepper, and grated onion and keep stirring for a few minutes. Add sour cream and heat. <u>Do not boil.</u>
4. Remove from heat and gradually add 1½ cup of the shredded cheese until it is all melted. Add the cooked beans to the saucepan.
5. Pour into a 2-quart greased casserole dish.
6. Sprinkle the remaining ½ cup of grated Swiss cheese on top.
7. In a separate small pan, melt the remaining 2 tablespoons of butter and add corn flake crumbs and mix.
8. Sprinkle buttered corn flake crumbs over the cheese.
9. Bake for 20-25 minutes, until cheese melts and the string beans are heated through.

Makes 10-12 servings

## Tips

- *Can be prepared ahead of time and baked just before serving.*
- *Makes a great side dish for buffet dinners.*

# Sautéed Green Beans with Red Pepper

*Sautéed Green Beans are easy to prepare, colorful and make a tasty vegetable side dish.*

## Ingredients
1 lb fresh string beans
1 red bell pepper
1 onion, chopped
1 Tbsp butter
1 Tbsp olive oil
Salt and pepper to taste

## Preparation
1. Cut off the ends of the string beans, then cut them into 1½-2 inch pieces. Blanch them, drain and set aside. Do not overcook. They should be slightly soft but firm.
2. Cut red pepper into strips.
3. Heat butter and oil together and sauté chopped onion and pepper for a few minutes. Add the blanched string beans and continue sautéing until the beans are heated through. Season with salt and pepper.
4. Serve as a side dish.

## Tips
- *You may want to sprinkle the top with toasted pine nuts or toasted slivered almonds.*
- *Instead of red pepper, cherry tomatoes are also good with the string beans.*

# Green Beans with Sautéed Onions and Tomatoes
*A nice vegetable dish which can be served cold or hot.*

## Ingredients
1 lb fresh string beans
1 onion, diced
2 cloves garlic, sliced
3 Tbsp olive oil
2 large ripe tomatoes, diced
Salt and pepper to taste

## Preparation
1. Cut the ends of the string beans, then cut them into 1½-2 inch pieces.
2. Heat olive oil in a saucepan and sauté chopped onion and garlic for a few minutes. Add the string beans and continue sautéing until the beans are coated with the olive oil and start turning bright green.
3. Add diced tomatoes, salt and pepper to taste. Add water to cover the beans. Bring water to a boil, then reduce heat and cook until string beans are tender.
4. Serve as a side dish.

# Pureed Lentils (Moujadara)

*This is a Lebanese dish made with pureed cooked lentils, rice and onions.*

## Ingredients
2 cups black lentils known as French lentils
6 cups water
1/3 cup short grain (Cal Rose) rice
2 medium onions
½ cup olive oil + 2 Tbsp butter
1½ tsp salt
¼ tsp black pepper

## Preparation
1. Rinse the lentils in a 4-5 quart saucepan. Cover with 6 cups of water and bring to a boil. Skim the foam and discard. Reduce the heat to medium and let lentils cook until tender. (About 15 minutes).
2. Add the rice and reduce heat to simmer. Cover the pan and let it cook until the rice is cooked, the liquid is reduced, and the mixture has thickened (approximately 15 minutes). If too dry, add a little more water. Add the salt and remove pot from the heat. With a hand held electric food processor, puree the lentil and rice mixture. Set aside.
3. Cut the onions in half and slice them thin. Put olive oil, butter, and sliced onion in a frying pan and cook until they turn dark brown and caramelized.
4. Take out ½ of the browned onions and drain on a paper towel. Pour the remaining onions in oil into the lentil mixture. Stir well. Put the pot back on low heat and stir occasionally to prevent the lentils from sticking to the bottom of the pot until the liquid comes to a boil. Remove from the heat.
5. While hot, pour 'moujadara' in a serving dish and garnish with the reserved drained onions.
6. Cool completely before serving.

Makes 5-6 servings

## Tips
- *This dish can be served warm or at room temperature.*
- *Keeps well refrigerated for 3-4 days.*

# Dhal Makhni
# (Lentils Seasoned with Butter Fried Spices)

*This dish is prepared with traditional Indian lentils. You can serve it with basmati rice as a family dinner, or use it as a side dish.*

## Ingredients
1 cup Channa dhal (lentils)
1 cup Urud dhal (lentil)
6 cups water
4 Tbsp butter
1 tsp mustard seeds
1 clove garlic, crushed
1 tsp crushed fresh ginger
1 onion, diced
1 tomato, diced
1 tsp garam masala
½ tsp red pepper flakes
½ tsp chili pepper
1 tsp cumin
Salt to taste

## Preparation
1. Rinse the dhals (lentils) and put in a slow cooker. Turn the heat on to medium and let it cook for 6-8 hours. You may cook it on the stove top as well; bring water to boil, reduce heat and let it simmer until lentils are soft and water has evaporated. With the back of a spoon, mash the lentils to make the mixture mushy.
2. Melt the butter in a frying pan, sauté mustard seeds for a minute, add garlic, ginger, and onion; sauté until onions are soft, add tomatoes and the rest of the spices. Mix well.
3. Pour the spices over the lentils and cover the pot. After five minutes, stir, adjust seasoning, and transfer to serving dish. Garnish with a piece of butter and fresh cilantro leaves. Serve with basmati rice (page 179 or 180)

Makes 6-8 servings

## Tips
- *Channa dhal is a yellow split lentil. You may purchase it in Indian or specialty grocery stores.*
- *Urud dhal is like pigeon peas, it comes with the black skin on or split. You may find them in Caribbean or Indian markets.*

# Fresh Spinach with Sautéed Onions in Olive Oil

*You may prepare this dish earlier in the day and just reheat before serving.*
*This wonderful healthy vegetable dish can also be served cold.*
*My mother always served this dish with her fried chicken.*

## Ingredients
1½ lb fresh spinach leaves
1 large onion, diced
3 Tbsp olive oil
2 tsp salt
½ tsp black pepper
¼ tsp red pepper flakes
2 Tbsp lemon juice

## Preparation
1. Rinse the spinach leaves in cold water and drain in a colander.
2. In a large saucepan bring 2 cups of water to boil and boil spinach for a few minutes, until leaves are soft. Drain and set aside.
3. In the same saucepan, heat 3 tablespoons of olive oil and sauté onions until soft. Add red and black pepper. Add the spinach and lemon juice and heat it through for 2 minutes. Adjust seasoning.

Makes 4-6 servings

## Tips
- *Spinach wilts considerably when cooked. For a side dish, make sure you buy 2 pounds of fresh spinach to serve six.*
- *I usually buy the 6 oz. packages of tender leaves of fresh spinach.*

# Okra with Cilantro in Tomato Sauce

*This dish is good served warm or at room temperature. An excellent dish for a buffet table because of its attractive presentation and advance preparation.*

## Ingredients
2 lb okra
3 Tbsp vegetable oil
2 medium size white onions, sliced thin
2 cloves garlic, sliced
1 tsp salt
¼ tsp black pepper
½ cup chopped cilantro
2 cups water
2 tsp lemon juice
1 (14.5 oz) can chopped tomatoes or 2 cups skinned and chopped fresh tomatoes

## Preparation
1. Remove the stems and hard caps of the okra by cutting them in a cone shape at their natural slant angle. Wash and drain the okra in a colander and spread them on a kitchen towel to dry completely.
2. Heat 2 tablespoons of oil in a pan and sauté the okras for 2 minutes in two or three batches until they are bright green and crisp. Do not let them start browning. Set aside.
3. Heat remaining 1 tablespoon of oil in a 4-quart pan and sauté the onions and garlic until they are wilted and start changing color.
4. Arrange sautéed okras in a deep frying pan in a circular pattern layering until all the okra is used. Leave an empty space in the center for the sautéed onions.
5. Mix chopped tomatoes, water, cilantro, salt and pepper and pour over the okra. Bring the liquid to a boil and lower the heat, cover the pan and cook on gentle heat until the okra is cooked and the liquid thickened. (Approximately 25-30 minutes). Turn off the heat. Let the okra cool in the pan.
6. To serve, place platter over the pan and invert.

Makes 8-10 servings

## Tips
- *Step 4 is done just to make an attractive presentation. You do not have to follow step 4 in layering the okra. You can just put everything in the pot and cook.*

# Succotash
*A tasty and colorful vegetable side dish that is good with any entrée.*

## Ingredients
1 (8 oz) pkg frozen lima beans
1 (8 oz) pkg frozen corn kernels
2 Tbsp butter
1 medium size onion, diced
½ red bell pepper, diced
½ tsp sugar
Pinch of black pepper

## Preparation
1. Cook lima beans and corn according to package directions. Drain and set aside.
2. In a saucepan melt butter and sauté diced onion until tender. Add diced bell pepper and sauté for another minute.
3. Add drained lima beans, corn, sugar and pepper into the saucepan. Heat it through and adjust seasoning.

Makes 4-6 servings

## Tips
- *If you like soy beans, substitute soy beans for the lima beans.*

# Banana Squash Puree

*This vegetable dish has a rich flavor and golden color. Preparation with brown sugar will add a little sweetness to it. Can be prepared several days in advance and reheated in a bowl over a pot of simmering water.*

## Ingredients
3 lbs banana squash
¾ tsp salt
4 Tbsp butter, melted
½ cup brown sugar
Dash of nutmeg

## Preparation
1. Peel the banana squash with a potato peeler and cut into 1½-inch pieces.
2. In a saucepan, cover the cut up squash with water and add the salt. Bring to a boil and cook until the squash is tender enough for smashing.
3. Drain all the liquid from the squash. Mash the squash with a potato masher. Add butter, sugar, and nutmeg. After mixing, taste and adjust seasoning. (If you wish to use a food processor, by all means do so; with the steel blade, just pulse until the squash is coarsely pureed then add the rest of the ingredients). Serve hot as a side dish.

Makes 5 cups

## Tips
- *Instead of banana squash, you may use butternut squash.*
- *Butternut squash is hard to cut and peel with a knife. I use a potato peeler to remove the hard shell making it easier to cut into cubes.*
- *This vegetable dish can be made several days in advance. Reheat it in a bowl of simmering water. It should have the consistency of mashed potatoes. If it is thick, thin it with milk or orange juice.*

# Carrot Puree

*It is wonderful to be able to prepare a vegetable side dish that is colorful and delicious and can accompany any dish. Especially good with fish.*

### Ingredients
1 pound carrots
½ tsp salt
½ cup cream
¼ tsp ground ginger
¼ cup sugar
Salt and pepper to taste

### Preparation
1. Peel and cut carrots crosswise into ½-inch slices.
2. In a saucepan of lightly salted boiling water, cook carrots 7-8 minutes, or until tender but not soft. Drain.
3. Transfer carrots to a food processor and process until finely chopped but not pureed. With the machine running add the cream and ginger and pulse until well blended.
4. Place the sugar in a small heavy saucepan over medium-low heat and cook while stirring occasionally until the sugar starts darkening and caramelizes. Remove from heat, and with the processor running, pour caramelized sugar down the feed tube of the food processor. Process until well blended. Season to taste.

Makes 4 servings

### Tips
- *This vegetable dish can be prepared in advance and reheated in a bowl over simmering water.*

# Carrot Crunch

*This simple preparation yields delicious results in this side dish. Orange zest adds tremendous flavor and the almonds add the crunch.*

## Ingredients
1 pound carrots
½ tsp salt
1½ Tbsp butter
2 Tbsp brown sugar
1 tsp orange zest
¼ cup toasted slivered
   or sliced almonds
Salt and pepper to taste

## Preparation
1. Peel and cut carrots crosswise into ½-inch slices.
2. In a saucepan of lightly salted boiling water, cook carrots 7-8 minutes, or until tender but not soft. Remove from pan and set aside.
3. In the same saucepan, melt butter, sugar, and orange zest. Add the almonds and mix well.
4. Return carrots to the pan and over low heat warm for a few minutes, stirring occasionally to coat with the almond mixture. Adjust seasoning.

Makes 4 servings

# Asparagus Parmesan
*This is a very easy first course or a side dish.*

## Ingredients
2 lb fresh asparagus (about 25)
2 Tbsp butter
½ cup Parmesan cheese, freshly grated
Salt and pepper to taste
1 lemon, cut into wedges

## Preparation
1. Preheat oven to 400°F before roasting.
2. Trim the asparagus and peel the thick part with a potato peeler.
3. Simmer the asparagus in water until the thick part can be pierced with a knife. Drain and plunge into ice water to stop the cooking. Remove from ice water, dry and set aside until ready to roast.
4. Butter a baking sheet and lay the asparagus in a single layer. Sprinkle with salt and pepper and half of the Parmesan cheese. Roast for 10 minutes, sprinkle remaining Parmesan cheese and return to the oven until the cheese melts. Serve with lemon wedges

Makes 5-6 servings

## Tips
- *Medium size asparagus are best for this dish.*

# Corn and Zucchini Casserole

*The combination of these summer vegetables flavored with oregano and topped with cheddar cheese makes a perfect side dish to any meal. It is colorful and can make an attractive addition to a buffet table.*

## Ingredients
2 zucchinis
2 yellow squashes
1 (14¾ oz) can creamed corn
1 (15¼ oz) can whole corn
8-10 cherry tomatoes
¼ tsp black pepper
¾ tsp salt
1 tsp crushed oregano
½ cup grated cheddar cheese

## Preparation
1. Slice the zucchinis and yellow squashes into ¼-inch thick round slices.
2. In a medium size saucepan, bring water to a boil and blanch the zucchini and squash. Do not overcook. They should be slightly soft but firm.
3. In greased 8x10-inch baking dish, spread the creamed & whole corn on the bottom. Arrange the zucchini slices alternating with the yellow squash.
4. Slice the cherry tomatoes into ¼-inch round slices and place them randomly in between the squash slices.
5. Sprinkle the top with salt, pepper, and oregano. Then sprinkle with grated cheddar cheese.
6. Bake in preheated oven 350°F for 15-20 minutes until heated through and cheese is melted.

Makes 6-8 servings

## Tips
- *Use firm and uniform size zucchini for best flavor and looks. This can be assembled ahead of time and baked in the last minute.*

# Spinach and Cheese Strata

*A versatile make-ahead breakfast strata is a good option for brunch or lunch. You can create your own version with any vegetable, meat and cheese combination.*

## Ingredients

1 (10 oz) pkg frozen chopped spinach, thawed and liquid squeezed out
¾ cup chopped onion
1½ Tbsp butter
½ tsp salt
¼ tsp black pepper
1/8 tsp grated nutmeg
5 cups 1-inch cubed (French or Italian) bread
1½ cups grated Gruyere cheese
1 cup grated Parmigiano Reggiano
1½ cups milk
5 eggs
1 Tbsp Dijon mustard

## Preparation

1. Saute chopped onion in butter in a skillet over moderate heat until soft. Add ¼ teaspoon salt, 1/8 teaspoon pepper and 1/8 teaspoon nutmeg and stir for a minute. Then stir in the spinach. Remove from heat.
2. Butter an 8x8-inch glass or ceramic baking dish. Spread 1/3 of the bread cubes evenly then top with 1/3 of the spinach. Sprinkle 1/3 of each cheese. Repeat layers twice ending with the cheese on top.
3. In a large bowl whisk milk, eggs, mustard remaining ¼ tsp salt and 1/8 tsp pepper. Pour over the strada. Cover and refrigerate overnight.
4. Preheat oven to 350°F before baking. Let strada stand at room temperature for 30 minutes then bake uncovered in the middle shelf of the oven for 45 minutes until it is puffed and the top is golden brown. Let stand 5 minutes before serving.

Makes 3-4 servings

## Tips

- *Variation:* Use a (10 oz) package of chopped frozen broccoli and 4 oz cooked ham cubed instead of the spinach.

## Special Cornbread

*This is a special cornbread; it is sweeter than most cornbreads, lighter, and tastier. A favorite with our grandchildren. Good with chili and crock pot stews.*

### Ingredients
2 cup buttermilk baking mix
5 Tbsp cornmeal
¾ cup sugar
2 eggs
1 cup milk
½ cup melted butter

### Preparation
1. Preheat oven to 350°F before baking.
2. Grease a 9-inch square pan and set aside.
3. In a mixing bowl, combine baking mix, cornmeal, and sugar
4. Add eggs and milk. Beat until well blended.
5. Mix in melted butter.
6. Pour in prepared pan and bake for 35-40 minutes or until a wood pick comes out dry. Cool slightly. Cut into squares.

Makes 12 pieces

### Tips
- *Double the recipe and bake in a 9 x13-inch pan.*
- *If you do not like your cornbread sweet, then use less sugar.*

# Quick and Easy Brioche

*Thanks to modern technology, a food processor makes preparation of brioche a cinch.*

## Ingredients
1 pkg active dry yeast
½ cup warm water
1 tsp sugar
3¾ cups flour
1/3 cup sugar
¾ tsp salt
4 oz frozen butter
3 large eggs
1 egg for egg-wash

## Preparation
1. Mix together dry yeast, ½ cup warm water and 1 teaspoon sugar. Set aside for 10 minutes for the yeast to start fermenting.
2. Attach the metal blade in a food processor. Put in flour, sugar, salt and frozen butter; cut into 8 pieces. Process for 20 seconds until mixture resembles corn meal.
3. Gradually add yeast mixture, then the eggs one at a time and process until the dough comes together.
4. Turn out onto a lightly floured board and knead until smooth. Place dough in a greased bowl, cover and refrigerate overnight.
5. Next day, take the dough out of the refrigerator and let it rest at room temperature for half an hour.
6. Punch down and knead several times. Cut and shape into small brioches. Place them in a greased muffin tin. Let rise until doubled in size.
7. Beat the one egg with one tablespoon water and brush on top of the brioches before baking.
8. Bake in a preheated oven at 400°F for 15 minutes. Reduce heat to 350°F and bake for another 15-20 minutes until golden brown.

Makes 18 brioches

## Tips
- *Brioche dough should rise in the refrigerator for best taste and texture. Start preparing this dough the day before you plan to use it.*

# Braided Brioche Bread

*Easter celebrations are very important in the Middle East, and lots of pastry and bread preparations are involved. The traditional Easter bread is delicious; it is similar to brioche but flavored and braided. During Easter, it is sold in bakeries as well as made at home. There are many recipes around and I have tried a lot of them, but this one is my family's favorite. Bake it and share it!*

## Ingredients

5 lb bag of flour
2 tsp baking powder
6½ cubes of butter
2½ pkg yeast plus 1 tsp sugar
½ cup warm water
13 eggs
1 tsp vanilla
3 cups sugar
½ tsp salt
2 Tbsp mahlab
1 tsp pulverized Mastik (optional)
1¾ cup whole milk
2 cups raisins
2 eggs beaten + 2 tsp milk
    for egg-wash
Sesame seeds to sprinkle on top

## Preparation

1. Sift flour and baking powder in a very large bowl. Set aside.
2. Melt butter and set aside to cool.
3. Dissolve yeast with 1 teaspoon sugar and ½ cup warm water and set aside for 10 minutes to start fermenting.
4. In a large bowl, beat the eggs and add vanilla, butter, sugar, salt, mahlab, mastik and milk; plus the fermented yeast.
5. Gradually add the mixture to the sifted flour. Knead well.
6. Add raisins and knead some more until smooth and satiny.
7. Place dough in an extra large greased bowl, cover and set in a warm place until it doubles in size. Depending on the temperature in the room, it can take from 4-6 hours and maybe longer.
8. When dough is ready, divide into portions and braid them into loaves, or shape them any way you wish. Arrange them on a non-stick baking tray 3-4 inches apart and let them double in size before baking. Brush the tops with the egg-wash and sprinkle sesame seeds on top.
9. Bake in a preheated oven 350°F until the tops are golden brown (approximately 30 minutes). Cool on a wire rack.

Makes 13-14 (12-inch) long braided loaves

## Tips

- *If you knead the dough late at night, it will be ready for shaping early in the morning.*
- *Mahlab and mastik are flavorings sold in Middle Eastern grocery stores.*

# Sticky Buns

*These wonderfully gooey buns are best served warm. Everyone's favorite! They make a special treat for breakfast on a weekend or on a special day. They are scrumptious!*

## Ingredients
1 recipe Brioche dough (page 235)
1 cup brown sugar
1 tsp cinnamon
1 cup chopped pecans
1 egg for egg-wash

<u>Caramel sauce</u>
6 oz butter
2 cups packed brown sugar
4 oz honey
½ cup cream
½ cup water

## Preparation
1. <u>*Prepare Caramel Sauce*</u>: In a saucepan over medium heat, melt butter and brown sugar together. Remove from heat, let cool. Whisk in the honey, cream, and water. Set aside.
2. Preheat oven to 350°F before baking.
3. <u>*Assemble buns:*</u> Roll out brioche dough to ¼-inch thick rectangle.
4. Combine 1 cup brown sugar, cinnamon and ½ cup of chopped pecans and sprinkle evenly over the dough.
5. Roll up the brioche in jelly-roll style and cut into 1-inch thick slices.
6. Spread the prepared sauce in the bottom of a 9 x13-inch pan, and sprinkle evenly with the remaining ½ cup chopped pecans over the sauce.
7. Over the sauce place the sliced brioche rolls, evenly spaced out, cover with plastic wrap and let it rise for 2-3 hours until doubled in size.
8. Whisk the egg with one tablespoon water and brush over the buns. Bake for 15-20 minutes until buns are golden and the sauce is bubbly. Cool in pan for 5 minutes. Invert onto a serving plate and serve while warm.

Makes 14-16 buns

## Tips
- *When pressed by time, use refrigerated flaky biscuits or crescent rolls instead of brioche. That will be your second best choice.*

# Zucchini Bread

*Children who will not even taste squash will love this cake. It is one way to get them to eat zucchini. Some restaurants serve zucchini bread, banana bread, or pumpkin bread with their luncheon salads. It is versatile. I like a slice of this bread spread with cream cheese along with a cup of coffee.*

## Ingredients
3 eggs
2 cups sugar
1 cup vegetable oil
1 tsp vanilla
½ cup drained crushed pineapple
3 cups flour
1 tsp salt
1 tsp baking soda
1 tsp baking powder
1 tsp cinnamon
¼ tsp nutmeg
2 cups grated zucchini
1 cup chopped walnuts or pecans

## Preparation
1. Preheat oven to 350°F before baking.
2. Grease and flour a 9x5x3-inch loaf pan.
3. In a mixing bowl, beat eggs, sugar, oil, and vanilla until creamy. Add pineapple and mix.
4. Sift together flour, salt, baking soda, baking powder, cinnamon, and nutmeg. Add to the egg mixture and mix until well incorporated. Fold in zucchini and walnuts.
5. Pour the batter into prepared loaf pan and bake for 50-60 minutes or until cake tester comes out clean. Cool on wire rack.

Makes 1 large or 2 small loaves

## Tips
- *When shredding zucchini, do not remove the skin. It adds color to the bread.*
- *Zucchini bread is good to serve with salads, or afternoon tea.*
- *Keeps in the refrigerator for over a week.*
- *Keeps in the freezer for several months. The flavor does not change.*
- *Bake in several disposable 4x6-inch pans and share with friends.*

# Pumpkin Bread

*You don't have to wait for Halloween to make this cake. It is good all year round for a snack, with coffee or with salads.*

## Ingredients
4 eggs
2¾ cups sugar
1 cup vegetable oil
1/3 cup water
1 tsp vanilla
2 cups canned pumpkin
3 1/3 cups flour
1 tsp salt
2 tsp baking soda
½ tsp baking powder
1 tsp cinnamon
1 tsp nutmeg

## Preparation
1. Preheat oven to 350°F before baking.
2. Grease and flour 2 (6x4.5-inch) disposable foil loaf pans.
3. In a mixing bowl, beat eggs, sugar, oil, water and vanilla until creamy.
4. Mix in canned pumpkin.
5. Sift together flour, salt, baking soda, baking powder, cinnamon, and nutmeg. Add to the egg mixture and mix until well incorporated.
6. Pour the batter into prepared loaf pans and bake for 60 minutes or until cake tester comes out clean. Cool on wire rack.

Makes 2 loaves

# Cheddar Cheese Bread

*A bread that does not need kneading. A delicious treat with any meal!*

## Ingredients
2½ cups flour
1 Tbsp sugar
½ tsp black pepper
1½ tsp baking powder
½ tsp baking soda
¾ tsp salt
2 eggs
1 cup sour cream
½ cup vegetable oil
¼ cup milk
4 oz shredded cheddar cheese

## Preparation
1. Preheat oven to 350°F before baking.
2. Grease the bottom and 1-inch sides of an 8x4-inch loaf pan.
3. In a large bowl stir together flour, sugar, black pepper, baking powder, baking soda and salt.
4. In another large bowl beat the eggs then add sour cream, oil and milk. Mix until well combined.
5. Add dry mixture along with the cheese to the wet mixture. Stir until just moistened. Do not beat or over stir.
6. Pour batter into the prepared pan and spread evenly. Bake for 45-50 minutes until a wooden pick inserted near the center comes out clean. Cool on a wire rack for 10 minutes then remove from the pan and continue cooling on a wire rack. Serve warm or at room temperature.

Makes 1 loaf

## Tips
- *The reason we do not grease the sides of the pan all the way up is to give a chance for the dough to adhere to the sides of the pan to rise.*

# Olive bread

*This is the shortcut version of the olive bread my aunt Sara used to make when we were little. She used to bake them in a clay oven in Kessab (a village in Syria). This makes a great accompaniment for a salad, or just a snack.*

## Ingredients
- 1 pkg Pillsbury's Grands buttermilk biscuits or 2 Pillsbury's refrigerated bread sticks dough.
- ¼ cup crumbled Feta cheese
- ½ cup chopped black Kalamata olives
- 2 Tbsp chopped green onion
- 1 small tomato chopped (without the seeds)
- 1 small jalapeño pepper deveined, chopped

## Preparation
1. Preheat oven to 350°F before baking.
2. Mix Feta cheese, olives, onion, tomato and pepper.
3. Separate the biscuit and split open each biscuit. On one half, spread one tablespoon of olive mixture. Cover with the other half, spread 1 teaspoon more of the olive mixture on top and with your fingers, press on it to seal and flatten.
4. Place them on a cookie sheet one inch apart and bake for 13-15 minutes, until they start browning.

Makes 8 breads or 16 breadsticks

## Tips
- *If using breadstick dough, follow the instructions on the package for twisting the breadsticks.*
- *You may also try making it with Pillsbury's Crescent rolls.*
- *You may use black cured olives, but if they are too salty, rinse them in cold water and squeeze dry before using.*

# Shankelish Bread

*This bread is another shortcut version of the variety of breads that reminds me of my childhood.*

## Ingredients
1 cup crumbled shankelish cheese (page 18)
2 cups shredded Jack cheese
1½ cup crumbled French Feta cheese
1½ cup chopped onion
3 Tbsp dried zahtar
3 Tbsp tomato paste
3 Tbsp pepper paste
1 cup olive oil
3 (14 oz) refrigerated Pillsbury's pizza dough

## Preparation
1. Preheat oven to 400°F before baking.
2. In a large mixing bowl; mix shankelish, Jack cheese, Feta cheese, onion and zahtar.
3. In another small bowl; mix tomato paste, pepper paste, and olive oil together. Pour over dry ingredients and mix well.
4. Unroll pizza dough on a cookie sheet. Press to desired thickness, or cut into 12-inch pieces and then roll each piece to desired thickness.
5. Top the crust with shankelish mixture and spread to the edges of the dough.
6. Bake for approximately 13 to 18 minutes, until the edges of the dough start turning golden brown.

Makes 36 pieces

## Tips
- *Just like pizza this small shankelish bread freezes very well. Could be served as an appetizer or for snacks.*

# Cakes

## Fudge Ribbon Cake

*This cake recipe was adapted from a Pillsbury Bake-Off award winning cake.
This is another family favorite cake.*

### Ingredients
1 box Pillsbury's Devils Food Cake Mix
3 eggs
1¼ cup water
½ cup vegetable oil
1 can Pillsbury's Whipped
   Chocolate Frosting

*Filling*
2 Tbsp butter
1 (8 oz) pkg cream cheese
¼ cup sugar
1 Tbsp cornstarch
1 egg
2 Tbsp milk
½ tsp vanilla extract

### Preparation
1. Preheat oven to 350°F before baking.
2. *Filling Preparation:* Cream 2 tablespoons of butter with cream cheese, add ¼ cup sugar and corn starch. Add 1 egg, 2 tablespoons milk and ½ teaspoon vanilla extract. Beat until smooth and creamy. Set aside.
3. *Cake preparation:* Combine cake mix, eggs, water, and oil. Beat for 2 minutes, until light and fluffy.
4. Spread half of the batter in a greased and floured 9x13-inch baking pan. Spoon cream cheese mixture over the batter and spread gently. Top with remaining batter and spread to cover the cheese mixture.
5. Bake for 50-60 minutes until cake springs back when touched lightly in center. Cool completely and frost with the canned frosting. Cut into squares.

Makes 12-15 servings

### Tips
- *This cake when decorated, makes a nice birthday or special party cake.*

# Pound Cake with Candied Fruits

*This Venetian fruitcake recipe was given to me by a friend of my father in 1965 who was a French pastry chef in Beirut, Lebanon. Rum soaked dried fruits are the goodies featured in this fruitcake. Bake at least eight days before you plan on serving to allow the flavors to mellow.*

## Ingredients
1 lb mixed candied fruits
½ cup rum, plus ½ cup for glazing
4 cups flour, plus 2 Tbsp
1 Tbsp baking powder
1 lb butter at room temperature
2¼ cup sugar
9 eggs at room temperature
1 tsp vanilla

## Preparation
1. Place the mixed fruits in a covered container and pour ½ cup of rum over them. Cover and let the fruits soak in rum for at least 24 hours, preferably 2-3 days.
2. Preheat oven to 375°F before baking. Butter and flour 3 (4x6-inch) loaf pans.
3. In a large bowl, sift 4 cups of flour and 1 tablespoon baking powder and set aside.
4. Cream the butter and sugar until light and fluffy. Add the eggs to the mixture 2 at a time alternating with flour and making sure not to overwork the batter.
5. Mix 2 tablespoons flour into the macerated fruit mixture to prevent the fruits from sinking to the bottom of the cake.
6. Gently fold in the macerated fruits, being careful to evenly distribute the fruits without over mixing.
7. Spoon the batter into prepared loaf pans.
8. Bake for 15 minutes then reduce heat to 350°F and bake 45 minutes longer or until cake tester comes out clean.
9. While cake is warm, brush the top with remaining ½ cup of rum. Let it cool, then wrap in plastic wrap and keep it in a cool place. Let the cake age for a week before serving. This cake tastes better when it has aged.

Makes 3(4x6-inch) loaves; or 2(5 x 9-inch) loaves.

## Tips
- *Mixing flour into the macerated fruit mixture prevents the fruits from sinking to the bottom of the cake pan. This will also keep the fruits from drying out while baking.*
- *This cake will keep well refrigerated for several weeks; in the freezer for several months.*

# White Chocolate Sour Cream Pound Cake

*A popular bundt cake that is moist and delicious. Attractive presentation without fussing with frosting.*

## Ingredients
4 oz white baking chocolate, melted
4 oz white baking chocolate, chopped
1 cup butter at room temperature
2 cups sugar
5 eggs at room temperature
2 tsp vanilla
3 cups flour
1 tsp baking powder
¼ tsp baking soda
½ tsp salt
1 cup sour cream

*Glaze*
4 oz. white baking chocolate, melted
4 oz. semisweet chocolate, melted

## Preparation
1. Preheat oven to 350°F before baking.
2. Butter and flour a 10-inch fluted pan.
3. In a large mixing bowl, cream the butter and sugar until light and fluffy. Add eggs one at a time beating well after each addition. Stir in vanilla and melted white chocolate.
4. Combine flour, baking powder, baking soda and salt; add to the creamed mixture alternating with sour cream. Mix until just combined.
5. Pour a third of the batter into the prepared pan. Sprinkle with half of the chopped white chocolate. Repeat this step. Pour the remaining batter on top.
6. Bake for 55-60 minutes or until cake tester comes out clean.
7. Cool for 10 minutes; remove from pan to a wire rack to cool completely.
8. When the cake is cool, drizzle with semisweet and white chocolate.

Makes 16 servings

## Tips
- *If you don't want to bother glazing the cake, before baking sprinkle the top of the batter with semisweet and white chocolate chips.*

# Fresh Apple Cake

*This wonderful cake makes an excellent desert served with ice cream or a dollop of whipped cream. The glaze is poured over the cake while it is hot, and that gives this dessert a rich moist texture. Preparation is easy and the taste is delicious.*

## Ingredients
2 cups sugar
3 cups flour
1 tsp baking soda
½ tsp baking powder
¼ tsp salt
1 tsp cinnamon
3 eggs at room temperature
1½ cup vegetable oil
1/3 cup orange juice
2 tsp vanilla
3 cups peeled and chopped apples
1 cup shredded coconut
1 cup chopped pecans

### *Glaze*
4 Tbsp butter
½ cup sugar
½ cup buttermilk
½ tsp baking soda

## Preparation
1. Preheat oven to 325°F before baking.
2. Butter and flour a 10-inch fluted pan.
3. In a large mixing bowl, combine the sugar, eggs, oil, orange juice, flour, baking soda, baking powder, salt, cinnamon and vanilla; mix well. Fold in apples, coconut, and pecans.
4. Pour batter into prepared pan and bake in preheated oven at 325°F for 1 hour 20 minutes or until a cake tester comes out clean.
5. Shortly before the cake is done, make the glaze. Melt the butter in a saucepan, stir in the sugar, buttermilk, and soda and bring to a boil, stirring constantly. Boil for 1 minute.
6. As soon as you remove the cake from the oven, make a few holes with a skewer to absorb the glaze, and pour the glaze over the hot cake in the pan. Let stand for at least 1 hour, then turn out onto a rack to cool completely.

Makes 16 servings

## Tips
- *If you do not have buttermilk available mix 1 tsp white vinegar in ½ cup milk and let it stand for 5-10 minutes.*

# Apple Sour Cream Coffee Cake

*This cake was one of the most popular cakes in the late sixties. Apple and cinnamon are flavors that go very well together. This cake is a round-the-clock favorite. Using raw apple gives a fresh flavor. Have it for breakfast or afternoon tea, or for dessert with a scoop of ice cream.*

## Ingredients

½ cup butter at room temperature
1 cup granulated sugar
2 eggs
1 tsp vanilla
1 cup sour cream
2 cups flour
1 tsp baking soda
1 tsp baking powder
½ tsp salt

### *Filling*

½ cup granulated sugar
1/3 cup brown sugar
1 tsp cinnamon
¼ cup walnuts, chopped fine
1 large green apple, peeled, cored and sliced thin.

## Preparation

1. Preheat oven to 350°F before baking.
2. Butter and flour a 10-inch fluted pan.
3. Cream together butter and sugar. Add the eggs one at a time and beat well. Add vanilla.
4. Sift dry ingredients together and fold in egg mixture alternating with sour cream. Mix thoroughly.
5. Spread half the batter in the prepared pan. Layer the apple slices on the batter. Sprinkle half of the sugar-cinnamon mixture over apples. Spread the remaining batter over the cinnamon mixture and sprinkle the rest of the cinnamon mixture on top of batter in the pan.
6. Bake the cake for 45 minutes or until a toothpick inserted in the cake comes out clean. Cool and unmold.

Makes 12 servings

# Date Nut Cake

*This is a rich, dense date cake perfect for the holidays. The rum adds a subtle flavor to it. You have to love dates to appreciate this cake.*

## Ingredients
1 cup boiled water
1 tsp baking soda
1 lb chopped dates
¾ cup butter
1½ cups brown sugar
3 eggs
½ cup rum
2¼ cups flour
½ tsp salt
1 lb chopped pecans

## Preparation
1. Preheat oven to 300°F before baking. Grease and flour a 10-inch tube pan.
2. Boil 1 cup of water, add the baking soda and pour over the chopped dates. Set aside.
3. Cream together butter and sugar, add the eggs and beat well. Add the rum and mix.
4. Sift flour and salt, and add to the egg mixture. Fold in the dates and nuts.
5. Pour into prepared pan and bake for 1 hour 20-30 minutes.
6. Cool and store the cake for several days before serving.

Makes 16 servings

## Tips
- *This cake tastes better when it ages.*
- *Keeps for several weeks in the refrigerator; several months in the freezer.*

# Flourless Chocolate Cake

*A decadent dessert! Sinfully rich chocolate taste with creamy texture, combined with the raspberry and mint colors make a dramatic presentation. This cake is a must if you wish to impress your guests. A coulis is just pureed sweetened fruit which is the perfect companion to this cake.*

## Ingredients
1¼ stick unsalted butter
½ cup sugar
12 oz semi-sweet chocolate chips
1 Tbsp brandy
4 large eggs separated,
    room temperature
1 tsp vanilla
¼ tsp salt
Confectioner's sugar

*Raspberry coulis*
1 pkg of frozen raspberries, thawed
½ cup confectioner's sugar
2 tsp lemon juice.

## Preparation
1. *Prepare Coulis:* Put ingredients in a blender or food processor and blend until smooth. Using a strainer, strain the mixture in order to get a nice smooth sauce, discard the seeds. Preheat oven to 425°F before baking.
2. Butter a spring form pan. Coat with sugar and tap out the extra sugar.
3. Melt butter and ¼ cup sugar in heavy medium saucepan over low heat, stirring until sugar is dissolved.
4. Stir in chocolate chips, stirring until chocolate is melted. Remove from heat. Add brandy.
5. Whisk egg yolks and vanilla about 4 minutes until light and frothy. Gradually whisk in melted chocolate. (Mixture may appear broken).
6. Beat egg whites with salt and beat until frothy; gradually add in the remaining ¼ cup sugar.
7. Fold 1/3 of the egg white into the chocolate mixture. Gradually fold in the remainder.
8. Bake in preheated oven for 15 minutes. Cool completely.
9. Sprinkle top with confectioner's sugar and decorate as you wish. Serve with raspberry coulis.

Makes 10-12 servings

## Tips
- *Beat egg whites at room temperature, they whip better.*
- *If you have both a hand-held mixer and a stand mixer, you may want to use the hand held mixer for the egg yolks and the stand mixer for the egg whites. This will save you time washing the mixer in the midst of your preparation.*
- *To make chocolate leaves, melt semi-sweet chocolate and spread in a thin layer on the back of waxy leaves, like camellia flower leaves. Do not forget to wash and completely dry the leaves before using. When chocolate is set, peel the leaves and discard them. You will have beautiful realistic looking chocolate leaves. Arrange as you wish to form a flower.*

# Carrot Cake

*This cake is one of our favorites. Children who do not like cooked carrots love this cake, even though the presence of carrots in the cake is quite obvious. The list of ingredients looks long but it comes together in just minutes.*

## Ingredients
1½ cups vegetable oil
2 cups sugar
4 eggs
1 tsp vanilla
½ cup crushed pineapple, drained
2 cups flour
1 tsp baking soda
½ tsp baking powder
1 tsp ground cinnamon
3 cups shredded carrots
1 cup chopped walnuts
1 cup shredded coconut

*Frosting*
1 (8oz) pkg cream cheese, room temperature
1 tsp vanilla
½ stick butter at room temperature
1 box confectioner's sugar

## Preparation
1. *Prepare Frosting:* Beat cream cheese and vanilla with a mixer on medium speed until creamy. Add butter and beat until incorporated. Gradually add confectioner's sugar, and beat until fluffy and smooth. Frosting can be refrigerated in an airtight container for several days. Bring to room temperature before using.
2. Preheat oven to 350°F before baking. Butter and dust with flour 2 (9-inch) round cake pans.
3. In a large mixing bowl, beat sugar, oil, eggs, and vanilla. Add crushed pineapple.
4. Sift flour, baking soda, baking powder, and cinnamon.
5. Add sifted flour mixture to the creamed mixture.
6. Fold in shredded carrots, nuts, and coconut.
7. Pour prepared batter into prepared pans, dividing evenly.
8. Bake for 35-40 minutes, or until a toothpick inserted in the cake comes out clean. Cool on a wire rack. If using a ring pan, bake for 60-65 minutes.
9. Place one cake on a serving platter and spread with 1 cup of frosting. Top with second cake and use remaining frosting over top and sides.

Makes 12 servings

## Tips:
- *The cake may be prepared in advance and frozen without the frosting. Bring the cake to room temperature and frost the day you serve the cake.*

# Key Lime Cake

*Key limes are smaller than regular limes and they have a unique strong lime flavor.
This cake has a tangy key lime flavor that reminds you of the Florida Keys.
With its green color it makes a good St. Patrick's Day cake.*

## Ingredients
1 box Lemon Velvet cake mix
1(3 oz) pkg Lime gelatin
¾ cup vegetable oil
¾ cup water
4 eggs
1 tsp lime zest

### Glaze
1¾ cup confectioner's sugar
½ cup lime juice
1 tsp lime zest
1 drop green food coloring

## Preparation
1. Preheat oven to 350°F before baking.
2. In a mixing bowl, put the cake mix, gelatin powder, oil, water, eggs, and lime zest.  Beat for 3-4 minutes.
3. Pour into a non-stick 9 x13-inch baking pan or a large round ring pan.
4. Bake for 30-35 minutes, until the top browns and a cake tester comes out clean.
5. While the cake is baking, prepare the glaze.  Combine sugar, lime juice and zest and keep stirring until the sugar is dissolved.
6. When the cake is done and while it is still hot, prick the cake with a fork and drizzle the top with the glaze.
7. Let the cool completely and absorb the glaze.
8. *Decorative glaze:* Use 2 teaspoons of lime juice, 1 drop of green food coloring and add confectioners' sugar to give sour cream consistency to the glaze.  Drizzle over the cake.

Makes 12 servings

## Tips
- *This cake keeps well for several days at room temperature.*
- *You may use a bundt cake pan too.  It works well.  I sometimes use 2 (9-inch) pans.  I use one and freeze the other.*
- *If the cake is made in a rectangular pan, cut into squares and serve.*

# Lemon Cake

*This cake is a hit every time I serve it. Its luscious lemon taste makes an ideal finish to a meal. The sugar and lemon juice brushed over the top after baking gives this cake an extra tangy flavor as well as a smooth sugary glaze. Frosting is not necessary. Yummy!*

## Ingredients
1 box Lemon Velvet cake mix
1 (3 oz) pkg Lemon gelatin
¾ cup vegetable oil
¾ cup water
4 eggs
1 tsp lemon zest

### *Glaze*
1¾ cup confectioner's sugar
½ cup lemon juice
1 tsp lemon zest

## Preparation
1. Preheat oven to 350°F before baking.
2. In a mixing bowl, put the cake mix, gelatin powder, oil, water, eggs, and lemon zest. Beat for 3-4 minutes.
3. Pour into a non-stick 9 x13-inch baking pan or into a large round ring pan.
4. Bake for 30-35 minutes, until the top browns and a cake tester come out clean.
5. While the cake is baking, prepare the glaze. Combine sugar, lemon juice and zest and keep stirring until the sugar is dissolved.
6. When the cake is done and while it is still hot, prick the cake with a fork and drizzle the top with the glaze.
7. Let it cool completely.
8. *Decorative glaze:* Use 2 teaspoons lemon juice, 1 drop of yellow food coloring and add confectioners' sugar to give sour cream consistency to the glaze. Drizzle over the cake.

Makes 12 servings

## Tips
- *This cake keeps well for several days at room temperature.*
- *You may use a bundt cake pan too. It works well. I sometimes use 2 (9-inch) round pans. I use one and freeze the other.*
- *If the cake is made in a rectangular pan, cut into squares and serve.*

# Almond Cake

*This cake is for almond lovers; it is dense but moist and has an intense almond flavor. Excellent with coffee. Serve with some fresh strawberries or raspberries.*

## Ingredients
10 oz baking almond paste
1 1/3 cups sugar
6½ oz butter
1/3 cup Amaretto liquor
5 egg whites
2/3 cup flour
Confectioners' sugar for dusting

## Preparation
1. Preheat oven to 350°F before baking.
2. Grease and flour a 10-inch tart pan or a 9-inch round pan.
3. In a bowl, beat the almond paste until it is soft. Add butter piece by piece and keep beating until the mixture becomes creamy. Add sugar and beat until smooth. Add amaretto and continue beating until it is all well incorporated.
4. In another bowl beat the egg whites until they are light and form stiff peaks.
5. Fold in 1/3 of the egg whites into the almond mixture alternating with 1/3 of the flour. Repeat until all mixed.
6. Spread into the prepared pan and bake for 40-50 minutes, until top browns and a cake tester comes out clean.
7. Cool on a wire rack for 10 minutes, then invert to a plate. Dust the top with confectioners' sugar.

Makes 12 servings

## Tips
- *Beat egg whites at room temperature, they whip better.*
- *This cake keeps well for several days at room temperature; a week to 10 days in the refrigerator; and several months in the freezer.*

# Tangy Lemon Cheesecake

*This rich lemon cheesecake is the best! It has a refreshing lemony taste and is unbelievably good. Make it a day or two in advance and refrigerate until serving time.*

## Ingredients
2 cups Graham cracker crumbs
½ cup butter, melted
4 Tbsp sugar
2 (14 oz) can Eagle brand condensed sweet milk
2 eggs
4 (8 oz) pkg cream cheese, room temperature
1 cup sugar
½ cup fresh lemon juice
2 tsp lemon zest

## Preparation
1. Preheat oven to 375°F before baking.
2. Mix together Graham cracker crumbs, melted butter, and sugar. Press in the bottom and sides of a 10-inch springform pan. Bake 6-8 minutes. Remove from the oven and reduce oven temperature to 350°F.
3. In an electric mixer, beat condensed milk, egg, cream cheese and sugar for 5 minutes, until fluffy.
4. Add lemon juice, and lemon zest, and continue beating for another 5 minutes.
5. Pour mixture into prepared crust. Bake at 350°F for 25-30 minutes. (Center of the cheesecake will still be soft. Do not over bake). Remove from the oven and let it cool on a wire rack. Refrigerate overnight before serving.

Makes 20-22 servings

## Tips
- *Make sure you do not bake longer than 30 minutes. The center will still be soft when you take it out of the oven, but it will set when chilled. If you bake longer than 30 minutes, the top will crack and it will lose its creamy texture.*

# Chocolate Mousse Brownie Cake

*This sinfully delicious dessert with a wonderfully smooth, rich and creamy texture mousse will have your guests begging for the recipe. The mousse recipe was given to me by my friend Juachim Caula, a well known Swiss chef. The recipe was his mother's recipe.*

## Ingredients
1 pkg Brownie mix
1 recipe of chocolate mousse
   (page 349)

## Preparation
1. Prepare brownie according to its package direction. Cool completely and cut into rectangular shapes, or triangles.
2. In a spring form pan arrange the cut pieces of brownie along the sides of the pan.
3. Cut the leftover brownie pieces into bite size pieces to use with the mousse in the filling.
4. Prepare the chocolate mousse per recipe directions on (page 349) pour half of the mousse into the spring form pan, sprinkle cut up pieces of brownie over it, pour remaining mousse over brownie pieces, and smooth the top. Cover and refrigerate overnight.

Makes 14-18 servings

## Tips
- *Begin preparing at least a day ahead to allow enough time for thorough chilling.*

# Banana Chocolate Chip Loaf Cake

*The banana flavor is strongest when you use over-ripe bananas. A great excuse using very ripe bananas. This easy-to-make cake includes everyone's favorite ingredients - bananas, chocolate chips and walnuts.*

## Ingredients
1 cup mashed bananas
3 Tbsp milk
½ cup butter
1 cup sugar
1 egg
2 cups sifted flour
¼ tsp salt
1 tsp baking powder
½ tsp baking soda
1 tsp vanilla
1 cup chocolate chips
½ cup chopped walnuts

## Preparation
1. Preheat oven to 350°F before baking. Grease and flour a 9x5x3-inch loaf pan.
2. Mash the bananas to measure 1 cup and mix with the milk. Set aside.
3. Sift flour, salt, baking powder and baking soda. Set aside.
4. In a bowl, cream butter and sugar, add the egg and vanilla; beat until light and fluffy.
5. Stir the flour by hand into the creamed mixture alternating with mashed bananas.
6. Fold in chocolate chips and nuts.
7. Pour batter into prepared loaf pan.
8. Bake for 1 hour, or until a toothpick inserted in the center comes out clean. Cool in pan for 10 minutes. Remove from pan and cool on a wire rack.

Makes 1 (9x5x3-inch) loaf

## Tips
- *Over-ripe bananas can be peeled and frozen in plastic bags until you are ready to make the cake.*
- *This cake freezes very well.*
- *The cake can be made several days in advance and it will stay fresh.*
- *If you wish to give this cake as a gift, make them in smaller foil pans and shorten baking time.*
- *If you wish you can substitute chopped macadamia nuts or pecans in place of the walnuts.*

# Banana Pineapple Coconut Loaf Cake

*This cake is very moist with tropical flavors. Good for a snack or served with coffee or tea.*

## Ingredients
3 cups flour
2 cups sugar
1 tsp baking soda
½ tsp salt
1 tsp cinnamon
3 eggs beaten
2 cups mashed ripe bananas
1½ cup vegetable oil
1 cup drained crushed pineapple
2 tsp vanilla
1 cup chopped walnuts or pecans
½ cup coconut flakes

## Preparation
1. Preheat oven to 350°F before baking. Grease and flour a 9x5x3-inch loaf pan.
2. Mix flour, sugar, baking soda, salt, and cinnamon in a large bowl. Set aside.
3. In another bowl, beat the eggs and add mashed bananas, oil, pineapple, and vanilla.
4. Add the flour by hand into the creamed mixture until flour is just moistened. Don't over mix.
5. Fold in the nuts and coconut.
6. Pour the batter into prepared loaf pan.
   Bake for 1 hour or until toothpick inserted in center comes out clean.
7. Cool in pan for 10 minutes. Remove from pan and cool on a wire rack.

Makes 1 loaf

## Tips
- *This cake freezes very well.*
- *If you wish to put them in gift baskets, bake them in smaller foil pans and reduce baking time.*

# Pineapple Zucchini Loaf Cake

*This cake is wonderful for breakfast or afternoon tea, even good served with salads.*

## Ingredients
2 cups vegetable oil
2½ cup sugar
4 eggs
2½ tsp vanilla
1 cup crushed pineapple
4¼ cups flour
1 Tbsp baking soda
½ tsp baking powder
¾ tsp cinnamon
½ tsp nutmeg
½ tsp salt
2 cups shredded zucchini
1 cup chopped walnuts or pecans

## Preparation
1. Preheat oven to 350°F before baking.
2. Grease and flour 3 (4x6-inch) disposable loaf pans and set aside.
3. Beat sugar and oil, then add eggs and vanilla and beat some more until all emulsified.
4. Add crushed pineapple and mix well.
5. Sift flour with baking soda, baking powder, cinnamon, nutmeg, and salt. Add to the egg mixture. Mix until flour is incorporated. Fold in zucchini and chopped nuts.
6. Pour into prepared disposable foil loaf pans and bake for 45-55 minutes, or until the top is browned and the cake tester comes out clean.

Makes 3 loaves

## Tips
- *When shredding zucchini, do not remove the skin. It adds color and texture to the cake.*
- *To make this cake more appealing to kids, you may want to add 1 cup of chocolate chips to the batter.*

# Chocolate Zucchini Loaf Cake

*The combination of ingredients is unusual but the result is a successful, tasty and moist cake. You can actually see the green flecks of zucchini in the cake.*

## Ingredients
½ cup unsalted butter, room temperature
½ cup vegetable oil
2 cups sugar
2 large eggs
½ cup buttermilk
1 tsp vanilla
2¾ cups flour
1/3 cup cocoa powder
1 tsp baking soda
½ tsp baking powder
¾ tsp cinnamon
¼ tsp ground clove
½ tsp salt
2 cups shredded zucchini
¾ cup chopped walnuts or pecans
1 cup semisweet chocolate chips

## Preparation
1. Preheat oven to 350°F before baking.
2. Grease and flour 2 (4x8-inch) disposable foil loaf pans and set aside.
3. Beat sugar, butter and oil, then add eggs, buttermilk, and vanilla and beat until well mixed.
4. Sift flour with cocoa powder, baking soda, baking powder, cinnamon, clove, and salt. Add to the above mixture. Mix until flour is incorporated with the egg mixture. Fold in zucchini, chocolate chips, and chopped nuts.
5. Pour into prepared disposable foil loaf pans and bake for 45-55 minutes, or until the cake tester comes out clean.
6. Cool cakes for 10 minutes in their pans, then turn them out onto racks to cool completely.

Makes 2 loaves

## Tips
- *When shredding zucchini, do not remove the skin. It adds color and texture to the cake.*
- *If buttermilk is not available, you can get the same result by mixing ½ cup milk and 1 tsp white wine vinegar. Let it sit for 5-10 minutes before using.*

# Sfouf (Turmeric Cake)

*This is a popular Middle Eastern cake. Basically a dense cake similar to corn bread but the addition of turmeric makes it exotic by adding a bright yellow color to the cake and a mild spicy flavor.*

## Ingredients
1 Tbsp tahini (sesame seed paste)
2½ cups farina (semolina)
1 1/3 cups flour
1½ tsp turmeric
1½ tsp baking powder
¼ tsp salt
1 cup sweet butter, room temperature
1 cup + 3 Tbsp lukewarm water
2½ cups sugar
¼ cup pine nuts, or blanched almonds

## Preparation
1. Preheat oven to 350°F before baking.
2. Spread tahini in the bottom of a 9x13-inch pan and set aside..
3. In a large mixing bowl, measure farina, flour, turmeric, baking powder and salt. Whisk all dry ingredients together to evenly mix them.
4. Add the butter, and rub with your fingers until mixture resembles coarse meal.
5. In another bowl, measure sugar and add warm water. Mix until sugar is dissolved. Add dissolved sugar into the dry ingredients and mix until well-blended. Pour the batter into the prepared pan, sprinkle the top with pine nuts or almonds and let it stand at room temperature for half an hour for the farina to absorb the water.
6. Bake for approximately 30-35 minutes until top starts browning.
7. Let it cool completely before cutting into squares.

Makes 24 servings

## Tips:
- *This cake keeps well for over a week at room temperature. It freezes well for several months.*

# Carrot Cupcakes

*Moist and delicious, these cupcakes will be a hit with your family every time you serve them.*

## Ingredients

½ cup vegetable oil
1¼ cups sugar
2 eggs
1 tsp vanilla
¼ cup crushed pineapple, drained
1½ cups shredded carrots
2 cups flour
½ tsp baking soda
2 tsp baking powder
1 tsp cinnamon
¼ tsp salt
½ cup shredded coconut
½ cup chopped pecans

### *Frosting*

4 Tbsp butter at room temperature
1 (8 oz) pkg cream cheese at room temperature
1 tsp vanilla
3½ cups confectioners' sugar

## Preparation

1. Preheat oven to 350°F before baking.
2. Grease and flour 2 muffin pans or line with paper muffin cups and set aside.
3. In a large mixing bowl, beat vegetable oil, sugar, eggs, and vanilla. Add crushed pineapple and shredded carrots. Mix well.
4. Sift together flour, baking soda, baking powder, cinnamon and salt. Gently fold into the wet mixture.
5. Fold in coconut and pecans.
6. With an ice cream scoop, fill in the muffin cups ¾ full.
7. Bake for 20-22 minutes or until a toothpick inserted in the cupcakes comes out clean. Let it cool on a wire rack for 5 minutes, and then remove from the muffin pans. Cool completely on a wire rack.
8. Prepare the frosting by beating butter, cream cheese and vanilla. Gradually add the sugar until well incorporated. Frost the cupcakes and decorate them as you wish.

Makes 18 cupcakes

## Tips

- *Save the cupcakes, without frosting, in a cake saver for up to 3 days at room temperature or in the refrigerator up to a week. Frost them before serving.*
- *These cupcakes also keep well in the freezer.*

# Chocolate Sour Cream Cupcakes

*Bake these cupcakes for children's birthday parties. Kids love chocolate cupcakes.*

## Ingredients
24 paper muffin pan liners
1 (18.25 oz) box devil's food cake mix with pudding
½ tsp baking powder
¾ cup water
1 cup sour cream
½ cup vegetable oil
3 large eggs at room temperature
1 tsp vanilla

### *Frosting*
1 (8 oz) pkg cream cheese at room temperature
4 Tbsp butter at room temperature
4 oz semi-sweet chocolate chips, melted
1 tsp vanilla
3½ cups confectioners' sugar

## Preparation
1. Preheat oven to 350°F before baking.
2. Line 24 muffin cups with paper liners and set aside.
3. In a large bowl, place the cake mix, baking powder, water, sour cream, vegetable oil, eggs, and vanilla. Blend with an electric mixer at low speed for 1 minute. Scrape the sides of the bowl and beat at medium speed until the batter is well combined.
4. With an ice cream scoop fill the muffin cups ¾ full.
5. Bake in the middle shelf of the oven for 20-25 minutes until a toothpick inserted in the center comes out clean. Remove from the oven and place the trays on a wire rack to cool for 5 minutes. Remove the cupcakes from the tray and place them on a wire rack to cool completely.
6. *Prepare frosting*. With an electric mixer, cream butter and cream cheese. Add melted chocolate, vanilla, and confectioners' sugar. Continue mixing at low speed until all the ingredients are well mixed together and the frosting is smooth.
7. Use a spatula to frost the top of the cupcakes, or a decorative pastry tube to make rosettes. Sprinkle with cupcake decorating sprinkles of your choice.

Makes 24 cupcakes

## Tips
- *When in a hurry, use any canned cake frosting that you like.*
- *Unfrosted cupcakes keep for a week in the refrigerator, or covered 3 days at room temperature.*
- *These cupcakes also keep well in the freezer.*

# Chocolate Chip Cupcakes

*This is a simple yellow cupcake full of chocolate chips. Frost them with your favorite frosting and decorate them as you wish. They are good even without frosting.*

## Ingredients
2¼ cup flour
1 1/3 cup sugar
3 tsp baking powder
½ tsp salt
2 eggs
½ cup vegetable oil
¾ cup milk
1 tsp vanilla
¾ cup semi-sweet chocolate chips

## Preparation
1. Preheat oven to 350°F before baking.
2. Grease and flour muffin pan or line with paper cups.
3. In a large bowl, combine flour, sugar, baking powder and salt.
4. In another bowl slightly beat the eggs, add vegetable oil, milk, and vanilla.
5. Add the wet mixture to the flour mixture and beat for 1 minute. Fold in the chocolate chips.
6. Spoon batter into the muffin paper liners ¾ full.
7. Bake for 23-25 minutes or until toothpick inserted in center comes out clean.
8. Cool for 5 minutes in pan then remove and place on wire rack to cool completely.
9. Decorate as you wish.

Makes 12 cupcakes

## Tips
- *Use any canned cake frosting that you like to frost the cupcakes.*
- *Using an ice cream scoop to fill in the muffin cups is easier, faster and does not make a mess.*

# Fresh Blueberry Muffins

*On a visit to Martha's Vineyard these muffins were served at a Bed and Breakfast. The owners were kind enough to share the recipe with us. Blueberries fresh or frozen are an ideal ingredient for muffins. They add moistness to the muffins.*

## Ingredients
1½ cups all purpose flour
1 cup sugar
2 tsp baking powder
½ tsp salt
½ cup butter, melted and cooled
1 egg, lightly beaten
1 tsp vanilla
¾ cup sour cream
2 cups fresh blueberries

## Preparation
1. Preheat oven to 400°F before baking.
2. Grease and flour muffin pan or line with paper cups.
3. In a large bowl, measure flour, sugar, baking powder and salt. Set aside.
4. In a small bowl combine together the egg, butter, vanilla and sour cream.
5. Add the wet ingredients to the flour mixture and stir just combined.
6. Add blueberries and toss gently to not crush them.
7. Spoon into prepared muffin cups ¾ full and sprinkle the tops with raw sugar.
8. Bake for 18-20 minutes, until the tops brown and a cake tester comes out clean.

Makes 12 muffins

## Tips
- *If using frozen sweetened blueberries, reduce sugar to ¾ cup and add a few minutes longer to the baking time. Toss the blueberries in the batter while still frozen - it will prevent staining the batter.*
- *If you wish to save time in the morning, mix the dry ingredients the night before, cover and refrigerate until morning. In the morning mix dry and liquid ingredients, fill muffin cups and bake.*

# Macadamia Nut White Chocolate Chip Muffins

*White chocolate chips, coconut, and macadamia nuts work well together giving you a taste of the tropics.*

## Ingredients
2 cups flour
½ cup packed brown sugar
2 tsp baking powder
¼ tsp salt
1 egg, room temperature
½ cup butter, melted and cooled
2 tsp vanilla
1 cup milk, room temperature
1½ cup white chocolate chips
¾ cup chopped macadamia nuts
¾ cup coconut flakes

## Preparation
1. Preheat oven to 400°F.  Grease and flour 2 muffin pans or line with paper cups.
2. In a large bowl, measure flour, sugar, baking powder and salt.  Set aside.
3. In a medium bowl, whisk together the egg, butter, vanilla and milk.
4. Add the wet ingredients to the flour mixture and stir until just combined.
5. Fold in white chocolate chips, macadamia nuts, and coconut.
6. Spoon into prepared muffin cups ¾ full.  Bake approximately for 20 minutes, until the tops are a very light brown color and a cake tester comes out clean.  Cool on a wire rack for 5 minutes and then remove them from the cups.  Serve warm or at room temperature.

Makes 18 regular size muffins

# Banana Chocolate Chip Muffins
*Make and freeze the extras. They make an easy breakfast on a day when you are pressed by time.*

## Ingredients
2 ripe bananas
¾ cup sugar
½ cup vegetable oil
1 egg, beaten
1 tsp vanilla
1 cup all purpose flour
½ cup whole wheat flour
2 tsp baking powder
1 tsp salt
¾ cup chocolate chips

## Preparation
1. Preheat oven to 425°F before baking.
2. Grease and flour muffin pan or line with baking paper cups.
3. In a small bowl mash bananas and set aside.
4. In a large bowl, cream together sugar and oil, then add egg and vanilla, and mashed bananas and mix well.
5. Sift together flour, whole wheat flour, baking powder and salt. Fold in wet mixture. Add chocolate chips.
6. Spoon batter into prepared muffin cups ¾ full.
7. Bake for 15-20 minutes, until tops start browning.

Makes 12 muffins

# Lemon-Poppy Seed Muffins

*Enjoy the crunch of poppy seeds with their nutty flavor. Make a batch and freeze the extras. They make an easy breakfast on a day when you are on the run.*

## Ingredients
¼ cup vegetable oil
¾ cup sugar
2 eggs
¼ cup milk
1 cup sour cream
1/3 cup poppy seeds
1 tsp lemon rind
2 cups flour
3 tsp baking powder
½ tsp salt

## Preparation
1. Preheat oven to 425°F before baking.
2. Grease and flour muffin pan or line with baking paper cups.
3. In a bowl, cream together oil, sugar and eggs. Add milk, sour cream, poppy seeds, and lemon rind.
4. In another bowl, sift together flour, baking powder and salt. Fold into the creamed mixture. The mixture will be thick and lumpy. Do not over mix.
5. Spoon batter into prepared muffin cups ¾ full. Bake for 15 minutes.

Makes 12 muffins

# Date Muffins
*Muffins are handy for those hurried mornings.  Make and freeze the extras.*

## Ingredients
1 cup chopped dates
1/3 cup butter, room temperature
½ cup sugar
1 egg, beaten
¾ cup milk
1 tsp vanilla
2 cups flour
3 tsp baking powder
½ tsp salt

## Preparation
1. Preheat oven 400°F before baking.
2. Grease and flour muffin pan or line with baking paper cups.
3. Chop dates and dust one tablespoon of flour over them, separating the pieces.
4. In a bowl, cream butter and sugar.  Add egg, milk, and vanilla; beat well.
5. In another bowl, sift together flour, baking powder and salt.  Add to the creamed mixture.  Add the dates and gently mix all together.
6. Spoon batter into prepared muffin cups ¾ full.  Bake for 20-25 minutes.

Makes 12 muffins

# Savory Cheese Muffins

*Muffins don't have to be sweet. We like these muffins with soups and salads. They are easy enough to make often. Great in lunch boxes too.*

## Ingredients
2 cups grated cheddar cheese
1½ cups of self-rising flour
1 Tbsp sugar
½ tsp salt
¼ tsp cayenne pepper
1 egg, slightly beaten
1 cup milk

## Preparation
1. Preheat oven 400°F before baking.
2. Grease and flour muffin pan or line with baking paper cups.
3. In a large bowl, combine grated cheese, flour, sugar, salt and pepper. Mix lightly to combine.
4. In another bowl, slightly beat the eggs and milk until evenly combined. Sprinkle the flour and cheese mixture over the liquids, then fold the two mixtures together, taking care not to over mix.
5. Spoon batter into prepared muffin cups ¾ full. Bake for 12-15 minutes.

Makes 12 muffins

## Tips
- *For optional topping; you may sprinkle muffins with a little extra cheese, cayenne pepper, or paprika before baking.*
- *For variety, you may add ½ cup of chopped ham or crisp bacon bits into the dry ingredients.*

# Hawaiian Ham Savory Muffins

*The combination of ham, cheese, and pineapple seem to be the Hawaiian trio.*
*Use these savory muffins for lunch with a salad, or with a cup of soup for a light and complete meal.*
*Also good for school lunches.*

## Ingredients
2 cups flour
4 tsp baking powder
½ tsp salt
1½ cup diced ham
1½ cup grated cheese
2 scallions, chopped
1 small can crushed pineapple
¾ cup milk
2 Tbsp vegetable oil
1 egg

## Preparation
1. Preheat oven to 400°F before baking.
2. Grease and flour muffin pan or line with baking paper cups.
3. Measure dry ingredients into a large bowl. Add diced ham and grated cheese. Add chopped scallions including the green leaves. With a fork, toss everything together.
4. Drain pineapple, reserving the liquid. Increase the juice to one cup by adding milk to it. In another bowl, using a fork, mix together pineapple, juice, milk, oil and egg until well combined. Sprinkle the flour mixture over the liquids and fold together until the flour is just moistened. Do not over mix.
5. Spoon batter into prepared muffin cups ¾ full. Bake for 18-22 minutes or until tops brown. Cool in the pan for a few minutes before removing to a cooling rack.

Makes 12 muffins

## Tips
- *These muffins freeze well and thaw fast.*
- *You may use Jack cheese, mozzarella, or gruyere cheese.*
- *If you like you may want to top it with more grated cheese before baking.*

# Broccoli and Cheese Savory Muffins

*Neither the broccoli nor cheese flavors are strong in the muffin.*
*Use these muffins for lunch with or without a salad, or with a cup of soup for lunch or dinner.*

## Ingredients
1½ cups plain yogurt
¼ cup vegetable oil
1 egg
¾ cup milk
2 cups cooked broccoli, chopped
1½ cups any grated cheese
  or 1 cup blue cheese
2 cups self-rising flour
½ tsp salt

## Preparation
1. Preheat oven to 400°F before baking.
2. Grease and flour muffin pan or line with baking paper cups. .
3. Place the yogurt, oil, egg, and milk in a bowl; with a fork combine them together. Add cooked and chopped broccoli and grated cheese.
4. Measure the flour and salt, sprinkle over the liquids and fold together until the flour is just moistened. Do not over mix. If needed, add an extra tablespoon of milk.
5. Spoon batter into prepared muffin cups ¾ full. Bake for 20-22 minutes or until the tops brown. Let them cool in the pan for a few minutes before moving to a cooling rack.

Makes 12 muffins

## Tips
- *You may use Jack cheese, mozzarella, or gruyere cheese. Blue cheese is good too but use only ½ cup.*

# Rock Cakes

*On my first visit to Stonehenge in England, I tasted a rock cake from one of the kiosks; I loved it and tried to find a recipe for it. This cake is similar to a scone. It is good for afternoon tea or for a snack or even for breakfast.*

## Ingredients
2 cups all purpose flour
½ tsp salt
1½ tsp baking powder
4 Tbsp butter
½ cup sugar
1 egg
1 tsp lemon rind
1/3 cup whole milk
¾ cups currants
2 Tbsp raw sugar to sprinkle on top

## Preparation
1. Preheat oven to 400°F before baking.
2. Sift flour, salt, and baking powder. Set aside.
3. In a mixing bowl, cream butter and sugar, add egg, lemon rind and milk. Mix until all incorporated.
4. Add the flour mixture and currants to the creamed mixture. Mixture should be crumbly. Add a little milk at a time to make stiff dough.
5. Drop on a tray with a tablespoon and sprinkle the tops with raw sugar. Bake for approximately 18-20 minutes, until the tops brown. Cool completely.

Makes 12 rockcakes

## Tips
- *Keeps fresh for several days in an air-tight container.*

# Blueberry Scones

*These moist scones are a scrumptious breakfast or brunch treat. Minimal hand mixing is required for these delicate fresh blueberry scones.*

## Ingredients
2 cups flour
1 Tbsp baking powder
¼ cup sugar
1 tsp grated lemon rind
6 Tbsp cold butter cut into
    ¼-inch squares
1 cup heavy cream
½ fresh blueberries

## Preparation
1. Preheat oven to 425°F before baking.
2. In a large bowl, measure flour, baking powder, sugar, and lemon rind. Whisk to mix them.
3. Cut in the butter until mixture resembles coarse meal. Add the blueberries and mix to distribute.
4. Add the cream and with a fork or spatula incorporate with the flour mixture until the dough starts forming, about 30 seconds. It will be lumpy.
5. Transfer the dough and all the flour bits to a countertop and knead by hand just until it comes together. (Do not over-handle the dough). Gently pat into a 1 inch thick square or rectangle.
6. For an attractive sheen, brush the top with one tablespoon of cream, and sprinkle with sugar. With a knife, cut into 4 or 6 pieces and then cut them diagonally to form triangles. Transfer to a baking sheet.
7. Bake on the top shelf for 13-15 minutes, until the top starts browning. Cool on a wire rack for 10 minutes before serving or serve at room temperature.

Makes 8-12 scones

## Tips
- *The less you handle the dough the lighter the scones.*
- *The success of this recipe is using heavy cream instead of milk.*

# Date Scones

*Minimal hand-mixing is required for these delicate date scones.
They stay fresh for several days in a covered container.*

## Ingredients
2 cups flour
1 Tbsp baking powder
¼ cup sugar
1 tsp grated lemon rind
4 Tbsp cold butter cut into
    ¼-inch squares
1 egg, lightly beaten
¾ cups heavy cream
½ cup chopped dates

## Preparation
1. Preheat oven to 425°F before baking.
2. In a large bowl measure flour, baking powder, sugar, and lemon rind. Whisk to mix them.
3. Cut in the butter until mixture resembles coarse meal. Add the dates and mix to distribute.
4. Add the cream to the beaten egg. With a fork or spatula, incorporate with the flour mixture until the dough starts forming. About 30 seconds.
5. Transfer the dough and all the flour bits to a countertop and knead by hand just until it comes together. (Do not over-handle the dough). Gently pat into a 1-inch thick circle.
6. For an attractive sheen, brush the top with one tablespoon of cream and sprinkle with sugar. With a knife cut into 8 to 12 wedges and transfer to a baking sheet.
7. Bake on the top shelf for 13-15 minutes, until the top starts browning. Cool on a wire rack for 10 minutes before serving, or serve at room temperature.

Makes 8-12 scones

## Tips
- *The less you handle the dough the lighter the scones.*
- *The success of this recipe is using heavy cream instead of milk.*

# English Breakfast Scones

*For a successful scone, minimal hand-mixing is required. You may prepare all the dry and wet ingredients the night before. Just mix the two together in the morning and bake. They stay fresh for several days in a covered container.*

## Ingredients
2¾ cups flour
1½ Tbsp baking powder
6 Tbsp sugar
½ tsp salt
½ cup cold butter cut into
    ¼ inch squares
1 tsp grated lemon rind
2 eggs, lightly beaten
1 cup chilled heavy cream
¾ cups raisins

## Preparation
1. Preheat oven to 400°F before baking.
2. In a large bowl measure flour, baking powder, sugar and salt. Whisk to mix them.
3. Cut in the butter until mixture resembles coarse meal. Add raisins and mix to distribute.
4. Add the cream and lemon rind to the beaten eggs. With a fork or spatula incorporate with the flour mixture until the dough starts forming. About 30 seconds.
5. Transfer the dough and all the flour bits to a countertop and knead by hand just until it comes together. (Do not over-handle the dough). Gently pat into a 1 inch thick circle. With a knife cut into 10 to 12 wedges, or with cookie cutter cut into 2-inch circles, and transfer to a baking sheet. For an attractive sheen, brush the top with one tablespoon of cream and sprinkle with sugar.
6. Bake on the top shelf for 10 minutes, reduce heat to 350°F and continue baking for 15-18 minutes longer or until the top starts browning. Cool on a wire rack for 10 minutes before serving, or serve at room temperature.

Makes 12-16 scones

## Tips
- *The success of this recipe is using heavy cream instead of milk.*
- *For variety, instead of raisins use chopped dates, dried cranberries or cherries.*

# Cookies

## Apricot Coconut Bars
*These delicious bars are at their best the day they are made.*

### Ingredients

*Crust*
1 cup all-purpose flour
1 tsp baking powder
½ cup butter
1 egg
1 Tbsp whole milk or cream

*Filling*
1 cup apricot preserve

*Topping*
1 egg, slightly beaten
2/3 cup sugar
2 Tbsp butter, melted
1 tsp vanilla
2 cups shredded coconut

### Preparation
1. Preheat oven to 350°F before baking.
2. In a bowl, combine flour and baking powder. Cut in butter until mixture resembles coarse crumbs.
3. Slightly beat the egg with the milk and add to the flour mixture. Spread the dough in a greased 9-inch square baking pan.
4. Spread apricot preserve over the crust.
5. Combine topping ingredients; carefully drop by the tablespoonful over the apricot layer, covering the apricot preserve completely.
6. Bake for 25-30 minutes or until the top is golden brown.
7. Cool completely and cut into squares or rectangles. Store in an air-tight container.

Makes 18-24 bars

### Tips
- While storing in a container, place wax paper between layers of bars to prevent the bars from sticking to each other.

# Chocolate Coconut Pecan Bars
*These bars are unbelievably good for a pecan bar. Chocoholic's delight!*

## Ingredients
*Crust*
1½ cups all purpose flour
½ cup firmly packed brown sugar
¾ cup coconut
¾ cup butter

*Filling*
1 cup semi-sweet chocolate chips
3 eggs, slightly beaten
1 cup light corn syrup
1/3 cup firmly packed brown sugar
1½ tsp vanilla
1½ cups chopped pecans

## Preparation
1. Preheat oven to 350°F before baking.
2. Combine flour, sugar and coconut in a bowl and mix well.
3. With a fork or pastry blender, cut in butter until mixture is crumbly.
4. Press evenly in the bottom of a greased 9 x13-inch pan.
5. Bake for 12 minutes or until lightly browned.
6. *Prepare filling:* Melt the chocolate chips in the microwave or over a double boiler. Set aside.
7. In a large bowl, slightly beat the eggs, add corn syrup, brown sugar, and vanilla.
8. Blend in melted chocolate. Fold in pecans and pour over warm crust.
9. Bake for 25-30 minutes or until the top is puffed and set. Let it cool completely then cut and store in an air-tight container.

Makes 36 bars

## Tips
- *While storing in a container, place wax paper between layers of bars to prevent the bars from sticking to each other.*

# Ultimate Chocolate Pecan Bars

*These bars make great summer backyard barbeque dessert.  Easy to pack for picnics or lunch boxes.*

## Ingredients

*Crust*
1 cup all purpose flour
½ cup unsweetened cocoa
2/3 cup sugar
¼ tsp salt
2/3 cup butter
1 beaten egg

*Filling*
1 (14 oz) can sweetened condensed milk
1 egg
1½ tsp vanilla
2 cups pecan halves or pieces

## Preparation
1. Preheat oven to 350°F before baking.
2. In a large bowl, combine flour, sugar and cocoa and salt; mix well.
3. With a fork or pastry blender, cut in butter until mixture is crumbly.
4. Stir in 1 beaten egg.  Press evenly in the bottom of a greased 9 x13-inch pan.
5. Bake for 25 minutes.
6. Meanwhile, in a medium bowl slightly beat the condensed milk, egg and vanilla.
7. Stir in pecans and pour over warm prepared crust.
8. Distribute the pecan halves evenly.
9. Bake 25 minutes longer or until golden brown.  Cool.  Cut into bars.

**Makes** 36 bars

## Tips
- *While storing in a container, place layers of wax paper between layers of bars to prevent the bars from sticking to each other.*

# Amazing Butterscotch Bars

*I had these amazing bars in a Café in New Zealand where they are called "Tan" bars. My search for the recipe led me to a bookstore where I met this kind lady who shared with me her grandmother's treasured recipe for these bars. As she said, certainly her grandmother's recipe is the best.*

## Ingredients
*Crust*
½ cup butter, room temperature
½ cup sugar
1 egg
1 tsp vanilla
2 cups all purpose flour
1 tsp. baking powder

*Filling*
½ cup butter
2 Tbsp light Karo syrup
1 (14 oz) can sweetened condensed milk

## Preparation
1. Preheat oven to 350°F before baking.
2. Beat together butter and sugar. Add egg and vanilla, mix until evenly mixed.
3. Add flour and baking powder. Using a fork or pastry blender mix until mixture is crumbly.
4. Press ¾ of the dough in a 9x13-inch pan.
5. Put the rest of the dough in the refrigerator.
6. *Prepare filling:* Melt the butter and add to it Karo syrup and condensed milk. Mix thoroughly.
7. Pour mixture over prepared unbaked crust.
8. Crumble the refrigerated portion of the dough over the top.
9. Bake for 25-30 minutes or until golden brown. Let it set 2 hours then cut into pieces using a sharp knife dipped in hot water.

Makes 36 bars

## Tips
- *To prevent dough from sticking to hands, put a piece of plastic wrap on dough then press it down.*
- *While storing in a container, place layers of wax paper between layers of bars to prevent the bars from sticking to each other.*

# Caramel Pecan Bars

These bars are one of my favorites. They are rich with a caramel filling. Yummy!

## Ingredients

*Crust*
2 cups flour
½ cup light brown sugar
1 egg, beaten
½ cup butter, cold
1 tsp vanilla
¾ cups chopped pecans

*Filling*
¼ cup butter
1 (14 0z) can sweetened condensed milk
24 pieces of caramels, unwrapped

## Preparation

1. Preheat oven to 350F before baking.
2. In a large bowl, combine flour, sugar and egg; cut in butter until mixture is crumbly. Stir in pecans.
3. Reserve 2 cups of the mixture for topping and press the remainder in a 9 x13-inch baking pan. Bake for 12-15 minutes.
4. While the crust is baking, prepare the filling. In a heavy saucepan, over low heat, melt the caramels with the milk and butter.
5. Pour melted caramel over the crust and top with reserved crumb mixture. Bake for 20-25 minutes. Cool completely before cutting into bars. Store loosely covered at room temperature.

Makes 36 bars

## Tips

- *For variation, melt 2 (one oz) squares unsweetened chocolate with the caramels, and instead of pecans, use walnuts. Prepare as instructed above.*
- *While storing in a container, place wax paper between layers of bars to prevent the bars from sticking to each other.*

# Championship Chocolate Chip Bars

*These are the best of the bar cookies. If you taste them, only then will you know why they are called "Championship Bars"*

## Ingredients

*Crust*
1½ cups all purpose flour
½ cup firmly packed brown sugar
½ cup cold butter
½ cup chocolate chips

*Filling*
1 egg
1 (14 oz) can sweetened condensed milk
1½ tsp vanilla
1 cup chopped nuts, walnuts or pecans
1½ cups chocolate chips

## Preparation

1. Preheat oven to 350°F before baking.
2. In a medium bowl, combine flour and sugar.
3. With a fork or pastry blender, cut in butter until mixture is crumbly. Add ½ cup chocolate chips
4. Press evenly in bottom of a greased 9x13-inch pan.
5. Bake at 350°F for 15 minutes.
6. Meanwhile, in the same bowl, slightly beat the egg and add condensed milk and vanilla.
7. Stir in chopped nuts and chocolate chips and pour over warm prepared crust.
8. Bake for 20-22 minutes longer or until light golden brown. Cool completely. Cut into bars. Store covered at room temperature.

Makes 24 to 36 bars

## Tips

- *While storing in a container, place wax paper between layers of bars to prevent the bars from sticking to each other.*

# Date Bars

*These bars are a great healthy addition to lunch boxes. It is very light, almost cake-like. A favorite with date lovers! No pun intended.*

## Ingredients
2 cups chopped dates
1/3 cup boiling water
½ cup butter, softened
1 cup granulated sugar
2 eggs
1/3 cup milk
1 tsp vanilla
1¾ cups flour
½ tsp baking soda
½ tsp baking powder
½ tsp salt
1/8 tsp ground nutmeg
½ tsp ground cinnamon
½ cup chopped nuts, optional
Confectioners' sugar to dust
   on top of the bars

## Preparation
1. In a medium size bowl, pour boiling water over dates and let them cool. Do not mix so the dates do not get mushy.
2. Preheat oven to 350°F before baking.
3. Grease and flour a 9 x13-inch baking pan.
4. In a bowl, beat butter and sugar until light and fluffy. Beat in eggs, one at a time. Stir in milk and vanilla.
5. Combine flour, baking soda, baking powder, salt, nutmeg and cinnamon. Mix into the mixture.
6. Mix chopped nuts with the dates, and then gently fold into the batter. Pour into prepared pan.
7. Bake for 25-30 minutes, until top browns and cake tester comes out clean.
8. Cool on a wire rack. Sprinkle with confectioners' sugar and cut into bars. Store bars in an airtight container.

Makes 24 bars

## Tips
- *Mixing the nuts with the dates before folding into the batter helps keep even distribution of the dates and nuts and prevents the dates from sinking into the bottom of the pan while baking.*
- *To keep the confectioners' sugar undisturbed, dust on the bars before serving.*

# Deluxe Date Squares

*This recipe was published in the LA Times as one of the best recipes of the year.*
*I changed it slightly to please my mother-in-law, Ethel. It became another one of her favorite cookies.*
*If you like dates, you will enjoy these cookies.*

## Ingredients

*Filling*
1 lb pitted dates, chopped
½ cups light brown sugar, packed
1 cup water
1 tsp vanilla
2 tsp lemon juice
1 tsp lemon zest

*Crust*
1½ cups flour
1½ cups oatmeal
1 cup brown sugar, packed
½ tsp baking soda
½ tsp cinnamon
¼ tsp salt
1 cup cold butter, cut into cubes

## Preparation

1. Preheat oven to 350°F before baking.
2. Combine dates, ½ cup brown sugar, water, vanilla, lemon juice, and lemon zest in a 2-quart saucepan. Bring to simmer over medium high heat. Cook until dates are softened, 2 minutes. Remove from heat and cool.
3. Place flour, oatmeal, sugar, baking soda, salt and cinnamon in a food processor. Pulse to combine. Add cold butter cubes and pulse until mixture is crumbly.
4. Pat half of the mixture in a lightly greased 9-inch baking pan. Spread date mixture evenly over it. Top with remaining crumb mixture, spreading evenly. Press down lightly.
5. Bake for 35-40 minutes, until top starts browning. Cool completely before cutting. Store in an air-tight container.

Makes 16 squares

## Tips

- *To obtain clean cut squares, freeze for 20 minutes then cut into squares.*
- *While storing in a container, place wax paper between layers of bars to prevent the bars from sticking to each other.*

# Eight-Layer Bars

*Sometimes these bars are called magic bars. Extraordinarily easy to make. It does not require any mixing. Just layer the ingredients in the baking pan and bake.*

## Ingredients
1 cube butter
2 cups Graham cracker crumbs
1 cup chocolate chips
1 cup butterscotch chips
1 cup coconut
1 cup chopped walnuts
1 egg
1 (14 oz) sweetened condensed milk
1 tsp vanilla

## Preparation
1. Preheat oven 350°F before baking.
2. Melt the butter in a 9 x 3-inch pan and spread evenly over the bottom of pan. Then sprinkle 1 cup of Graham cracker crumbs over the butter. Press down onto the bottom of the pan and bake for 6-7 minutes. Remove from the oven and let it cool.
3. Over baked crust sprinkle chocolate chips, butterscotch chips, remaining 1 cup Graham cracker crumbs, coconut, and walnuts in layers in the mentioned order.
4. In a small bowl, beat the egg, condensed milk, and vanilla until well incorporated. Pour over the layered mixture.
5. Bake for 30 minutes. Cool completely before cutting.

Makes 36 bars

## Tips
- *While storing in a container, place wax paper between layers of bars to prevent the bars from sticking to each other.*

# Cream Cheese Layer Bars

*These bars will satisfy the cravings for cheesecake. You need to keep them refrigerated because of the cream cheese.*

## Ingredients
1½ cups graham cracker crumbs
¼ cup sugar
¼ cup melted butter
1 (8 oz) pkg cream cheese, room temperature
½ cup sugar
1 egg
1 tsp vanilla
¾ cup coconut
¾ cup chopped walnuts
1 cup chocolate chips

## Preparation
1. Preheat oven 350°F before baking.
2. Combine graham cracker crumbs, ¼ cup sugar and melted butter; press down into the bottom of 9 x13-inch baking pan. Bake at 350°F for 10 minutes.
3. Combine cream cheese, ½ cup sugar, vanilla, and egg. Beat until well blended.
4. Spread over baked crust. Combine together coconut, nuts and chocolate chips; sprinkle over cream cheese mixture and press lightly into the surface. Bake for 25-30 minutes until lightly browned. Cool completely before cutting. Store cookies in an air-tight container in the refrigerator.

Makes 36 bars

## Tips
- *To obtain clean cut squares, refrigerate before cutting into squares.*
- *While storing in a container, place wax paper between layers of bars to prevent the bars from sticking to each other.*

# Chocolate Nut Bars
*This is such a simple preparation yielding delicious results.*

## Ingredients
1¾ cups graham cracker crumbs
½ cup melted butter
1 (14 oz) can sweetened condensed milk
1 tsp vanilla
2 cups chocolate chips
1 cup chopped walnuts

## Preparation
1. Preheat oven to 375°F before baking.
2. Combine Graham cracker crumbs with melted butter and press firmly on bottom of ungreased 9x13-inch baking pan.
3. Bake for 8 minutes. Remove from the oven. Reduce oven temperature to 350°F.
4. In a small saucepan, melt one cup of chocolate chips with condensed milk and add vanilla.
5. Spread over baked crust. Sprinkle with remaining chocolate chips and nuts; press down firmly. Bake at 350°F for 25-30 minutes. Cool completely before cutting into bars. Store loosely covered at room temperature.

Makes 36 bars

## Tips
- *While storing in a container, place wax paper between layers of bars to prevent the bars from sticking to each other.*

# Chocolate Graham Break-aways

*Believe me it does not get any easier than this, or tastier than this.
A very simple, fast, and delicious preparation.*

## Ingredients
12 (4½ x 2½-inch) graham crackers
¾ cup butter
½ cup brown sugar
1½ cup semi-sweet chocolate chips
1 cup chopped walnuts

## Preparation
1. Preheat oven to 375°F before baking.
2. Line a 10x15-inch baking pan with foil and arrange the graham crackers fitting them tightly.
3. Melt butter over moderate heat; add brown sugar, whisking until mixture is well combined.
4. Immediately spread evenly on crackers and bake for about 8 minutes until it is lightly browned and bubbly.
5. Remove from the oven, sprinkle chocolate chips evenly, and return to the oven for an additional 1-2 minutes or until chocolate is melted.
6. Remove from oven; immediately spread chocolate evenly over the crackers. Sprinkle with nuts and press nuts lightly into chocolate. Cool completely.
7. Refrigerate 15 minutes until chocolate is set. Carefully lift crackers from pan. Peel off foil and break crackers into serving pieces.

Makes 48 servings

## Tips
- *If you use sweet butter, add a pinch of salt to the recipe*
- *For variety; instead of walnuts, you may substitute pecans, almonds, or peanuts.*
- *Use white chocolate instead of semi-sweet, and sprinkle with slivered almonds.*

# Apricot and Almond Florentines

*Freezer friendly bars. Delicious! You will always be ready for surprise visitors. One of the most popular cookies on the Silverseas cruiseship. I had befriended the pastry chef, and the night before we disembarked, she sent a plate of these cookies with the recipe to our suite.*

## Ingredients

### Sweet Paste Dough
3 1/3 cups flour
¾ cup butter
1 cup confectioners' sugar
2 eggs
1 tsp vanilla

### Topping
¾ cup whipping cream
6 Tbsp butter
1/3 cup honey
1/3 cup Karo syrup
1½ cups sugar
2 cups diced dried apricots
3 cups sliced almonds

## Preparation

1. Preheat oven to 375°F before baking. Line 13 x18-inch shallow baking pan with foil paper.
2. Cream butter and powdered sugar. Add eggs, one at a time, add vanilla and blend well. Gradually add flour and mix until just incorporated. Wrap dough in plastic wrap, press into a flat square and refrigerate for several hours.
3. Roll out dough and transfer prepared pan. Press dough into the pan trimming edges to fit pan. Using scraps fill gaps in dough pressing seams together to seal. Prick all over with fork. Bake for 15-18 minutes. Remove from oven and let it cool.
Reduce oven temperature to 350°F.
4. *Prepare topping:* Melt butter in a saucepan over medium heat. Add cream, honey, syrup, and sugar; bring to a boil and boil until candy thermometer reads 235°F. Quickly add sliced almonds and apricots. Spread evenly over pre-baked crust.
5. Bake at 350°F until topping bubbles and turns golden brown, 15-20 minutes. Cool completely. Cut into bars.

Makes 48 bars

## Tips

- *If you use sweet butter, add a pinch of salt to the recipe.*
- *Keeps well in the freezer in an airtight container for several months.*
- *While storing in a container, place wax paper between layers of bars to prevent the bars from sticking to each other.*

# Almond Bars
*This recipe was printed in the Los Angeles Times. The bars are excellent!*

## Ingredients
*Sugar Dough*
- ½ cup butter
- ½ cup confectioners' sugar
- 1 egg
- 1 tsp vanilla
- 1¾ cups flour
- ½ tsp baking powder

*Topping*
- ½ cup butter
- 1/3 cup honey
- ½ cup granulated sugar
- 2 cups sliced almonds

## Preparation
1. Preheat oven to 350°F before baking. Line a 9x13-inch baking pan with parchment paper.
2. Cream butter until pale and fluffy, add confectioners' sugar and blend. Add egg and vanilla and blend well. Gradually add flour and baking powder and mix until smooth. Wrap dough in plastic wrap and refrigerate for several hours.
3. Roll out dough and transfer to prepared pan. Press dough into the pan, trimming edges to fit pan. Using scraps, fill gaps in dough pressing seams together to seal. Prick all over with a fork. Bake for 12-14 minutes. Remove from oven and let it cool.
4. *Prepare topping*: Melt butter in a saucepan over medium heat. Add honey and sugar and bring to a boil. Add sliced almonds, return to a boil then remove from heat and let it cool slightly.
5. Pour warm filling over baked shell, spreading evenly. Bake at 350°F until topping bubbles and turns golden brown, 12-15 minutes. Cool completely, and then cut into bars.

Makes 24 bars

## Tips
- *If you use sweet butter, add a pinch of salt to the recipe*
- *While storing in a container, place wax paper between layers of bars to prevent the bars from sticking to each other.*

# Pecan Honey Bars
*Another freezer friendly bar. Delicious and addictive.*

## Ingredients
<u>Sugar Dough</u>
½ cup butter
½ cup confectioners' sugar
1 egg
1 tsp vanilla
1¾ cups flour
½ tsp baking powder

<u>Topping</u>
½ cup butter
1/3 cup honey
½ cup granulated sugar
2 cups chopped pecans

## Preparation
1. Preheat oven to 350°F before baking. Line a 9 x13-inch baking pan with parchment paper.
2. Cream butter until pale and fluffy, add confectioners' sugar and blend. Add egg and vanilla and blend well. Gradually add flour and baking powder and mix until smooth. Wrap dough in plastic wrap and refrigerate for several hours.
3. Roll out dough and transfer to prepared pan. Press dough into the pan trimming edges to fit the pan. Use scraps of dough to fill gaps, pressing seams together to seal. Prick all over with a fork. Bake for 12-14 minutes. Remove from oven and let it cool.
4. *Prepare topping:* Melt butter in a saucepan over medium heat. Add honey and sugar and bring to a boil. Add chopped pecans, return to a boil then remove from heat and let it cool slightly.
5. Pour warm filling over baked shell, spreading evenly. Do not overfill. Bake until topping bubbles 14-15 minutes. Cool completely, and then cut into bars.

Makes 24 bars

## Tips
- *If you use sweet butter, add a pinch of salt to the recipe*
- *While storing in a container, place wax paper between layers of bars to prevent the bars from sticking to each other.*

# Jumbo Raisin Cookies

*These moist and spicy cookies are real adult crowd pleasers. Bake them and share them. They are a hit every time I serve them.*

## Ingredients
2 cups golden raisins
1 cup water
4 cups all-purpose flour sifted
1 tsp baking soda
1 tsp baking powder
1 tsp salt
1½ tsp cinnamon
¼ tsp nutmeg
¼ tsp allspice
l cup butter, room temperature
2 cups sugar
3 eggs
1 tsp vanilla
1 cup coarsely chopped walnuts

## Preparation
1. Add 1 cup water to 2 cups raisins and boil on low heat for 5 minutes. Cool completely.
2. Preheat oven to 375°F before baking.
3. Sift the flour together with baking powder, baking soda, salt, cinnamon, nutmeg, and allspice. Set aside.
4. Cream butter and sugar. Add the eggs and vanilla and beat well.
   Mix in cooled raisin mixture with its liquid and the walnuts.
5. Add the sifted flour to the creamed mixture. Mix until all is well-blended.
6. Drop with a tablespoon on a greased cookie sheet.
7. Bake for 12-14 minutes, until golden brown.
8. Cool on wire rack and store in an air tight container.

Makes 45-50 cookies.

## Tips
- *Use the same amount of dough for each cookie, either a teaspoon or a tablespoon, whatever size you want your cookies to be. I use a small ice cram scoop with a release bar and the cookies come out in uniform size.*

# Irresistible Peanut Butter Cookies
*I bet you cannot eat just one. These cookies melt in your mouth.*

## Ingredients
1¼ cups light brown sugar
½ cup butter room temperature
¾ cup creamy peanut butter
3 Tbsp milk
1 tsp vanilla
1 egg
1¾ cups all-purpose flour sifted
½ tsp baking soda
1 tsp baking powder
¼ tsp salt
¼ cup chocolate chips (optional)

## Preparation
1. Preheat oven to 350°F before baking.
2. Cream butter, peanut butter, milk, vanilla and sugar. Add the eggs and beat well.
3. Sift the flour together with the salt, baking powder, and baking soda. Add the sifted flour to the butter mixture. Mix until just blended. Refrigerate the dough for half an hour before baking.
4. Drop with a tablespoon, 2 inches apart, on an ungreased cookie sheet. With the fork tines, flatten slightly in a crisscross pattern, or sprinkle a few chocolate chips and flatten cookies by hand.
5. Bake for 7-8 minutes. Do not over bake. Cookies will be very soft when you first take them out of the oven.
6. Cool on a baking sheet for a few minutes, then transfer to a wire rack to cool completely. Store cookies in an air-tight container.

Makes 36 cookies.

## Tips
- *Use a small ice cream scoop to drop the cookies on a cookie sheet. They turn out evenly sized and shaped nicely.*

# Chocolate Chip Cookies
*America's favorite cookies. Need I say more?*

## Ingredients
1 cup butter at room temperature
¾ cup sugar
¾ cup brown sugar
1 tsp vanilla
2 eggs
2¼ cups flour
1 tsp baking soda
½ tsp baking powder
2 cups chocolate chips
1 cup chopped walnuts

## Preparation
1. Preheat oven to 375°F before baking.
2. In a large mixing bowl, beat together butter, sugar, vanilla, and the eggs.
3. In a separate bowl sift together flour, baking soda, baking powder, and salt. Gradually mix in the wet mixture.
4. Fold in the chocolate chips and walnuts.
5. Drop with rounded tablespoon on a cookie sheet. Bake for 10 minutes. Do not over bake.
6. Cool on a wire rack. Store cookies in an air-tight container.

Makes 4 dozen cookies

## Tips:
- *This cookie dough can be frozen up to 2 months. To bake, thaw out for an hour then bake as directed.*
- *Baked cookies keep well in the freezer as well.*

# Ultimate Chocolate Chocolate-Chip Cookies

*These cookies are for those who never get enough chocolate in a chocolate chip cookie. Very intense chocolate flavor and addictive. Yummy!*

## Ingredients
1 cup butter, room temperature
1 cup brown sugar
¾ cup sugar
1 tsp vanilla
2 eggs
2¼ cups flour
2/3 cup unsweetened cocoa powder
1 tsp baking soda
½ tsp baking powder
¼ tsp salt
1 lb chocolate chips (2½ cups)

## Preparation
1. Preheat oven to 350°F before baking.
2. In a large mixing bowl, beat together butter, brown sugar and sugar until creamy. Add the eggs and vanilla and beat until well incorporated.
3. Sift together flour, cocoa powder, baking soda, baking powder, and salt. Gradually mix into the butter mixture.
4. Fold in the chocolate chips.
5. With and ice cream scoop drop on a cookie sheet 3-inches apart. Bake for 10-11 minutes. Do not over bake.
6. Cool on a wire rack. Store cookies in an air-tight container.

Makes 24 large cookies

## Tips
- *If you do not have a sifter, use a whisk to mix the dry ingredients for even distribution of the flour and the cocoa powder.*
- *This cookie dough can be frozen up to 2 months. To bake, thaw out for an hour then bake as directed.*
- *Baked cookies keep well in the freezer as well.*

# Coconut Macaroons

*These are the best of the best macaroons. They are moist and chewy and drizzled with melted chocolate makes them m-m-m yummy!*

## Ingredients
1 (14 oz) pkg sweetened shredded coconut
1 (14 oz) can sweetened condensed milk
1 tsp vanilla
2 egg whites at room temperature
¼ tsp salt
Chocolate glaze (optional)

## Preparation
1. Preheat oven to 325°F before baking.
2. In a large bowl, combine coconut, condensed milk, and vanilla.
3. In a separate bowl whisk the egg whites with the salt until it forms soft peaks.
4. Gently fold the egg whites into the coconut mixture.
5. Line a baking pan with parchment paper and drop the batter 2 inches apart on the parchment paper, using a tablespoon or a small ice cream scoop (1½-inch diameter).
6. Bake for 25 to 30 minutes, until edges are slightly browned. Cool completely before glazing.
7. <u>Chocolate Glaze:</u> Melt ¾ cup semi-sweet chocolate chips plus 1 tablespoon shortening in the microwave or in a double boiler. Dip the bottom of each macaroon in the melted chocolate and arrange them on parchment paper.
8. Put remaining melted chocolate in a small plastic bag and snip one of the corners. Squeeze the melted chocolate through the hole across the macaroons making decorative squiggly lines. Let the chocolate set then store in an air tight container.

Makes 50-60 macaroons

## Tips
- *These macaroons are equally good without the chocolate glaze.*
- *Macaroons freeze well and they taste good even when eaten frozen.*

# Mexican Wedding Cookies

*These cookies have been given more names than any other cookies. Shaped differently and given a different name like; Greek Wedding Cookies, Buttery finger, Pecan crescents, Christmas snowballs, etc. They are delicious, very easy to prepare and keep well.*

## Ingredients
1 cup butter, softened
½ cup confectioners' sugar
2 tsp vanilla
¼ tsp salt
2 cups flour
¾ tsp baking powder
1 cup chopped pecans or walnuts
¼ cup confectioners' sugar for the top

## Preparation
1. Preheat oven to 350°F before baking.
2. Cream butter, sugar, salt and vanilla until light and fluffy.
3. Mix in flour and baking powder.
4. Add chopped nuts. Mix well.
5. Take a tablespoon of dough at a time, shape into a ball and place on a cookie sheet, or use a small 1-1½ inch diameter ice cream scoop and drop the cookies on a non-stick baking sheet.
6. Bake for 14-15 minutes or until the top starts turning light brown.
7. While warm, sprinkle the top with confectioners' sugar.
8. Cool completely and store in an airtight container.

Makes 45-50 cookies.

## Tips
- *For variety, to make spiced snowballs, add ¾ tsp cinnamon or ground cardamom to the flour.*
- *These cookies keep very well for several weeks; they also freeze well for several months.*
- *Shape into crescents and dip the ends in melted chocolate.*
- *So as not to disturb the confectioners' sugar, I like to put them in paper candy cups before storing them.*

# Pecan Shortbread
*Simple and delicious cookies. Good any time of the day.*

## Ingredients
1½ cups unsalted butter at room temperature
1 cup sugar
1 tsp vanilla
½ tsp almond extract
3½ cups sifted flour
¼ tsp salt
1½ cup chopped pecans

## Preparation
1. Preheat oven to 350°F before baking.
2. In a bowl mix together butter and sugar until just combined. Add vanilla and almond extracts.
3. Add sifted flour and salt to the butter mixture and mix until the mixture comes together.
4. Add pecans and mix. With your hands, combine the crumbly dough together and divide into two portions. Wrap in plastic wrap and chill for at least half an hour.
5. On a floured board or in between two sheets of wax paper roll out the dough to half inch thickness and cut into 2-inch circles. Place cookies on an ungreased baking pan and bake for 20-25 minutes or until the edges begin to brown. Cool and store in an air tight container.

Makes 5 dozen cookies

## Tips
- *If pressed by time, you may slice the cookies instead of rolling out the dough. When refrigerating the dough, form them into logs and then wrap in plastic wrap to chill. Use a very sharp small knife to slice the dough, and make sure you slice them evenly so they bake evenly.*
- *You can refrigerate rolled and wrapped cookie dough for up to one week or freeze up to 2 months.*
- *Baked cookies keep well in the freezer as well.*

# Apricot Jam Sablé Cookies

*It is well worth the effort making these cookies. They are flaky, light and have a luscious apricot jam filling. I have been making them every Christmas for the past 45 years.*
*My family thinks Christmas will never be the same without them.*

## Ingredients
1¼ cups butter at room temperature
½ cup Crisco shortening
2/3 cup sugar
4½ cups flour
½ tsp baking powder
2 eggs
1 tsp vanilla
¾ cup apricot jam
2 Tbsp confectioners' sugar

## Preparation
1. Preheat oven to 375°F before baking.
2. Sift flour and baking powder and set aside.
3. In a large bowl, cream butter, shortening, and sugar together. Add the eggs and vanilla. Mix.
4. Gradually add the flour and knead until soft dough is formed. Refrigerate dough for ½ hour.
5. On a floured board, or in between sheets of waxed paper, roll out the dough into a ¼-inch thickness. With a 2-inch cookie cutter cut into rounds. Cut out a ¾-inch hole in half of the cookies.
6. Bake for 10-15 minutes. Cool completely.
7. After cookies are cooled, spread apricot jam on the whole cookies and top them with the cookies with the holes. Sprinkle confectioners' sugar on top.

Makes 48-50 cookies

## Tips
- *By using a little shortening with the butter, the cookies stay crisper longer than if I use only butter.*
- *Keeps for several weeks in an airtight container, and several months in the freezer.*

# Chocolate Sablé Cookies

*These cookies are the companion to the Apricot Jam Sablé cookies. They are also a must for our Christmas Eve party. Chocolate lovers prefer them over any other cookies. Well worth the effort making them.*

## Ingredients
6 cups flour
3 oz cocoa powder
1 tsp baking powder
2¼ cups butter at room temperature
1/3 cup Crisco shortening
1¼ cups sugar
3 eggs
1 tsp vanilla
1½ cups chocolate chips, melted

## Preparation
1. Preheat oven to 375°F before baking.
2. Sift flour, cocoa powder and baking powder. Set aside.
3. In a large bowl, cream butter, shortening, and sugar together. Add the eggs and vanilla. Mix.
4. Gradually add the flour mixture and knead until soft dough is formed. Refrigerate dough for 30 minutes.
5. On a floured board, or in between sheets of waxed paper, roll out the dough into ¼-inch thickness. With a 2-inch cookie cutter, cut out into rounds.
6. Bake for 12 -15 minutes. Cool completely.
7. After cookies are cooled put a dollop of melted chocolate on half of the cookies, and top them with another cookie. Brush melted chocolate on top of each cookie and let it set either at room temperature, or 15 minutes in the refrigerator.
8. Store in an air tight container.

Makes 60-75 cookies

## Tips
- *You may cut these cookies larger or smaller, as you wish.*
- *Cookies keep well for several weeks at room temperature or several months in the freezer.*
- *By using a little shortening with the butter, the cookies stay crisper longer than if I use only butter.*

# Oatmeal Raisinets Cookies

*Raisinets are chocolate covered raisins. You get both the chocolates and the raisins in these delicious cookies.*

## Ingredients
1 cup butter, softened
1 cup firmly packed brown sugar
½ cup granulated sugar
2 eggs
2 tsp vanilla
1½ cups flour
1 tsp baking soda
½ tsp baking powder
1 tsp ground cinnamon
½ tsp salt
3 cups quick cooking oatmeal
1½ cups raisinets

## Preparation
1. Preheat oven to 350°F before baking.
2. Beat together butter and sugar until creamy. Add eggs and vanilla; beat well.
3. Add flour, baking soda, baking powder, cinnamon and salt; mix well.
4. Fold in oats and raisinets.
5. Using an ice cream scoop, drop onto a cookie sheet and press them down with your hands to a 1-inch thickness rounds.
6. Bake for 11-12 minutes until light golden brown.
7. Cool in pan for 1 minute and with a spatula gently remove to a wire rack.
8. Cool completely. Store in an air-tight container

Makes 24-30 cookies

## Tips
- *These cookies are just as good made with just plain raisins or just chocolate chips, either way they make great kids' lunch box surprises.*

# Oatmeal Chocolate Chip Cookies

*One way to make kids eat their cereal. Just add chocolate chips in the preparation.*

## Ingredients
¾ cup butter, chilled
1¼ cups firmly packed brown sugar
1 egg
1/3 cup milk
1½ tsp vanilla
3 cups quick cooking oats
1 cup flour
¾ tsp baking soda
¾ tsp ground cinnamon
½ tsp salt
1 cup chocolate chips
½ cup chopped nuts (optional)

## Preparation
1. Preheat oven to 375°F before baking.
2. In a large bowl, combine butter, brown sugar, egg, milk, and vanilla. Beat until well blended.
3. Fold in oats, flour, baking soda, cinnamon, salt, chocolate chips and nuts; mix well.
4. Drop with a rounded tablespoonful onto a cookie sheet.
5. Bake for 10-12 minutes or until light golden brown.
6. Cool in pan for 2 minutes and with a spatula gently remove to a wire rack.
7. Cool completely. Store in an air tight container

Makes 36 cookies

## Tips
- *For a chewy cookie you may want to eliminate the chocolate chips and instead use raisins.*

# Sesame-Pistachio Cookies (Barazik)

These Middle Eastern cookies have become quite popular in America.

## Ingredients
- ¾ cup sesame seeds
- ½ cup chopped pistachio nuts
- 1 egg white
- 1 Tbsp water
- ½ cup sweet butter, melted and cooled
- ½ cup sugar
- 1 egg, plus 1 egg yolk
- 1 tsp cider vinegar
- 1 tsp vanilla
- 1¾ cups flour
- 1¼ tsp baking powder
- ¼ tsp salt

## Preparation
1. Preheat oven to 375°F before baking.
2. Measure sesame seeds and spread them on a baking sheet. Toast seeds in the oven for 10 minutes stirring occasionally to prevent burning. Cool.
3. Place sesame seeds and pistachio nuts in separate dishes and set aside.
4. Mix water with the egg white in a separate dish and set aside.
5. In a mixing bowl, cream butter, sugar, egg, egg yolk and vinegar. Add vanilla. Stir in flour and baking powder and salt; mix until combined and forms soft dough. Wrap in plastic wrap and refrigerate for 30 minutes.
6. When dough is ready, take a teaspoon of dough at a time and form into a ball in your hands. Flatten it with your hands to form a 2 x ¼ in circle. Press gently, coarsely chopped pistachio nuts, on one side of the dough. Brush the other side with the egg white and press into the sesame seeds. Arrange cookies on a baking sheet and bake for 10-12 minutes, or until the cookies are golden.
7. Cool completely and store in an air tight container.

Makes 4 dozen cookies

## Tips:
- *A ¼ teaspoon of cinnamon adds extra flavor to the cookies.*

# Ma'moul

*These Middle Eastern semolina cookies with either walnut, pistachio nut, or date fillings are especially associated with holidays. Traditionally the dough is pressed in a carved wood cookie mold called 'tabi', sold in Middle Eastern stores, which shapes the cookies and presses designs on them.*

## Ingredients
1 pkg yeast
1 tsp sugar
½ cup warm water
3 cups farina
¾ cup semolina
1/3 cup sugar
½ tsp mahlab
1 cup unsalted butter, melted
1/3 cup milk
Confectioners' sugar for dusting cookies
<u>Nut filling</u>
3 cups chopped walnuts,
    or pistachio nuts
1 cup sugar
3 Tbsp Ma'Zahr (rose water)
<u>Date Filling</u>
2 cups chopped dates
½ cup boiling water
1 Tbsp Ma'Zahr (rose water)

## Preparation
1. *Prepare Nut filling:* Mix nuts, sugar, and Ma'Zahr together and set aside.
2. *Prepare Date Filling:* Pour boiling water over the dates and set aside to cool. Add rosewater, mix.
3. Preheat oven to 375°F before baking.
4. *Prepare dough:* In a small bowl put the yeast, 1 tsp sugar and ½ cup warm water and let the yeast start fermenting.
5. In a large bowl sift together farina, semolina, sugar and mahlab. Add melted butter and mix. Add yeast and milk and knead until the dough pliable dough is formed. If needed add a little more milk. Cover dough with plastic wrap and let it rest for at least 2 hours.
6. *Assemble Ma'moul:* Roll a walnut-size piece of dough into a ball and holding it in your left cupped palm, make a depression to hold one tablespoon of filling. Spoon in the filling in the depression and pinch the edges of the opening to enclose the filling.
7. If using the mold, press the smooth side of the cookie into the mold to get the design impression. Tap the mold into your tray to release the cookie. (If not using a mold, after enclosing the filling in the dough, roll cookie between your palms to form a ball, then slightly flatten to shape). Use the remaining dough and filling the same way and arrange cookies on a non-stick cookie sheet 1-inch apart. Let them rise for an hour in a warm spot before baking.
8. Bake until cookies are pale golden, 18-20minutes. Transfer to a wire rack to cool. Dust the nut filled ma'mouls with confectioners' sugar.

Makes 36-40 cookies

## Tips
- *To prevent the cookies from sticking to the mold, Flour the mold before each cookie is pressed in. Just spoon in some flour, then tap it out.*
- *Cookies keep fresh in an airtight container at room temperature for a week and in the freezer for several months.*

# Ethel's Kahkés

*This is an old country recipe and happens to be my mother-in-law's favorite recipe. They are rich, flaky, and crisp. In her last weeks, the only thing she cared to eat were these kahkés. I have named them in her honor.*

## Ingredients
6 cups sifted flour
1 cup farina
1½ Tbsp ground mahlab
1½ pkg yeast
1 tsp sugar
½ tsp salt
½ cup warm water
2¼ cups butter
½ cup Crisco shortening
½ cup milk
1 egg for egg-wash
Sesame seeds to sprinkle on top
Date filling (optional)

## Preparation
1. Preheat oven to 375°F before baking.
2. In a large mixing bowl, mix together flour, farina and mahlab. Set aside.
3. In a small bowl, mix yeast, sugar, salt and water. Set aside for 5 minutes to start fermenting,.
4. Melt the butter and shortening, add to the flour mixture and mix. Then add fermenting yeast and milk and knead to form soft dough. Set aside in a warm place to double in size.
5. When dough is ready, take a walnut size piece and roll on a board (approximately 2/3-inch thick and 6 inches long). Bring the two ends together and press forming a circle. Place on a baking sheet. Let it rest for ½ an hour before baking.
6. Beat the egg with 1 tablespoon of water and brush tops with egg-wash. Sprinkle with sesame seeds.
7. Bake for approximately 20 minutes or until top starts browning. Cool on a wire rack and store in an air tight container.

Makes 50 kahkés

## Tips
- *These kahkés keep 3-4 weeks in an air-tight container, and several months in the freezer.*
- *<u>Variation:</u> Flatten a piece of the dough into a circle and into the center place a tablespoon of the date mixture. Fold over and seal the edges. Brush top with egg wash and sprinkle sesame seeds. Transfer to baking sheet.*
  *<u>Date filling</u>: Pour 1 cup hot water over 2 cup chopped dates and mix until date is softened and all the water is absorbed.*

# Cream Cheese Cookies

*There are numerous varieties of these cookies, each having their own taste and texture.
These are made with cream cheese and are great with coffee or tea.*

## Ingredients
2 eggs
¾ cup sugar
1½ cups butter, softened
¼ cup vegetable oil
1 (8oz) pkg cream cheese, softened
5-5¼ cups flour
1½ tsp baking powder
1 tsp mahlab
1 egg for egg-wash
Sesame seeds

## Preparation
1. Preheat oven to 350°F before baking.
2. Beat eggs, add sugar, oil, softened butter, and softened cream cheese.
3. Add flour, baking powder and mahlab. Knead to form soft dough. If too soft, add a little more flour.
4. Roll ½ inch thick and 6 inches long and twist. You may braid or make circles, as you wish. Place on a greased or non stick baking sheet.
5. Beat the other egg and one tablespoon of water for egg-wash. Brush tops with the egg-wash and sprinkle with sesame seeds.
6. Bake approximately 20-25 minutes or until golden in color.
7. Cool and store in an air tight container. These cookies will keep fresh for three weeks.

## Tips
- *If you wish the cookies to be extra crispy, after they are all baked and you turn off the oven, let the oven cool down a little and place the cookies in the warm oven for a while to crisp them.*
- *These cookies keep a long time in the freezer.*

# Grace's Simit

*Grace was one of my mother-in-law's friends. This recipe was one of her family's favorite and my mother-in-law liked it very much.*

## Ingredients
6 cups flour
1 Tbsp baking powder
½ tsp salt
1 cube butter, melted
¼ cup Crisco shortening, melted
¾ cup vegetable oil
½ cup milk
3 eggs, slightly beaten
1 tsp vanilla
¾ cup sugar
1 egg for egg-wash
Sesame seeds

## Preparation
1. Preheat oven to 350°F before baking.
2. In a large bowl sift flour, baking powder and salt. Set aside.
3. In another bowl, mix together melted butter, shortening, vegetable oil, and milk.
4. Add the eggs, vanilla and sugar.
5. Add the liquid mixture to the flour and knead to form soft dough. Add more flour if needed. Cover dough and set aside for 20 minutes to rest.
6. On a floured board, roll the dough to ½-inch thickness and 6-inches long and create the desired shapes. You may braid, or twist, or make circles, as you wish. Place on a greased or non stick baking sheet.
7. Beat the other egg and 1 tablespoon of water for egg-wash. Brush tops with the egg-wash and sprinkle with sesame seeds.
8. Bake approximately 20-25 minutes or until golden in color.
9. Cool and store in an air tight container.

## Tips
- *These cookies will keep fresh at room temperature for three weeks and longer in the freezer.*

# Crisp Aniseed Sweet Rings

*A Greek cookie, flavored with aniseed that is good for snacks or with coffee or tea.*

## Ingredients
1 cup sweet butter, room temperature
½ cup vegetable oil
1 cup sugar
½ cup milk
1½ Tbsp crushed aniseed
5½ cups flour
2 tsp baking powder
½ tsp salt
1 egg for egg-wash

## Preparation
1. Preheat oven to 350°F before baking.
2. In a large mixing bowl, cream together butter, oil and sugar. Add the milk and crushed aniseed.
3. Sift together flour, baking powder and salt. Add to the butter mixture and knead to form soft dough.
4. Beat the egg with 1 tablespoon water. Set aside.
5. Take a piece of dough in your hands and roll on a board to form a 5-inch strip approximately ¾-inch in diameter.
6. Place on a baking sheet and brush the top with egg-wash.
7. Bake for 20-22 minutes or until the top and bottom turn golden brown.

Makes 70 cookies

## Tips
- *If you do not care for the aniseed flavor, eliminate the aniseed and flavor it with vanilla, and sprinkle sesame seeds over the egg-wash.*

# Sugar Cookies (Ghureybia)

*All Middle Eastern countries have a version of these cookies. They are made with only three ingredients - butter, sugar and flour. They are very good and of course rich in butter, and simply melt in your mouth*

## Ingredients
1 cup clarified butter
1 cup baker's sugar (fine granulated)
2 cups flour
¼ tsp vanilla (optional)
Pistachio nuts for garnish

## Preparation
1. Preheat oven to 300°F before baking.
2. Clarify the butter and measure 1 cup. Refrigerate for half an hour until it is solidified but not hard.
3. Cream sugar and butter by hand until well creamed.
4. Gradually add the flour until well incorporated. Refrigerate dough for an hour.
5. Shape walnut size pieces into S shapes or circles. Top with a pistachio nut.
6. Bake for 23-28 minutes or until the cookies are firm. Use your judgment; they will still be white but firm. Undercooking will make them very brittle, overcooking will make them chewy. If you can lift one up with a spatula, the underside should be light pink.
7. Remove from the oven and let them cool completely before removing out of the tray.

Makes 32 cookies

## Tips
- *These cookies are very delicate. They will be soft when they come out of the oven but they will set as they cool down. They should not be browned.*
- *If you make these cookies on a hot day, make sure to refrigerate the dough before shaping, for easier handling. Also refrigerate before baking to prevent them from spreading out too much.*
- <u>*Clarified butter*</u>*: In a saucepan melt sweet butter over low heat. Skim the milk solids off the top and carefully pour the clarified butter into another container without disturbing the remaining milk solids and water that are in the bottom of the pan. Clarified butter keeps up to 6 months in the refrigerator.*

# Austrian Rugelach

*These rugelachs compete with the bakery made rugelachs. Trust me these taste better.*

## Ingredients
1 cup butter, room temperature
1 (8 oz) pkg cream cheese, room temperature
1 tsp vanilla
2 cups flour
¼ cup sugar
¼ tsp salt

### Filling
¼ cup sugar
¼ cup brown sugar
1 tsp ground cinnamon
¾ cup raisins, or chocolate chips
¾ cup walnuts, chopped fine
1 cup pureed apricot jam
   or strawberry jam
1 egg, beaten for egg-wash

## Preparation
1. Preheat oven to 350°F before baking.
2. Cream butter and cream cheese together until well combined, add vanilla and mix.
3. In a separate bowl, sift together flour, sugar and salt. Add the flour mix to the cream cheese mixture and mix until well combined. Dump the dough on a floured board and roll into a ball. Divide dough into four pieces, and wrap each piece in plastic wrap and refrigerate for at least 1 hour.
4. To prepare the filling, combine brown sugar and cinnamon. Set aside. Have handy your preferred jam, chocolate chips, raisins or walnuts.
5. On a well floured board roll out each piece of dough into an 8x12 inch rectangle. Arrange dough on a parchment paper, the long side of the rectangle towards you. Spread over the dough evenly with ¼-cup of the jam and then 2 tablespoons of sugar-cinnamon mixture. Sprinkle your preferred raisins or chocolate chips and/or nuts. Using parchment paper as an aid, roll up dough into a log.
6. Beat the egg with 1 tablespoon water and brush logs with egg-wash and sprinkle the tops with the remaining sugar.
7. With a sharp knife, cut log into 1-inch slices and arrange them 1-inch apart on parchment paper lined baking pan   Repeat the same procedure with the other three pieces.
8. Bake for 18-20 minutes, until lightly browned. Cool completely.

Makes 36-40 cookies

## Tips
- *You can use your imagination and use any nut or jam combination for the filling, like coconut, hazelnut, almond, seedless raspberry jam, orange marmalade etc.*

# Date-Nut Coconut Sticks

*I saw these cookies prepared on television by Paula Dean. When I made them at home, I found them to be too sweet and too buttery. I have adapted the recipe to please my family.*

## Ingredients
1¼ stick butter
1¼ cup sugar
2 eggs, slightly beaten
8 oz chopped dates
1 tsp vanilla
l cup chopped pecans
1¾ cups Rice Krispies
1 cup coconut flakes

## Preparation
1. In a medium size saucepan melt the butter over medium heat.
2. Add sugar, eggs and chopped dates. Bring mixture to a boil stirring constantly. Reduce heat and cook for 8 minutes, stirring constantly.
3. Remove from heat and stir in vanilla. Add pecans and Rice Krispies. Stir to mix together and set aside to cool.
4. When mixture is cool, take a walnut size piece and shape into a 3-inch long by 1-inch diameter sticks.
5. Roll the sticks in coconut.

Makes 30-34

## Tips
- *To prevent dates sticking to the knife while chopping, coat the blade with a little vegetable oil before chopping the dates.*

# Lace Oatmeal Cookies

*These are ultra-thin delicate cookies, crisp and buttery.   Good served with ice cream.*

## Ingredients
1 cup butter
1 cup quick cooking oatmeal
1 cup sugar
1 egg
1 tsp vanilla
1 cup flour
1 tsp baking powder
½ tsp salt
1 cup chopped nuts

## Preparation
1. Preheat oven to 350°F before baking.
2. Melt butter, pour oatmeal over melted butter and set aside.
3. In a mixing bowl, beat sugar and egg until creamy, add vanilla and mix.
4. Add, flour, baking powder, salt, oatmeal mixture and walnuts.  Mix well.
5. Drop the batter on a greased cookie sheet, 3-inches apart and bake for 12-15 minutes or until the edges of start browning.  Remove cookies from oven and let them cool slightly before removing them to a wire rack to cool completely.
6. Store in an airtight container.

Makes 36-40 cookies

## Tips
- *As the melted butter cools, the cookie dough gets stiffer.  In that case, try to flatten them in the baking tray to get the nice lacy look when they bake.*
- *They will keep fresh and crisp for a few weeks in an air-tight container.*

# Florentines with Milk Chocolate
*These are very delicate, lacy cookies sandwiched with milk chocolate.*

## Ingredients
2/3 cup unsalted butter
2 cups quick cooking oats
1 cup granulated sugar
¼ cup corn syrup
¼ cup milk
1 tsp vanilla
¼ tsp salt
2/3 cup sifted flour
1 cup milk chocolate chips

## Preparation
1. Preheat oven to 375°F before baking.
2. In a medium saucepan, melt the butter; remove from heat. Stir in oats and mix.
3. Add flour, sugar, corn syrup, milk, vanilla and salt. Mix thoroughly.
4. Drop with a level teaspoon onto prepared cookie sheets 3 inches apart and then spread them thinly with the back of the spoon or a spatula.
5. Bake for 6-8 minutes or until the edges are golden brown. Cool completely on baking sheets on a wire rack. Remove from pan very gently as they are very fragile.
6. Melt chocolate chips in the microwave or in a double boiler. Spread a thin layer of melted chocolate onto the flat side of half of the cookies and top them with remaining cookies.

Makes 3-4 dozen sandwiched cookies.

## Tips
- *These cookies are extremely delicate, handle them gently.*

# Chocolate Chip Biscotti

*These twice-baked crisp Italian cookies have a subtle anise flavor and are great with coffee. Traditionally they are served with espresso or cappuccino for dipping. Kids love them because of the chocolate chips.*

## Ingredients
4½ cups all purpose flour
1 tsp baking powder
1 tsp baking soda
½ tsp salt
2 large eggs
1½ cups sugar
¾ cup vegetable oil
½ cup sour cream
1 tsp vanilla
½ cup chopped walnuts
½ cup chocolate chips

## Preparation
1. Preheat oven 350°F before baking.
2. Sift flour, baking powder, baking soda and salt. Set aside.
3. In a mixing bowl, beat together eggs, sugar and oil until well combined.
4. Add to the above mixture: sour cream, ~~anise seeds~~, vanilla and ~~anise extract~~.
5. Gradually add flour mixture until the mixture becomes dough.
6. Add to the dough, ½ cup chopped walnuts and ½ cup chocolate chips.
7. On a floured surface, use your hands to form 3 logs (12-inches long and 2½-inches in diameter).
8. Place the logs on a greased baking sheet and bake until the edges are browned and the center is firm. Approximately 30-35 minutes. Remove from oven and let them cool for 10 minutes.
9. Reduce oven temperature to 300°F. Slice the logs crosswise on a slight diagonal into ½ - ¾ inches wide, lay them on a tray, and return to the oven for 10-15 minutes to lightly toast. Cool and keep in an airtight container.

Makes 45-50 slices

## Tips
- *Biscotti keep in an air-tight container for 1 month and in the freezer for up to 6 months.*
- *You may substitute almonds or pistachios for the walnuts and raisins or dried cranberries for chocolate chips.*
- *For variety you might want to dip one end of the biscotti in melted chocolate.*

# Aniseed Biscotti
*A classic Italian cookie, twice baked and crisp.
Perfect with ice cream or just enjoy with a cup of coffee.*

## Ingredients
4½ cups all purpose flour
1 tsp baking powder
1 tsp baking soda
½ tsp salt
2 large eggs
1¾ cups sugar
¾ cup vegetable oil
½ cup sour cream
¾ tsp anise seeds
½ tsp anise extract
1 tsp vanilla
½ cup blanched almonds

## Preparation
1. Preheat oven to 350°F before baking.
2. Sift flour, baking powder, baking soda and salt. Set aside.
3. In a mixing bowl beat together eggs, sugar and oil until well combined.
4. In another small bowl mix together sour cream, anise seeds, anise extract and vanilla. Pour into the egg mixture and mix well.
5. Gradually add flour mixture until the mixture becomes dough.
6. Add to the dough, ½ cup chopped almonds.
7. On a floured surface, use your hands to form 2 logs (12-inches long and 2½-inches in diameter.
8. Place the logs on a greased baking sheet and bake until the edges are browned and the center is firm. Approximately 30-35 minutes. Remove from oven and let them cool for 15 minutes.
9. Reduce oven temperature to 300°F. Slice the logs crosswise on a slight diagonal into ½ - ¾ inches wide, lay them on a tray, and return to the oven for 10-15 minutes to lightly toast. Cool and keep in an airtight container.
10. This step is optional. If you wish drizzle on top of the cake with melted white and dark chocolate.

Makes 45-50 slices

## Tips
- *Biscottis keep in an airtight container for 1 month and in the freezer for up to 6 months.*
- *You may substitute pistachios for the almonds.*
- *For variety you might want to dip one end of the biscotti in melted chocolate.*

# Double Chocolate Biscotti

*These crisp cookies have a rich chocolate flavor and they are not very sweet. Sometimes in Italy they are called **mostacchioli** because of their mustache shape. Traditionally they are served with espresso or cappuccino for dipping.*

## Ingredients
4 cups all purpose flour
2/3 cup unsweetened cocoa powder
1 tsp baking powder
1 tsp baking soda
½ tsp salt
1 cup butter, room temperature
2 cups sugar
3 large eggs
1½ tsp vanilla
½ tsp almond extract
1 cup Macadamia nuts, coarsely chopped
1 cup chocolate chips

## Preparation
1. Preheat oven to 350°F before baking.
2. Sift flour, cocoa powder, baking powder, baking soda and salt. Set aside.
3. In a mixing bowl, beat butter and sugar until creamy. Add the eggs, vanilla and almond extract.
4. Gradually add flour and cocoa mixture until the mixture becomes dough.
5. Add 1 cup chopped nuts and 1 cup chocolate chips. If the dough is too sticky, add a little more flour. Refrigerate dough for half an hour for easy handling.
6. On a floured surface, use your hands to form 3 logs (12-inches long and 2½-inches in diameter).
7. Place the logs on a greased baking sheet and bake at 350°F until the edges are browned and the center is firm. Approximately 35 minutes. Remove from oven and let them cool for 15 minutes.
8. Reduce oven temperature to 300°F. Slice the logs crosswise on a slight diagonal into ½ - ¾ inches wide, lay them on a tray, and return to the oven for 15 minutes to lightly toast. Cool and keep in an airtight container.

Makes 45-50 slices

## Tips
- *Biscotti keeps in an airtight container for 1 month and in the freezer for up to 6 months.*
- *You may substitute walnuts, almonds or hazelnuts for the macadamia nuts.*
- *You might want to drizzle melted white chocolate on them for an attractive look.*

# Banana-Walnut Chocolate Chip Cookies

*Our grandchildren love these cookies; a little banana, a little oatmeal and a little chocolate chip. What's there not to like?*

## Ingredients
1½ cups all purpose flour
½ tsp salt
½ tsp baking soda
¾ cup butter, softened
½ cup sugar
½ cup brown sugar
1 egg
1½ tsp vanilla
¾ cup mashed ripe bananas
1 cup quick cooking rolled oats
1 cup chocolate chips
½ cup coarsely chopped walnuts

## Preparation
1. Preheat oven to 375°F before baking.
2. Sift together flour, salt, baking soda. Set aside.
3. In a bowl, cream butter and sugars and beat until fluffy. Add egg and vanilla extract. Mix in mashed bananas. Mix well.
4. Fold in flour mixture until just combined.
5. Stir in oats, walnuts, and chocolate chips.
6. Drop dough with a full tablespoon onto a baking sheet and bake for 13-15 minutes or until the top starts browning. Transfer to wire rack and let cool completely. Store them in an airtight container. They will keep fresh for 2-3 days.

Makes 3 dozen cookies

## Tips
- *These cookies are a good choice for kids' lunch box surprise treats.*

# Zucchini Chocolate Chip Cookies

*Even though it is obvious that these cookies are loaded with zucchini, kids love them anyway as long as they have chocolate chips in them.*

## Ingredients
l cup butter room temperature
1½ cups sugar
2 eggs
1 tsp vanilla
2 cups shredded zucchini
3 cups all-purpose flour sifted
2 tsp baking powder
½ tsp salt
1½ tsp cinnamon
1 cup chopped walnuts
1 cup shredded coconut
1 cup chocolate chips

## Preparation
1. Preheat oven to 350°F before baking.
2. Cream butter and sugar. Add the eggs and vanilla and beat well. Mix in shredded zucchini.
3. Sift the flour together with the salt, baking powder, and cinnamon,
4. Fold in the flour. Add walnuts, coconut and chocolate chips.
5. Drop by a tablespoon on a greased cookie sheet.
6. Bake for 18-22 minutes, until golden brown.
7. Cool on wire rack and store in an air tight container.

Makes 5 dozen cookies

## Tips
- *To make Zucchini Chocolate Cookies, reduce the flour by ¼ cup and add 1/3 cup of Cocoa powder and 2 tablespoons of sugar.*

# Peanut Butter Chocolate Chip Bars

*These bars are deliciously rich with peanut butter and chocolate chips.
The thick layer of semi-sweet chocolate ganache makes it irresistible.*

## Ingredients
2 sticks unsalted butter, softened
1½ cup sugar
1 cup creamy peanut butter
2 large eggs
2 tsp vanilla
2 cups flour
1½ cups chocolate chips

*For Ganache*
1½ cups semi-sweet chocolate chips
½ cup heavy cream
1 Tbsp unsalted butter,
  room temperature

## Preparation
1. Preheat oven to 350°F before baking.
2. Lightly butter and flour a 9 x13-inch baking pan.
3. Beat together butter and sugar with an electric mixer until mixture is light and fluffy. Add the eggs and vanilla and beat until incorporated.
4. Add flour and mix until just combined. Do not over beat.
5. Fold in chocolate chips and spread batter in the prepared pan.
6. Bake at 350°F for 30-35 minutes, until top is golden brown. Cool completely in the pan on a wire rack.
7. *Prepare Ganache:* Bring cream to boil in a small pan. Remove from heat.
8. Add chocolate chips and let the mixture stand for one minute.
9. Add butter and gently whisk until chocolate is completely melted and the mixture is smooth.
10. Spread warm ganache on cooled cookie sheet and let stand until set. Cut into bars.

Makes 32 bars

# Chocolate Fudge Brownies

*Only three words will describe these brownies - ooey, gooey, chewy. It has an intense chocolate flavor because of the hot fudge sauce mixed in the batter. I do not think there is a specific test for the fudginess of brownies. Baked at maximum time will result in moist brownies, but not as moist and wet as baking at minimum time. You might want to experiment to obtain your preferred results.*

## Ingredients
½ cup butter
1 2/3 cups sugar
2 Tbsp water
4 (1 oz) squares unsweetened chocolate
½ cup any purchased hot fudge topping
2 large eggs
1 tsp vanilla
1 1/3 cups flour
½ tsp baking soda
Pinch of salt
½ cup chopped nuts (optional)

## Preparation
1. Preheat oven to 350°F before baking. Grease and flour a 9-inch square baking pan.
2. With a knife, break the chocolate squares into pieces.
3. In a microwave safe bowl or on the stove top, melt butter, sugar, and water until the mixture starts bubbling. Add the chopped chocolate and stir until melted.
4. Stir in hot fudge topping and vanilla. Add eggs one a time until incorporated.
5. Add flour, baking soda, and salt; stir until blended. If using nuts, stir in the nuts.
6. Pour into prepared baking pan.
7. Bake for 16-18 minutes or until toothpick inserted in center comes out with fudgy crumbs. Cool completely on a wire rack before cutting.

Makes 24 squares

## Tips
- *On the stove top method, heat sugar, butter and water in a medium saucepan just to boiling, stirring constantly. Remove from heat and add cut-up chocolate and stir until melted. Proceed as above.*
- *If you like cake-like brownies use 4 eggs and extra ½ cup flour.*

# Butterfinger Fudge Brownies
*These brownies are only for chocolate lovers.*
*Irresistibly rich flavor with ooey-gooey consistency will simply send you to heaven.*
*My daughters refer to these as "killer brownies". Pure decadence!*

## Ingredients
2 pkgs (8x8 pan size) Pillsbury's Traditional Fudge Brownie mix
2 eggs
½ cup water
2/3 cup vegetable oil
15 oz Nestle's Butterfinger bar, chopped

## Preparation
1. Preheat oven to 350°F before baking.
2. Grease bottom of a 9 x13-inch baking pan.
3. In a large bowl, combine brownie mix, eggs, water, and oil. Mix by hand until dry ingredients are moistened. Do not over mix. Mixture will be lumpy.
4. Spread in prepared pan.
5. Sprinkle the top with the chopped Butterfinger chocolate.
6. Bake for 28-30 minutes. Do not over bake.
7. Cool completely before cutting.

Makes 18-24 pieces

## Tips
- *You may use your favorite brand Fudge Brownie mix. Just follow the preparation instruction on the package and top it with chopped Butterfinger chocolate.*

# Caramel Brownies

*This is the ultimate chocolate lover's fantasy! It just can't get any better than this, or any chewier than this. These are simply sinfully rich, and what's wrong in sinning this way once in a while?*

## Ingredients
4 (1 oz) squares unsweetened baking chocolate
1½ cubes butter
2 cups sugar
4 eggs
1 tsp vanilla
1 cup flour
½ tsp salt
1 pkg (14 oz) caramels unwrapped
1/3 cup heavy cream
1½ cups chopped walnuts or pecans
1 cup chocolate chips

## Preparation
1. Preheat oven to 350°F before baking.
2. Grease and line with foil a 9x13-inch baking pan.
3. Melt unsweetened chocolate and butter in the microwave or over the stove on low heat, stirring until chocolate is melted and smooth.
4. Mix in sugar until well blended, add eggs, vanilla, flour and salt. Mix until well incorporated.
5. Divide batter in half and pour half of the batter in the prepared pan. Bake for 25 minutes.
6. Meanwhile, melt the caramels and cream in the microwave or over the stove on low heat, stirring until caramel is well melted. Add half of the nuts to the melted caramels.
7. Remove pan from oven and spread caramel mixture over baked brownies, keeping it away from the sides of the pan. Spread the remainder of the batter over caramel. Sprinkle the top with the remaining chopped nuts and chocolate chips. Return to the oven and bake for an additional 25-30 minutes. Cool completely before cutting.

Makes 24 pieces

## Tips
- *I personally think these brownies taste better the second day.*

# Banana Chocolate Chip Brownies
*Brownies are traditional American favorites. These are my grandchildren's favorite. These brownies are moist and have a pleasant banana flavor.*

## Ingredients
1 cup mashed ripe bananas
½ cup sugar
2 large eggs
8 oz semi sweet chocolate chips, melted
½ cup vegetable oil
1 tsp vanilla
½ cup flour
2 tsp cocoa powder
1½ tsp baking powder
¼ tsp salt
½ cup chocolate chips

## Preparation
1. Preheat oven to 325°F before baking.
2. Lightly butter and flour an 8 x 8-inch baking pan.
3. In a mixing bowl, mash the bananas; add sugar, eggs, melted chocolate, oil, and vanilla. Stir to combine.
4. Sift flour, cocoa, baking powder and salt. Fold into the wet mixture. Do not over mix.
5. Fold in chocolate chips.
6. Bake for 30 minutes. Cool completely before cutting.

Makes 9 large or 12 smaller pieces

## Tips
- *These brownies are at their best the day you make them.*

# Tangy Lemon Triangles

*These bars have a delicious tangy lemon flavored custard topping. Our granddaughter Taylor's favorite bars. Easy to prepare and, by the way, they disappear fast.*

## Ingredients
1¼ cups flour
¼ cup confectioners' sugar
3 tsp grated lemon rind
1 cube unsalted butter
2 large eggs
¾ cup sugar
6 Tbsp lemon juice
2 Tbsp flour
½ tsp baking powder
Pinch of salt

## Preparation
1. Preheat oven to 350°F before baking.
2. Combine flour, confectioners' sugar and 1 tsp lemon rind. Cut in butter. Press the mixture in the bottom of a 9 x13-inch baking pan. Bake the crust for 18-20 minutes.
3. Meanwhile combine the eggs, ¾ cup sugar, lemon juice and 2 teaspoons lemon rind,. Beat with an electric beater for 5 minutes.
4. Mix together 2 tablespoons flour, baking powder, and salt. Whisk into the egg-lemon mixture.
5. Pour filling over baked crust and continue baking 25 minutes longer.
6. While hot, sift confectioners' sugar over the mixture. Cool completely. Cut into triangles or bars. Store in an air-tight container.

Makes 24

## Tips
- *If some of the sugar is dissolved from the moisture of the bars, sprinkle some more confectioners' sugar before serving.*

# Peanut Brittle Marshmallow Treats
*Wow! Crunchy peanut brittle and crackling rice Krispies. Great combination.*

## Ingredients
½ cup sugar
¾ cup roasted peanuts
3 Tbsp butter or margarine
4 cups miniature marshmallows
¼ cup peanut butter
¼ cup peanut butter
6½ cups Rice Krispies cereal
2 cups peanut butter chocolate chips

## Preparation
1. In a skillet over low flames melt the sugar until it turns a light caramel color. Remove from the heat and add the peanuts; stir to coat them with the melted sugar. Transfer them to a greased tray and separate them to dry. Let them cool and chop them. Set aside for the topping.
2. Butter a 9 x13 x 2-inch pan and set aside.
3. Melt butter and peanut butter in a large saucepan over low heat. Add marshmallows and stir until completely melted and smooth. Remove from heat.
4. Add Rice Krispies cereal and stir until well coated.
5. Using a buttered spatula or waxed paper, press mixture evenly into the pan. Cool.
6. Melt peanut butter chocolate chips in the microwave or over a double boiler on the stove top.
7. Spread over cooled Krispies. Sprinkles prepared peanut brittle over melted chocolate and lightly press into chocolate. Refrigerate until chocolate is firm. Cut into squares.

Makes 24 bars

## Tips
- *For variety, you may use Cocoa Krispies instead of the Rice Krispies.*

# Cocoa Krispies Marshmallow Treats
*Even grownups like these treats. How can you go wrong with coco Krispies and chocolate?*

## Ingredients
3 Tbsp butter
4 cups miniature marshmallows
6 cups Coco Krispies
2 cups semi-sweet chocolate chips
1 Tbsp shortening

## Preparation
1. Butter a 15½ x10½ x1-inch pan and set aside.
2. Melt butter in a large saucepan over low heat. Add marshmallows and stir until completely melted and smooth. Remove from heat.
3. Add Coco Krispies cereal. Stir until well coated. Using buttered spatula or wax paper, press evenly into pan. Set aside to cool.
4. For filling, combine chocolate chips and shortening in a small saucepan over a double boiler. Stir until chocolate is melted and is smooth.
5. Cut cooled cereal mixture in the tray in half. Reserving 1/3 cup of melted chocolate for the top, spread remaining 2/3 over one half. Top with the other half and gently press halves together.
6. Drizzle reserved chocolate mixture over top. Let chocolate set.
7. Cut into 1½-inch squares. Store in an air-tight container.

Makes 35 bars

## Tips
- *If you do not have Coco Krispies around use Rice Krispies, they work just as well.*

# S'more Snacks
*Children love these for snack. I wonder why?*

## Ingredients
5 cups miniature marshmallows
4 Tbsp Karo syrup
5 Tbsp butter
1½ cup chocolate chips
½ tsp cinnamon (optional)
1 tsp vanilla
8 cups Golden Graham cereal
½ cup chopped nuts (any combination)
1 cup miniature marshmallows

## Preparation
1. Butter a 9 x13-inch pan and set aside.
2. In a 3 quart saucepan, over the stove top, heat 5 cups of marshmallows, corn syrup, butter, chocolate chips, and cinnamon. Stir until chocolate and marshmallow are melted. Remove from heat.
3. Add vanilla and stir.
4. Add 8 cups of cereal and mix until completely coated with the chocolate mixture.
5. Add nuts and 1 cup of marshmallows. Stir to mix then pour into the prepared pan. Let it cool.
6. Cut into squares. Store loosely covered. Will stay fresh for several days.

Makes 24 pieces

# Candies

## Old Fashioned Peanut Brittle
*An American favorite.*

### Ingredients
1 cup sugar
½ cup light corn syrup
¼ cup water
3 Tbsp unsalted butter
1½ cups lightly salted peanuts
¾ tsp baking soda
½ tsp vanilla

### Preparation
1. Combine sugar, corn syrup, and water in a heavy 2quart saucepan. Clip a candy thermometer to the saucepan touching the liquid in the pan.
2. Over medium high heat, stir the mixture until sugar is dissolved and it comes to a boil.
3. Add the butter and keep stirring until the candy thermometer reaches 280°F and the syrup starts turning brown.
4. Add the peanuts and keep stirring until the candy thermometer reads 305°F. Remove from heat and quickly stir in the baking soda and vanilla.
5. Pour hot mixture on a greased cookie sheet and spread it out to the edges of the pan.
6. Cool and break into pieces. Keep in an air-tight container at room temperature.

Makes 20 servings

### Tips
- *Peanut brittle will keep 2-3 weeks in an airtight container at room temperature.*

# Butter Toffee

*These crunchy toffees are a real treat. One Christmas, my friend Barbara Eden and I got together to make toffee to give to our friends. We each had a different recipe. We kept on tasting to see which one was better until half was gone and we had created a mess in the kitchen. Her husband Jon rescued us by helping to clean-up. This recipe is a simplified version of those two recipes.*

## Ingredients
- 1 cup butter
- 1½ cups sugar
- ¼ cup water
- ½ tsp salt
- 1 tsp vanilla
- 4 oz semi-sweet chocolate morsels
- 4 oz milk chocolate morsels
- ½ cup blanched almonds, toasted and chopped

## Preparation
1. Lline a 9x11½-inch pan with foil. Generously butter the foil and set aside.
2. Combine butter, sugar, water and salt in a heavy 2-quart saucepan. Cook over medium-high heat, stirring constantly, until candy thermometer reads 295°F, or until a drop of the syrup in cold water forms a firm ball. Remove from heat and stir in vanilla.
3. Immediately pour into prepared pan spreading to even out the thickness. When almost set, use a sharp knife to score the toffee into squares to make breaking easier after it is set. Cool completely.
4. Melt semi-sweet and milk chocolate together either in the microwave or in the top of a double boiler. Spread half of the chocolate over the toffee and sprinkle on half of the almonds. Press the almonds to set in the chocolate. Refrigerate until the chocolate is firm.
5. Reheat remaining chocolate, flip over the toffee, peel the aluminum foil, spread the other side with the melted chocolate and sprinkle with remaining almonds.
6. After the chocolate is set, break into squares and store in an air-tight container.

Makes 24-36 pieces

## Tips
- *These toffees are good to eat as they are, but they are much better with the chocolate.*

# Candied Apricots

*Fresh apricots are usually abundantly available in June and July. We can preserve and have them available all year round. Apricots preserved this way are very popular in Middle Eastern countries.*

## Ingredients
5 lb fresh apricots
3 cups sugar
2 cups water
1½ cups Karo syrup
3 Tbsp lemon juice

## Preparation
1. In a saucepan, cook sugar, water, Karo syrup, and lemon juice for 15 minutes.
2. Add apricots and cook 5 minutes. Do not stir. Remove from heat and leave apricots in the syrup to cool.
3. Second day, boil the apricots for 5 minutes more. Do not stir. Remove from the heat and leave the apricots in the syrup to cool.
4. On the third day, remove apricots from the syrup, take the pits out and place them back in the syrup. Boil for 5 minutes without disturbing them while boiling. Cool them in the syrup.
5. When completely cool, take them out of the syrup and drain them on a grill to get rid of the excess syrup.
6. Place them on a wooden board, center exposed, cover the apricots with a cheese cloth to keep insects away. Place the board in the sun to dry. On the next day close them and leave them in the sun all day. On the third day, turn them over to the other side and let them dry in the sun all day.
7. Store in an air tight containers. Refrigerate or freeze. Use as needed.

## Tips
- *In the freezer they keep for several months.*

# Crystallized Ginger

*Crystallized ginger is fragrant and spicy and is used as an after dinner digestive, or in desserts. It also has some medicinal value; it helps calm vertigo and nausea.*

### Ingredients
1 lb ginger root
2 cups sugar
3 Tbsp water
½ cup sugar to coating

### Preparation
1. With a potato peeler, peel ginger and slice, slightly thinner than ¼ inch, or cut into ½ inch cubes.
2. Cover with water and boil gently for 30-40 minutes or until tender.
3. Drain water. Add sugar and 3 tablespoons of water, bring to boil stirring often until ginger is transparent and the syrup has almost evaporated.
4. Remove from heat and keep stirring constantly until almost dry. The heat from the pan will cause the remaining sugar syrup to crystallize and the pieces of ginger to separate from each other.
5. Toss cooled mixture in a half cup of sugar to coat. Store crystallized ginger in an airtight jar and they will keep 2-3 months.

### Tips
- *Don't slice ginger too thin; they will dry up while crystallizing..*

# Honeyed Sesame Candy

*We grew up in Beirut, Lebanon eating these nutritious bars bought from street vendors. They are chewy, simply delicious and nutritious. It is easy to keep reaching for more.*

## Ingredients
½ cup honey
½ cup firmly packed brown sugar
¼ tsp salt
¾ tsp cinnamon
2 cups sesame seeds
1/3 cup roasted sunflower seeds
1/3 cup roasted peanuts
1/3 cup roasted slivered almonds

## Preparation
1. Toast the sesame seeds, in a baking pan, in a preheated oven 350°F for about 15 minutes.
2. In a 4-quart pan, combine honey, brown sugar, salt, and cinnamon. Bring to a boil over medium heat stirring constantly; cook for 2 minutes.
3. Remove pan from heat and immediately stir in sesame seeds, sunflower seeds, peanuts and almonds. Mix thoroughly.
4. Turn into a buttered 9 x 3-inch pan, and with a large buttered spatula, press down the candy firmly and evenly.
5. Cool for 15 minutes, and then lift out of pan with a spatula and cut into 1x2-inch rectangles. Store the candy in an air-tight container at room temperature.

Makes 48 pieces

## Tips
- *Place waxed paper between the layers of the sesame candy to prevent them from sticking to each other.*

# Assorted-Nut Crisp Bars

*These bars have more flavor than sweetness. A good source of energy, but I'll warn you they are addictive! You can use your favorite nuts all combined in a bar. The nuts have been toasted to enhance their flavor.*

## Ingredients

2 cups raw sesame seeds
1 cup raw sunflower seeds
1 cup raw peanuts
1 cup raw slivered almonds
1 cup raw pistachios
6 Tbsp butter
½ cup honey
1 cup sugar
¼ tsp salt
1 tsp cinnamon (optional)
A candy thermometer

## Preparation

1. Roast the nuts and seeds in a large skillet, one ingredient at a time, until they are very lightly browned. (Different nuts require different times for roasting, so roast them separately according to how much roasting is required for each kind of nut.)
2. Combine roasted nuts in a large bowl.
3. Oil a 1-inch deep 12x16-inch baking sheet. Place tray in a warm oven to just slightly heat it.
4. In a small saucepan, heat butter, honey, sugar, salt and cinnamon. Bring to a boil and cook until candy thermometer reaches 270°F. Immediately pour over the mixed nuts in the bowl and mix well until the nuts are well coated. (Make sure the bulb of the thermometer does not touch the bottom of the pan and is entirely in the liquid and not just the foam.)
5. Pour the nuts into the warm, oiled pan. Spread the nuts out evenly. Lay a sheet of parchment paper over the warm nuts and press down with the bottom of another tray to get a smooth even top.
6. Let cool somewhat, then using a knife score into squares. When fairly cool, break into pieces along the scored lines.
7. Cool completely, store in an-airtight container in a cool place.

Makes 48 pieces

## Tips

- *A warm tray will allow you to spread the mixture easily to obtain desired thickness.*
- *You can use pre-roasted, unsalted nuts to save the first step.*
- *You can use any combination of nuts; if you favor peanuts, eliminate the ones you don't like and double the amount of peanuts. It does not make any difference what kind of nuts you use, as long as you have 6 cups.*
- *If you like the bars crisp, keep them in the refrigerator and they stay crisp for a couple of months. If you like the bars chewier, keep them at room temperature and they will be good for 2 weeks.*
- *Seeds and nuts keep best and longest when stored in the freezer and they can be used directly from the freezer.*

# Cinnamon Seasoned Pecans
*A healthy snack food. Good any time of the day. It is a popular item at cocktail parties. Packed in a nice jar they make a nice hostess gift.*

## Ingredients
2 Tbsp butter melted
2 Tbsp light corn syrup
4 tsp sugar
1 tsp cinnamon
¼ tsp nutmeg
¼ tsp salt
4 cups pecan halves

## Preparation
1. Preheat oven to 250°F before baking.
2. In a saucepan, melt the butter; add corn syrup, sugar, cinnamon, nutmeg and salt.
3. Add the pecans and toss to coat with the mixture.
4. Spread on a non-stick cookie sheet in a single layer. Bake for 1 hour stirring every 15 minutes.
5. Remove from the oven and cool. Store them in an airtight container. It will keep fresh and crisp for two weeks.

Makes 4 cups

## Tips
- *You may wish to make the nuts spicier; add 1 teaspoon of crushed pepper with the spices.*

# Spiced Candied Walnuts

*Another healthy snack food. Good any time of the day. They are also good sprinkled on salads. Packed in a nice jar they make a nice hostess gift.*

## Ingredients
½ cup sugar
Pinch of salt
1 tsp crushed red pepper
3 cups water
2 cups walnut halves

## Preparation
1. Preheat oven to 300°F before baking.
2. Slightly grease a baking sheet. Set aside.
3. Combine sugar, salt, and pepper. Mix well. Set aside.
4. In a saucepan, bring 3 cups of water to a boil. Add walnuts and boil for 5 minutes. Drain.
5. Return walnuts to the saucepan and toss the hot walnuts to coat with the sugar mixture.
6. Spread the walnuts on the prepared baking sheet in single layer. Bake for 35-40 minutes or until walnuts start browning, stirring every 10 minutes. Cool completely and store in an air-tight container.

Makes 2 cups

## Tips
- *The secret to the success of this recipe is boiling the walnuts before baking.*
- *Walnuts taste better if made a day or two ahead.*
- *If you like the walnuts spicier, add cayenne pepper to your liking.*

# Milk Chocolate Fudge

*There is nothing as good as home-made fudge. This is delicious, soft and smooth fudge. The only tricky part is knowing the exact cooking time on your stove top. Five minutes is your guideline. Cook thirty seconds more or less depending on your standard of moderate heat.*
*These are a must during the holidays.*

## Ingredients
1 (7 oz) jar marshmallow cream
1½ cups sugar
2/3 cup canned evaporated milk
¼ cup butter
¼ tsp salt
1 cup semi-sweet chocolate chips
1 cup milk chocolate chips
1 tsp vanilla
½ cup chopped nuts, optional

## Preparation
1. In a 3-qt flat-bottom saucepan, combine marshmallow cream, sugar, evaporated milk, butter and salt.
2. Bring to a boil stirring constantly over moderate heat. Continue boiling 5 minutes stirring constantly.
3. Remove from heat. Add chocolate chips and stir until chocolate is melted.
4. Stir in vanilla. If using chopped nuts, add to the melted chocolate mixture.
5. Pour into greased 8-inch square pan. Chill until firm.
6. Cut into 1-inch squares.

Makes 64 squares

## Tips
- *A flat bottom wooden spoon is best for scraping all the surface of a flat-bottom saucepan.*
- *You may make this fudge a week in advance, but do not cut into squares so it does not dry out.*

# Easy Chocolate Truffle Squares

*These truffles are rich, smooth, and creamy and are easy to make. They keep well in the refrigerator. Shape into balls or cut into squares and dip in melted chocolate and they will keep even longer.*

## Ingredients
2 cups semi sweet chocolate chips
2½ cups confectioners' sugar
1 (8 oz) cream cheese, room temperature
1 tsp vanilla

## Preparation
1. Melt chocolate either in the microwave or over a double boiler. Stir until chocolate is completely, melted. Set aside.
2. In a food processor, beat cream cheese until smooth. Gradually add in confectioners' sugar, beating until well blended.
3. Add melted chocolate and vanilla. Mix well.
4. Line a 8x8-inch square pan with plastic wrap, pour mixture in the pan and smooth the top. Refrigerate for several hours or quick freeze for an hour.
5. Cut into desired shapes, squares or rectangles. Refrigerate until ready to dip in chocolate.
6. In a double boiler or microwave, melt 1 cup of semi sweet chocolate with 1 teaspoon of clarified butter or shortening. Dip the squares in the melted chocolate to coat and gently remove with a candy fork and lay them on a piece of wax paper to set.

Makes 64 squares

## Tips
- *For variation in presentation, you may dip them in cocoa powder, chopped nuts, or coconut flakes. You may want to shape them into balls and roll them in your preferred coating.*
- *For taste variation, you may divide truffle in thirds, eliminate the vanilla and use 1 tablespoon of your favorite liqueur like coffee, orange, almond, or even raspberry puree.*
- <u>*Tempering chocolate*</u>*: Melt the chocolate in a double boiler over hot water to reach 122°F. At this point all crystals will melt, Cool it down to 81°F, and then heat it slightly to 90°F. This temperature is the right temperature for working with the chocolate. If chocolate is not tempered properly, the cocoa butter will separate and you will have some white spots on the truffles.*

# Milk Chocolate Truffles

*If you use commercially produced hollow truffle shells, these truffles look and taste better than the best store bought truffles. Try to use the best chocolate you can find. The preparation of these truffles are a little work but well worth it. You need a candy thermometer for this recipe.*

## Ingredients
6 oz. heavy cream
14 oz. milk chocolate
60 hollow milk chocolate shells
1 tsp vanilla
Milk chocolate vermicelli

## Preparation
1. If using block chocolate, chop the chocolate into ¼ inch pieces and set aside.
2. *Prepare the ganache:* Over medium high heat bring the cream to a boil, remove from heat and add the finely chopped chocolate and stir until all are melted and smooth. Add 1 teaspoon vanilla or any other flavoring you wish. Set aside to cool to room temperature.
3. Using a pastry bag, fill the shells with the ganache. Let it set, then seal the openings with tempered chocolate.
4. When the seal is set, roll the truffles in tempered milk chocolate, then roll over a wire rack to give texture, or roll in milk chocolate vermicelli.
5. Keep in a well sealed container in a cool place.

Makes 60 truffles

## Tips
- *For variation in presentation, you may dip them in cocoa powder, chopped nuts, or coconut flakes.*
- *Tempering chocolate:* *Melt the chocolate in a double boiler over hot water to 122°F. At this point all crystals will melt, Cool down to 81°F, then heat slightly to 90°F. This temperature is the right temperature for working with the chocolate. If chocolate is not tempered properly, the coco butter will separate and you will have some white spots on the truffles.*
- *If you have leftover tempered chocolate and some plastic chocolate molds, such as lollipops, baskets, hearts, etc. use your tempered chocolate to make them.*

# Dark Chocolate Truffles

*These truffles have a higher content of cocoa. I have used commercially produced hollow truffle shells. These truffles look and taste better than the best store bought truffles. Try to use the best chocolate you can find. Preparing these truffles are a little work but well worth it. You need a candy thermometer for this recipe.*

## Ingredients
8 oz heavy cream
10 oz dark chocolate
60 hollow dark chocolate shells
1 tsp vanilla
Dark chocolate vermicelli

## Preparation
1. If using block chocolate, chop the chocolate into ¼ inch pieces and set aside.
2. <u>*Prepare the ganache:*</u> Over medium high heat bring the cream to boil, remove from heat and add the finely chopped chocolate and stir until all are melted and smooth. Add 1 teaspoon vanilla or any other flavoring you wish. Set aside to cool to room temperature.
3. Using a pastry bag fill the shells with the ganache. Let it set, then seal the openings with tempered chocolate.
4. When the seal is set, roll the truffles in tempered dark chocolate, roll in dark chocolate vermicelli.
5. Keep in a well sealed container in a cool place.

Makes 60 truffles

## Tips
- *For variation in presentation, you may dip them in cocoa powder, chopped nuts, or coconut flakes.*
- <u>*Tempering chocolate*</u>*: Melt the chocolate in a double boiler over hot water to 122°F. At this point all crystals will melt, Cool down to 81°F, then heat slightly to 90°F. This temperature is the right temperature for working with the chocolate. If chocolate is not tempered properly, the coco butter will separate and you will have some white spots on the truffles.*
- *If you have leftover tempered chocolate and some plastic chocolate molds, such as lollipops, baskets, hearts, etc. use your tempered chocolate to make them.*

# Nutella Chocolate Truffles

*These are hazelnut flavored truffles.*
*I use commercially produced hollow truffle shells. They look and taste better than the best store bought truffles. Try to use the best chocolate you can find. The preparation is a little work but well worth it. You need a candy thermometer for this recipe.*

## Ingredients
8 oz heavy cream
10 oz. dark chocolate
1 (13 oz) jar Nutella
60 hollow dark chocolate shells

## Preparation
1. If using block chocolate, chop the chocolate into ¼ inch pieces and set aside.
2. <u>*Prepare the ganache:*</u> Over medium high heat bring the cream to boil, remove from heat and add the finely chopped chocolate and stir until all are melted and smooth. Add Nutella and mix thoroughly. Set aside to cool to room temperature.
3. Using a pastry bag, fill the shells with the ganache. Let it set, then seal the openings with tempered chocolate.
4. When the seal is set, roll the truffles in tempered dark chocolate and set wax paper to set.
5. Keep in a well sealed container in a cool place.

Makes 60 truffles

## Tips
- *For variation in presentation, roll truffles in chopped hazelnuts, or roll them on a wire tray to give texture.*
- <u>*Tempering chocolate*</u>*: Melt the chocolate in a double boiler over hot water to 122°F. At this point all crystals will melt, Cool down to 81°F, then heat slightly to 90°F. This temperature is the right temperature for working with the chocolate. If chocolate is not tempered properly, the coco butter will separate and you will have some white spots on the truffles..*
- *If you have leftover tempered chocolate and some plastic chocolate molds, such as lollipops, baskets, hearts, etc. use your tempered chocolate to make them.*

# Apricot Jam

*My family's very favorite jam is apricot jam. My brother Jack's apricot tree provides us with enough apricots to make our yearly supply of jam. These apricots are the sweetest and tastiest apricots ever. You can just imagine how tasty the jams turn out.*

## Ingredients
8 cups pitted fresh apricots
4 cups sugar
2 tsp lemon juice

## Preparation
1. Prepare the apricots by removing the seeds and cutting them in half or quarters if they are large. Measure them into a pot.
2. Crush the first layer of fruits to provide moisture until the rest of the fruits release their juices.
3. Heat on low flames until they are warm and release some more of their juices, then add the sugar and lemon juice and stir until dissolved. Raise the heat to medium and bring the mixture to a boil. Skim the foam and discard. Stir occasionally to make sure there is no sticking to the bottom of the pan.
4. Reduce the heat and cook until mixture thickens and the apricots are soft. (Approximately 20-30 minutes.)
5. Fill in sterilized jars.

Makes 4 cups

## Tips
- When cooking the jam stay close to the kitchen to stir frequently and thoroughly. As the jam thickens it tends to stick to the pan.
- If the apricots are too juicy and produce a lot of liquid, spoon out some of the extra syrup and use it on pancakes and waffles.
- <u>To prepare jars</u> - wash jars and screw bands and lids in hot soapy water, rinse with warm water. Pour boiling hot water over them. To dry, carefully remove jars with tongs, empty the water out of them and invert them on a clean dry towel until ready to use.

# Strawberry Jam

*Home-made Strawberry jams are special treats with morning toasts or scones, also good with peanut butter sandwiches. This is the most popular jam with children. Make some extra and share with family and friends.*

## Ingredients
6 cups fresh strawberries
3 cups sugar
2 Tbsp lemon juice
1 (3 oz) pouch Certo (liquid pectin)

## Preparation
1. Wash and hull strawberries and cut the large ones in half or quarters. Place in a heavy bottom saucepan.
2. Crush the first layer of fruits to provide moisture until the rest of the fruits release their juices.
3. Add lemon juice and sugar. Place the saucepan on medium heat.
4. Bring to a boil. Skim the foam and discard. Stir occasionally to make sure there is no sticking to the bottom of the pan. Cook for approximately 15-20 minutes until strawberries are cooked and the jam starts thickening.
5. Add a pouch of Certo (liquid pectin) and bring to a full boil again.
6. Remove from the heat and immediately ladle the jam into prepared jars.

Makes 4-5 cups

## Tips
- *Using a heavy bottom saucepan will help prevent scorching.*
- *Adding ½ teaspoon butter to the jam while cooking will reduce foaming.*
- *If the strawberries are too juicy and produce a lot of liquid, spoon out some of the extra syrup and use it on pancakes and waffles.*
- *<u>To prepare jars</u> - wash jars and screw bands and lids in hot soapy water, rinse with warm water. Pour boiling hot water over them. To dry, carefully remove jars with tongs, empty the water out of them and invert them on a clean dry towel until ready to use.*

# Pepper Jelly

*Thirty-five years ago my neighbor introduced me to pepper jelly. Hot, spicy and sweet, it makes great accompaniment to lamb and pork dishes. Served with cream cheese and crackers, this jelly makes a good cocktail appetizer or a delicious afternoon snack.*

## Ingredients
1/2 cup finely chopped jalapeno peppers
1 cup finely chopped green bell peppers
1 small onion, finely chopped
1 cup cider vinegar or white vinegar
6 cups sugar
6 oz liquid pectin (preferably Certo)
6 drops green food coloring

## Preparation
1. Sterilize 6 (1/2-pint) canning jars.
2. Remove seeds from jalapeno and green peppers and chop them to measure.
3. In a food processor or blender, blend peppers, onion, and a little of the vinegar until well pureed. Transfer pepper puree to a saucepan, add sugar and remaining vinegar and bring mixture to a rolling boil. Boil for 2 to 3 minutes. Remove from heat and add pectin and food coloring. Mix well until pectin is dissolved and the food coloring is well distributed.
4. Pour into prepared sterilized jars and seal.

Makes 6 (½ pint) jars.

## Tips
- *I prefer canning them in small jars as using one jar at a time is more practical.*
- *<u>To prepare jars</u> - wash jars and screw bands and lids in hot soapy water, rinse with warm water. Pour boiling hot water over them. To dry, carefully remove jars with tongs, empty the water out of them and invert them on a clean dry towel until ready to use.*
- *If you prefer a hotter jelly, save the jalapeno seeds and tie them in a cheesecloth and put in the pot with the sugar and cook the jelly. Remove from pan cheesecloth and discard before adding the pectin.*

# Mint Jelly

*This jelly is a companion to lamb dishes. It adds a refreshing taste to the food.*

## Ingredients
1½ cups firmly packed mint leaves
2¼ cups water
2 Tbsp lemon juice
3½ cups sugar
1 (3 oz) pouch Certo liquid pectin
2-3 drops green food coloring

## Preparation
1. Sterilize 4 (8 oz) Mason jars. Set aside.
2. Rinse mint leaves with cold water, shake off excess moisture and chop finely.
3. In a 3-quart saucepan combine mint and water. Bring to a boil over medium-high heat. Remove from heat, cover and let steep for 10 minutes.
4. Strain the liquid in a strainer, lined with cheesecloth, over a large measuring cup. Let the liquid drain until you have 1¾ cup of mint flavored liquid.
5. In a large stainless steel saucepan, combine liquid, lemon juice and sugar. Stirring constantly bring to a full boil and boil for 5 minutes. Stir in a pouch of liquid pectin and continue stirring for another minute
6. Add food coloring one drop at a time. If you are not satisfied with the color, add one more drop. Remove from heat, skim off the foam, and pour into sterilized jars. Seal jars and keep in a cool dark place.

Makes 4 (8 oz) jars

## Tips
- *Make sure you use liquid pectin. Powder pectin does not work well.*
- *When jelly reaches to a boiling point, it will bubble and might boil over. So keep a close look.*
- *Cheesecloth can be found in grocery stores and kitchen supply stores where the kitchen utensils are displayed.*

## Applesauce

*Applesauce can't get any better than this. Once you make your own applesauce, you will never buy the commercial preparations. At a very young age, my granddaughter Taylor, after tasting this homemade applesauce, refused to eat the commercially prepared versions.*

### Ingredients
10 apples (your favorite kind)
½ cup brown sugar
2 Tbsp lemon juice
3 cinnamon sticks

### Preparation
1. Peel core and slice apples into thin slices.
2. On medium to low heat, cook the apples, with sugar, lemon juice, and cinnamon sticks, stirring occasionally to prevent sticking to the bottom of the pan.
3. Reduce heat and simmer until the apples are softened and mushy (approximately 30 minutes) If needed add a little water or apple juice.
4. Remove the cinnamon sticks. If you need pureed applesauce, use a hand-held blender to puree.
5. Cool and store in an airtight container in the refrigerator.
6. Serve as-is with a sprinkle of cinnamon, or with ice cream.

Makes approximately 4 cups

### Tips
- *Instead of brown sugar, you may want to use honey.*

# Peach Cobbler

*It certainly is much quicker to make a crumble topping then a pie crust.
With a scoop of ice cream makes a great dessert.*

## Ingredients
6 cups sliced fresh peaches
2 Tbsp cornstarch
½ cup sugar
½ tsp cinnamon

*Topping*
1½ cups flour
½ tsp baking powder
½ tsp cinnamon
½ cup sugar
½ cup butter
1 egg, slightly beaten

## Preparation
1. Preheat oven to 400°F before baking.
2. In a large mixing bowl, combine sugar and cornstarch. Add sliced peaches; toss to coat completely.
3. Pour peaches into a greased or non-stick 9 x13-inch baking pan.
4. In another mixing bowl, sift flour, baking powder, and cinnamon.
5. Use a fork to cut in butter and combine with sugar and egg.
6. Sprinkle mixture evenly over peaches.
7. Bake for 20 minutes or until the cobbler is golden brown and bubbly.
8. Serve with a dollop of whipped cream, or ice cream.

Makes 6-8 servings

## Tips
- *For variety, you may use apricots or plums to prepare this cobbler.*

# Apple Crisp
*A topping of oats gives a crunch to this dessert.*
*Great for breakfast or warmed with a scoop of ice cream or whipped cream for dessert.*

## Ingredients
6 golden delicious apples
3 Tbsp sugar
2 Tbsp orange juice
1 cup firmly packed brown sugar
6 Tbsp butter, softened
½ cup quick cooking oats
¼ cup flour
1 tsp cinnamon
Whipped cream
Mint for garnish

## Preparation
1. Preheat oven to 350°F before baking.
2. Peel and slice apples. Toss to coat with 3 tablespoons sugar and 2 tablespoons orange juice and arrange in a buttered 8x10-inch glass baking dish.
3. Combine brown sugar, oats, flour and cinnamon in a bowl. Add butter and rub with your fingers until pea size clumps are formed. Sprinkle the oat mixture over apples.
4. Bake for 45-50 minutes or until apples are tender and top is crisp.
5. Serve warm with ice cream or whipped cream.

Makes 8 servings

## Tips
- *For variety and to add color to this dessert, you may add 1 cup of fresh blueberries.*

# Custard Dessert (Cream Caramel)

*The perfect ending for an elegant dinner. Made in a bundt pan, it becomes a showpiece with a luscious creamy taste. For buffet tables the bundt pan presentation is outstanding.*

## Ingredients
1 cup sugar for caramelizing
6 eggs
Dash of salt
1 tsp vanilla
½ cup sugar for the custard
4 cups scalded milk
¼ tsp grated nutmeg

## Preparation
1. Preheat oven to 350°F before baking.
2. Melt 1 cup sugar in a skillet over moderate heat until it forms a light caramel colored syrup. Immediately pour the hot syrup in the mold of your choice and coat the bottom of the mold by rotating it around. You may use a bundt pan or individual custard dishes as the mold.
3. Scald the milk on the stove top.
4. In a bowl, beat the eggs with a pinch of salt and vanilla, and stir in the remaining ½ cup of sugar.
5. Gradually add one cup of scalded milk to the egg mixture (this will temper the egg mixture). Pour the tempered egg mixture into the scalded milk and mix well. Pour the custard in the prepared molds. Sprinkle with fresh grated nutmeg.
6. Set the molds in a baking dish and pour hot water around the molds to reach 1½ inches up the sides of the molds.
7. Bake the custard in the preheated oven for about 40-45 minutes, or until a knife inserted in the custard comes out clean. Remove custard molds from the water and let them cool on a wire rack.
8. Chill the custard several hours or overnight before unmolding.
9. To serve, run a sharp knife around the edge of the mold. Invert a serving dish on top of the mold and turn the mold upside down to release the custard.
10. If you choose to make it in a bundt pan, after inverting custard into a serving dish, decorate by whipping 1 cup of whipping cream with 3 tablespoons of sugar until stiff; put in a pastry bag fitted with a rosette tube and fill in the center. Decorate with fresh strawberries.

Makes 6-8 servings

## Tips
- *If using a large bundt pan, double the above recipe*

# Rice Pudding

*Rice pudding is a popular dessert throughout the world. Every culture has its own variation with a different flavoring. I categorize this pudding as real 'comfort food'. We loved it as children, and still do, and now our grandchildren love it. This creamy old-fashioned pudding is the very basic simple version. Arborio or short-grain rice are recommended for a delicious creamy textured pudding.*

## Ingredients
¾ cup Cal Rose rice
1½ cups water
½ tsp. salt
6 cups milk
½ cup sugar
Cinnamon

## Preparation
1. In a 5-quart saucepan, place the rice; add water and ½ teaspoon salt. Bring to boil. Reduce heat and simmer until all water is absorbed.
2. Heat the milk in the microwave and add to the rice.
3. Reduce heat to medium-low and continue to cook, stirring frequently with a flat bottom wooden spoon until the rice is tender, about 30-40 minutes. As the rice cooks and the milk is reduced, the mixture becomes thick. At this point, while the pudding is cooking do not leave it unattended. It is important to stir it gently and very often so the rice will not stick and burn onto the bottom of the saucepan.
4. Add the sugar and simmer a few minutes longer, stirring constantly until the sugar is completely dissolved. Taste for sweetness and adjust the sugar if necessary.
5. Remove saucepan from the heat and pour the pudding into the dishes. Sprinkle the top with cinnamon. Cool to room temperature before refrigerating. Chill several hours before serving.

Makes 8½ cup servings

## Tips
- *A heavy flat-bottom saucepan prevents the bottom of the pan from burning. An alternative is to use a heat diffuser between the flames and the pot.*
- *A flat bottom wooden spoon is best for scraping all the surface of a flat-bottom saucepan to prevent burning.*
- *Middle Eastern cooks like to add a tablespoon of rosewater/and or orange blossom water for flavoring.*
- *A Caribbean variation would be to substitute ½ of the milk with coconut milk and instead of cinnamon sprinkle the top with toasted coconut.*

# Chocolate Mousse

*Irresistible pleasure! Simply melts in your mouth. A sophisticated finale to any dinner.*

## Ingredients
10 egg yolks
½ cup sugar
2 tsp vanilla
10 oz good chocolate, melted
1/3 cup water
4 cups whipping cream, whipped

## Preparation
1. In an electric mixer, beat egg yolks, sugar and vanilla until light and fluffy.
2. Melt the chocolate in the microwave or over double boiler. While chocolate is still warm, pour over the beaten egg yolks and continue beating. Add water to bring the mixture to sour cream consistency. If needed, add more water one tablespoon at a time. Cool completely before adding the whipping cream.
3. Beat the whipping cream to form semi-stiff peaks. Fold in chocolate mixture.
4. Pour mousse into serving dishes, and garnish with more whipped cream, strawberry and mint leaves.

Makes 12-14 serving

## Tips:
- *Brownies and chocolate mousse combined make an irresistible cake. Look for the recipe "Chocolate Mousse Brownie Cake" (page 255)*
- *For a slightly lighter mousse you may substitute 1 cup of egg whites, at room temperature, stiffly beaten instead of 2 cups of whipping cream whipped; but you will sacrifice the real creamy texture.*
- *You may also use ½ the amount of water and use Grand Marnier for the other half.*

# Sticky Rice with Mango

*This glutenous rice dish happens to be one of Thailand's National dishes. It is served as a dessert or as a snack. When Haig and I we were visiting Thailand. we never missed an opportunity to eat this dish for a snack.*

## Ingredients
1 cup Cal Rose rice (gluttonous rice)
1½ cups coconut milk
¼ tsp salt
½ cup sugar
2 mangoes, peeled and sliced

## Preparation
1. Soak rice in water for 30 minutes to 1 hour. Drain.
2. Place rice in a cheesecloth or steamer and steam for 20-25 minutes until rice is cooked.
3. Meanwhile, in a small saucepan, bring coconut milk, salt, and sugar to boil and reduce heat and simmer until sugar is dissolved.
4. Remove cooked rice to a saucepan, pour coconut milk over it, and stir on low heat until most of the liquid is absorbed. Cover saucepan and set aside. Let it cool to lukewarm.
5. To serve, spoon rice in a serving dish and top with sliced mangoes. Garnish with mint leaves.

Makes 4 servings

## Tips:
- *If you like the rice sweeter, increase the amount of sugar to your liking.*
- *If you have extra sweetened coconut milk, you may add to the rice before serving.*
- *If coconut milk is not available, use 14 oz of shredded coconut soaked in hot water for 20-30minutes - drain, add sugar and proceed as in step #3.*

# Baklava

*This is a rich, sweet pastry prepared with layers of paper thin Filo dough. Each sheet of dough is spread with melted butter for flakiness. Half way through layering sheets it is spread with ground walnut. While hot, sugar syrup is poured over baked baklava.*

## Ingredients
1 pkg frozen Filo dough
1 cup clarified butter, melted
4 cups chopped walnuts
4 Tbsp sugar
2 tsp cinnamon

<u>Sugar Syrup</u>
4 cups sugar
3 cups water
2 Tbsp light Karo Syrup
2 tsp lemon juice
1 Tbsp ma-zahr
  (orange blossom water)

## Preparation
1. Preheat oven to 325°F before baking.
2. Mix nuts, sugar, and cinnamon and set aside.
3. <u>Prepare syrup:</u> Place sugar, water, and Karo syrup in a heavy pan and bring to a boil over medium heat. Simmer for 10-12 minutes, add lemon juice and continue boiling until syrup reaches 203°F on a candy thermometer or test by dropping a drop of syrup in cold water and see if it will form a soft ball. Set aside to cool.
4. Brush bottom and sides of a tray that is the same size as the filo sheets, with clarified butter.
5. <u>Assemble Baklava:</u> Spread 1 sheet of dough on the tray and brush the top with melted butter. Repeat this process until half of the dough is used, brushing butter on every sheet of dough.
6. Spread the prepared chopped nut mixture and continue to stack the rest of the filo sheets, buttering every sheet.
7. Brush the top sheet with butter. With a sharp and wet knife, proceed to cut into diamond shape (first cut into long strips, then diagonal strips). Spoon 4 tablespoons of melted butter on the cut pieces to prevent them from curling while baking.
8. Bake for 30-40 minutes until it starts browning then move up one shelf and cook further for another 25-30 minutes. If the top colors too fast, loosely cover the tray with aluminum foil to stop further browning while the rest is baking.
9. As soon as you take out baklava from the oven, pour 1¼ cups of the prepared cooled syrup over the cut lines and the surface. Save the rest of the syrup to use on other variations of the Baklava. Let it cool completely to absorb syrup. Serve after 8-10 hours.

## Tips
- *<u>Clarified butter:</u> In a saucepan, melt sweet butter over low heat. Skim the milk solids off the top and carefully pour the clarified butter into another container without disturbing the remaining milk solids and water that are in the bottom of the pan. Clarified butter keeps up to 6 months in the refrigerator.*
- *Filo dough dries out very fast - it is advisable while working to keep the stack of dough covered with a damp towel.*
- *Orange blossom water (ma-zaher) is a common flavoring used in Middle Eastern sweets. It can be purchased in most Middle Eastern grocery stores. It is optional to use in the syrup preparation.*
- *Best way to defrost filo dough is by leaving it overnight in the refrigerator to thaw out. Otherwise leave it at room temperature for 3-4 hours.*

# Birds Nest

*These basically are the same as baklava but shaped differently. Instead of walnuts, we use pistachio nuts.*

## Ingredients
1 pkg frozen Filo dough
1 cup clarified butter, melted
2 cups chopped pistachio
2 Tbsp sugar

<u>Sugar Syrup</u>
2 cups sugar
1 cup water
1 tsp lemon juice
1 Tbsp ma-zaher
   (orange blossom water)

## Preparation
1. Preheat oven to 350°F before baking.
2. Mix nuts, sugar, and cinnamon and set aside.
3. <u>*Prepare syrup:*</u> Place sugar, and water in a heavy pan and bring to a boil over medium heat. Simmer for 10-12 minutes, add lemon juice and continue boiling until syrup reaches 203°F on a candy thermometer or test by dropping a drop of syrup in cold water and see if it will form a soft ball. Set aside to cool.
4. <u>*Assemble Birds Nest:*</u> Take one sheet of dough and place on a work surface. Brush with butter and fold in half lengthwise. Brush again with a little butter.
5. Place a long ½ inch dowel on the folded edge and roll dough loosely over the dowel ¾ of the way, leaving the last part flat, approximately 1½-inches. Place your fingers at the two ends of the dough and gently push toward the center creating a ruffled look. Carefully pull out the dowel. Bring the rolled edges together, making a circle, and creating a base with the unrolled part. Tuck the loose ends under the nest.
6. Carefully place the nest on a buttered tray. Proceed the same way with the rest of the dough. Brush the tops of the nests lightly with melted butter before baking.
7. Bake for 20 minutes, reduce the heat to 300°F and bake for another 20-30 minutes or until light brown.
8. Remove from the oven, pour the cold syrup on the hot nests and let them cool to absorb syrup.
9. Fill centers with chopped pistachio nuts.

## Tips
- *<u>Clarified butter:</u> In a saucepan melt sweet butter over low heat. Skim the milk solids off the top and carefully pour the clarified butter into another container without disturbing the remaining milk solids and water that are in the bottom of the pan. Clarified butter keeps up to 6 months in the refrigerator.*
- *If you are using already prepared sugar syrup, use about 1-1¼ cups.*
- *For variety you may use chopped pine nuts for the center of the nests.*

# Bourma

These are another version of baklava individually rolled into cigar shapes.

## Ingredients
1 pkg frozen Filo dough
1 cup clarified butter, melted
3 cups chopped walnuts
3 Tbsp sugar
1 tsp cinnamon

<u>Sugar Syrup</u>
2 cups sugar
1 cups water
1 tsp lemon juice
1 Tbsp ma-zaher
   (orange blossom water)

## Preparation
1. Preheat oven to 350°F before baking.
2. Mix nuts, sugar, and cinnamon and set aside.
3. *Prepare syrup:* Place sugar, water and Karo syrup in a heavy pan and bring to a boil over medium heat. Simmer for 5-10 minutes, add lemon juice and continue boiling until syrup reaches 203°F on a candy thermometer or test by dropping a drop of syrup in cold water and see if it will form a soft ball. Set aside to cool.
4. *Assemble Bourma:* Take one sheet of dough and place on a work surface. Brush with butter and fold in half lengthwise. Brush again with a little butter and sprinkle one tablespoon of nut filling near the folded edge.
5. Place a long ½ inch dowel on the folded edge near the nuts and roll dough loosely over the dowel. Place your fingers at the two ends of the dough and gently push toward the center creating a ruffled look. Carefully pull out the dowel.
6. Carefully place the bourma on a buttered tray. Proceed the same way with the rest of the dough. Brush the tops of the bourmas lightly with melted butter before baking.
7. Bake for 20 minutes, reduce the heat to 300°F and bake for another 20-30 minutes until light brown.
8. Remove from the oven, pour the cold syrup on the hot bourmas and let it cool to absorb the syrup.

## Tips
- *<u>Clarified butter</u>: In a saucepan, melt sweet butter over low heat. Skim the milk solids off the top and carefully pour the clarified butter into another container without disturbing the remaining milk solids and water that are in the bottom of the pan. Clarified butter keeps up to 6 months in the refrigerator.*
- *Keeps well in an airtight container at room temperature for several weeks, in the freezer for several months.*
- *If you are using already prepared sugar syrup, use about 1-1¼ cups.*
- *For variety, you may use ground pine nuts or ground blanched almonds.*

# Walnut Parcels

This is another version of baklava. Individually shaped into parcels.

## Ingredients
1 pkg frozen Fllo dough
1 cup clarified butter, melted
3 cups chopped walnuts
3 Tbsp sugar
1 tsp cinnamon

*Sugar Syrup*
2 cups sugar
1 cup water
2 Tbsp Karo syrup
1 tsp lemon juice
1 Tbsp ma-zaher
   (orange blossom water)

## Preparation
1. Preheat oven to 350°F before baking.
2. Mix nuts, sugar, and cinnamon and set aside.
3. *Prepare syrup:* Place sugar, water, and Karo syrup in a heavy pan and bring to a boil over medium heat. Simmer for 5-10 minutes, add lemon juice and continue boiling until syrup reaches 203°F on a candy thermometer or test by dropping a drop of syrup in cold water and see if it will form a soft ball. Set aside to cool.
4. *Assemble parcels:* Stack 10-12 sheets of dough lightly buttering each sheet as you stack them. Cut the stack of buttered sheets into 3-inch squares. Place a tablespoon of nuts in the center and bring the four corners together. Do not pinch the corners. Carefully remove the parcel and place on a greased tray. Repeat with the rest of the dough and place them close to each other so that they will keep their shape.
5. Bake for 20 minutes. Take out the tray and drizzle the cut edges with hot butter so they puff out. Reduce the heat to 300°F and bake for another 20-30 minutes, or until light brown.
6. Remove from the oven, pour the cold syrup on hot the parcels and let them cool to absorb syrup.

## Tips
- *Clarified butter:* In a saucepan melt sweet butter over low heat. Skim the milk solids off the top and carefully pour the clarified butter into another container without disturbing the remaining milk solids and water that are in the bottom of the pan. Clarified butter keeps up to 6 months in the refrigerator.
- *If you are using already prepared sugar syrup, use about 1-1¼ cup.*

# Sha'abiat

*A luscious Middle Eastern dessert! The creamy custard filling enveloped in layers of crisp filo dough, paired with sugar syrup makes a perfect dessert. This dessert tastes best when served warm. It should be made days or weeks in advance and frozen, but baked one hour before you intend to serve.*

## Ingredients
1 pkg frozen Filo dough, thawed
1 cup clarified butter, melted
1 tsp cinnamon

*Filling*
1 qt half-and-half
1 cup whipping cream
¼ cup farina
½ cup sugar

*Sugar Syrup*
3 cups sugar
2½ cups water
1 tsp lemon juice
1 Tbsp ma-zaher
   (orange blossom water)

## Preparation
1. In a saucepan, combine half-and-half, cream, farina, and ½ cup sugar. Bring to a boil. Reduce heat and simmer, stirring constantly until mixture thickens. Takes approximately 20-25 minutes. Spread the hot mixture into a pan and let it cool. Refrigerate to firm it for easy handling.
2. Cut the filling into 1-1½ inch squares. Set aside.
3. Open filo dough package and cut the stack of sheets into four strips lengthwise. (2-2½ inches wide).
4. Working on one sha'abiat at a time; stack three strips on top of each other buttering each layer with a brush dipped in clarified butter. Place a square of filling at one end of the stacked strips and fold one corner over the filling making a triangle. Continue folding in triangles (flag-fashion) until the strip is all folded. Brush top with butter. Place on a tray.
5. Repeat with remaining dough and cream squares. Arrange all in a tray, cover loosely and freeze. After they are frozen, arrange them in a Tupperware with wax paper between each layer. (You can prepare them to this point and freeze them until ready to use at a later date).
6. When ready to bake, preheat oven to 400°F, place frozen Sha'abiat on a tray and bake for 20 minutes or until golden brown. Arrange Sha'abiat on a platter and pour syrup over the top. Sprinkle with cinnamon.
7. *Prepare syrup:* In a saucepan combine sugar, water, and lemon juice. Bring to a boil. Reduce heat and simmer for about 15-20 minutes. Remove from heat and add ma-zaher. Cool to room temperature. (The syrup can be prepared ahead of time and stored in a jar until serving time).

Makes about 40

## Tips
- *Clarified butter:* In a saucepan, melt sweet butter over low heat. Skim the milk solids off the top and carefully pour the clarified butter into another container without disturbing the remaining milk solids and water that is in the bottom of the pan. Clarified butter keeps up to 6 months in the refrigerator.
- *Sha'abiats keep in the freezer for up to 6 months.*

# Kadaif

*A favorite Middle Eastern dessert, often called Kunefe. Filling can be nuts or cream cheese.*

## Ingredients
2 (1 lb) pkg shredded Kadaif dough, thawed
1½ lb melted butter
¼ cup sugar to sprinkle over cheese
1 Tbsp cinnamon to sprinkle over cheese

*Filling*
½ pint cream
1 pint half and half
5 Tbsp corn starch
¼ cup sugar
1¼ cups milk
2 (8 oz) pkg cream cheese

*Sugar Syrup* V
4 cups sugar
3 cups water
2 tsp lemon juice
Rosewater to taste (optional)

## Preparation
1. *Prepare filling:* In a saucepan, combine cream, half and half, corn starch, sugar, milk, and cream cheese. Over medium heat, stirring constantly bring the mixture to a boil and cook for 15-20 minutes until mixture is thickened. Spread in a pan and let it cool completely.
2. *Prepare Kadaif:* With fingers, gently separate the strands of kadaif dough. Pour melted butter over the dough and toss gently to coat with butter.
3. *Assemble Kadaif:* Divide dough mixture into two equal parts Press one part of the dough in a 13 x16-inch baking pan. Top with the cheese mixture. Cut the filling into pieces and arrange over the dough. Sprinkle with cinnamon and sugar. Use the rest of the dough by spreading evenly to cover the cheese. Press down to smooth the top.
4. Preheat oven to 475°F before baking.
5. Bake for 10 minutes on the lowest shelf then move to the top shelf in the oven and bake for another 10-15 minutes until the top starts browning.
6. Remove from the oven and while still hot pour the cold syrup over it.
7. Cut into serving pieces and serve warm or cold.
8. *Prepare syrup*: in a saucepan, over medium high heat bring sugar, water, and lemon juice to boil, reduce heat and simmer for 15-20 minutes. If using rosewater add to syrup after you remove syrup from heat. Cool completely before using.

Makes 24-36 servings

## Tips
- It is possible to prepare Kadaif up to step 4 and freeze unbaked to be used at a later date.
- It is also possible to bake the Kadaif and not put the sugar syrup on it and freeze it. Just warm it up and pour syrup over before serving.
- I usually make two smaller pans and freeze one to use at another date.
- For variety, instead of the cheese filling, you may use chopped walnuts mixed with sugar and cinnamon. (3 cup finely chopped walnuts, ¾ tsp cinnamon, and 2 Tbsp sugar)

# Mamounia

*Mamounia can be served for breakfast or as a dessert.*

## Ingredients
10 oz Jack cheese
1½ cups sugar
4 cups water
½ cube butter
1 cup Cream of Wheat

## Preparation
1. Slice the cheese and set aside.
2. In a 3-quart saucepan bring sugar and water to a boil over medium heat and let it simmer until sugar is dissolved.
3. In a frying pan melt the butter and add Cream of Wheat stirring so it does not burn, until Cream of Wheat starts changing color.
4. Add the Cream of Wheat mixture into the sugar syrup stirring so it does not form lumps. Simmer until the mixture starts thickening.
5. Turn off the heat and add the sliced cheese to the hot mixture. Cover pan and let it rest for 5 minutes and until cheese is melted.
6. Stir to evenly distribute the melted cheese, and serve with a slice of cheese on top and a sprinkle of cinnamon.

Makes 6 servings

## Tips
- *Tastes good the next day served warm or cold.*
- *You may want to use almonds instead of pine nuts. Either work well.*

# Imrig Halva

*This is a sweet made with Cream of Wheat, milk and sugar. If you acquire a taste for it, you cannot stop eating it.*

## Ingredients
5 cups whole milk
2½ cups sugar
1½ cubes butter
¾ cup pine nuts
2 cups Cream of Wheat
1 Tbsp orange blossom water

## Preparation
1. In a saucepan, bring the milk and sugar to boil and let it simmer until the sugar is all dissolved.
2. In another saucepan, melt the butter and sauté the pine nuts until they are light brown.
3. Add the Cream of Wheat into the browning pine nuts and sauté, stirring until the cream of wheat starts changing color.
4. Add Cream of Wheat to the milk mixture and cook, stirring until the mixture thickens. Remove from heat and add orange blossom water. Pour hot mixture into serving dishes.

Makes 8-10 servings

## Tips
- *Imrig Halva keeps in the refrigerator for a week and in the freezer for 6 weeks.*
- *You may want to use almonds instead of pine nuts. It works well.*

# Chocolate Pudding Trifle
*Enjoy this dessert year-round. It is a crowd pleaser.*

## Ingredients
1 Angel Food Cake mix
1 (6 oz) pkg chocolate pudding mix, cook and serve not instant
3 cups milk
¾ cup strawberry or raspberry jam
2 cups whipping cream
3 Tbsp confectioners' sugar
Chocolate shavings for garnish
Strawberries or raspberries for garnish

## Preparation
1. Bake the cake according to package directions. Cool.
2. Prepare pudding as directed on the package with 3 cups of milk. Set aside.
3. Slice cake into 1-inch slices.
4. Whip the cream with the sugar until stiff. Set aside.
5. Cover the bottom of a 3-quart glass bowl with the cake slices.
6. Spread ½ of the jam over it. Pour 1/3 of the pudding over the jam. Top with ¼ of the whipped cream.
7. Repeat the layers of topping with the remainder of whipped cream.
8. Garnish with chocolate shavings and strawberries or raspberries.

Makes 12-15 servings

## Tips
- *If pressed by time, use store bought angel food cake.*
- *For variation, use fresh fruit in between the layers.*
- <u>*Brownie trifle:*</u> *Instead of angel food cake you can use brownies and instead of chocolate pudding use vanilla pudding.*

# Key Lime Pie

*Key limes also known as Mexican limes are smaller, and tastier and more aromatic than the regular limes. If you cannot find either one, use regular lime juice. It is just as good. Original Key Lime Pies are made with condensed sweetened milk. Before refrigeration, fresh milk was not readily available in the Florida Keys, thus they had to depend on sweetened condensed milk.*

## Ingredients

### *For the crust*
1½ cups graham cracker crumbs
½ cup granulated sugar
4 Tbsp butter, melted or use Ready Crust graham cracker pie crust

### *Filling*
½ cup lime juice
1 (14 oz)can Borden's sweetened condensed milk
2 eggs
1 egg yolk
1 Tbsp corn starch

### *Topping*
1 cup whipping cream or sour cream
¼ cup powdered sugar

## Preparation

1. Preheat oven to 375°F before baking.
2. In a bowl, mix graham cracker crumbs, sugar, and melted butter. Press mixture firmly into a 9-inch pie pan. Bake for 15-20 minutes. Remove from oven and let it cool.
3. Reduce oven temperature to 325°F.
4. Dissolve 1 tablespoon of cornstarch in the lemon juice.
5. In another mixing bowl, whisk the eggs and the egg yolk and add the lemon juice and condensed milk. Whisk them all together until well-blended. Pour into the prepared pie crust.
6. Bake at 325°F for 35 minutes, until the filling is firm. Remove from the oven and cool completely.
7. Refrigerate for at least 2 hours.
8. Whip the cream with the powdered sugar until stiff peaks form. Spoon cream over the top, or mix the sugar into the sour cream instead of the whipped cream and spread over the top of the pie. Chill pie at least 4 hours before serving.
9. To garnish the pie, sprinkle with lime zest and garnish the center with a lime wheel split in half.

Makes 8 servings

## Tips:
- *If you microwave the limes for 10-15 seconds, you can juice them more easily.*

# Pumpkin Pie

*Every Thanksgiving whenever the family gathered for a Thanksgiving dinner, my mother-in-law Ethel made her famous pumpkin pie which we always looked forward to. She was the best pie-maker.*

## Ingredients

*Pie Crust*
1¼ cups all purpose flour ¼ tsp salt
½ tsp baking powder
1/3 cup butter, very cold
2 Tbsp Crisco shortening
3-4 Tbsp ice cold water

*Filling*
¾ cup sugar
½ tsp salt
1 tsp cinnamon
½ tsp ground ginger
¼ tsp ground cloves
2 eggs, slightly beaten
2 cups canned pumpkin puree
1 (12 fl oz) can evaporated milk
Whipped cream for topping

## Preparation

1. *Prepare pie crust:* Combine flour, salt and baking powder. Add butter and shortening and cut into the flour with a fork or pastry blender until the mixture resembles coarse meal.
2. Add cold water 1 tablespoon at a time and stir with a fork to incorporate until dough is formed and can be handled. Do not over mix or knead.
3. Wrap dough in plastic wrap and refrigerate for half an hour.
4. Roll out dough on a floured board to ¼-inch thick. Fit in a 9-inch deep pie dish. Trim excess pastry and crimp the edges.
5. Preheat oven to 425°F before baking the pie.
6. *Prepare filling:* In a small bowl combine sugar, salt, cinnamon, ginger and cloves. Set aside.
7. In a large mixing bowl beat the eggs lightly, add pumpkin puree and sugar-spice mixture. Stir in evaporated milk. Pour into prepared pie pan.
8. Bake on middle rack for 15 minutes. Reduce oven temperature to 350°F and bake for 40-50 minutes or until knife inserted into the center comes out clean. Cool on wire rack. Serve at room temperature with a dollop of whipped cream.

Makes 8 servings

## Tips

- *This pie is at its best the day it is made. If you do not serve the same day, refrigerate it, but the crust will lose its crispiness from the moisture of the filling.*
- *If you have pumpkin pie mix, you may use 1¾ teaspoon of the mix instead of cinnamon, ginger and cloves.*

# Pumpkin Chiffon Pie

*This recipe was given to me by my sister-in-law, Rosalie Strauss. She prepared it for us for a Thanksgiving dinner and unanimously we all wanted her to share the recipe with us. It is an outstanding pie.*

## Ingredients

*Crust*
1½ cups (18 crackers) cinnamon graham crackers
¼ cup sugar
½ cup melted butter

*Filling*
1 envelope unflavored gelatin
½ cup sugar
½ tsp salt
½ tsp cinnamon
½ tsp allspice
¼ tsp ginger ½ tsp nutmeg
¾ cup milk
2 slightly beaten egg yolks
1 cup canned pumpkin
2 egg whites
¼ cup sugar
½ cup whipping cream, whipped
2 pints whipping cream for topping

## Preparation

1. In a food processor finely grind the graham crackers, add sugar and melted butter and mix until combined. Press firmly in a 9-inch pie pan. Bake in a preheated oven 375°F for 8 minutes until lightly browned. Cool completely before filling.
2. In a medium size saucepan combine gelatin, sugar, salt, cinnamon, allspice, ginger and nutmeg. Stir in milk, egg yolks and pumpkin and cook over medium heat stirring until mixture starts bubbling. Remove from heat and chill until partially set.
3. Beat egg whites until soft peaks form, gradually add sugar and beat until stiff. Fold into the pie mixture along with half a cup of whipped cream. Pour into the prepared pie crust and chill for at least one hour.
4. For topping, whip two pints of whipping cream, fill into a pastry bag and decorate the top of the pie with the whipped cream.

Makes 8-10 servings

# Fresh Peach Pie

*Make this delicious pie when fresh peaches are available during the summer months.*

## Ingredients

5½ cups peeled and sliced peaches (about 3½ lb)
1¼ cups sugar
¼ cup flour
¾ tsp ground cinnamon
3 Tbsp butter
1 tsp vanilla extract
Vanilla ice cream or
    whipped cream (optional)

### Pie Crust
2 cups flour
½ tsp salt
½ tsp baking powder
2/3 cup butter, very cold
2 Tbsp Crisco shortening
6-7 Tbsp ice cold water

## Preparation

1. *Prepare pie crust:* Combine flour, salt, and baking powder. Add butter and shortening and cut into the flour with a fork or pastry blender until the mixture resembles coarse meal.
2. Add cold water a few tablespoons at a time and stir with a fork to incorporate until dough is formed and can be handled. Do not over mix or knead.
3. Divide dough in half. Wrap in plastic wrap and refrigerate.
4. *Prepare peaches:* In a medium size saucepan, combine peaches, sugar and flour. Set aside until peaches start releasing their juices. Bring mixture to a boil, lower the heat and cook, stirring often, for 5-7 minutes until peaches start getting soft. Remove from heat, add butter and vanilla. Mix well.
5. *Assemble pie:* Roll each portion of the dough on a floured board. Fit one of them into a 9-inch pie pan. Trim off excess pastry along edges of the pie pan. Spoon peaches into pie shell.
6. Cut the other rolled out portion of the dough into ½-inch strips. Arrange strips in a lattice design over the peaches. Trim excess dough and with a fork crimp the edges to seal.
7. Bake in preheated oven at 425°F for 15 minutes, reduce heat to 350°F and continue baking for 25-30 minutes longer until the top browns and the filling is bubbling. Cool on a wire rack.
8. Serve warm or at room temperature with vanilla ice cream or whipped cream.

Makes 8 servings

## Tips

- *When fresh peaches are not in season, you may substitute 16 oz of unsweetened frozen peaches.*
- *You may also substitute fresh apricots for the peaches.*

# Chocolate Pecan Pie

*This is the perfect pecan pie with smooth texture and rich flavor.*

## Ingredients

*Pie Crust*
1¼ cups all purpose flour
¼ tsp salt
½ tsp baking powder
1/3 cup butter, very cold
2 Tbsp Crisco shortening
3-4 Tbsp ice cold water

*Filling*
3 eggs at room temperature
¾ cup sugar
1 cup corn syrup
5 oz semi-sweet chocolate, melted
2 Tbsp melted butter
1 tsp vanilla
1½ cups pecans

## Preparation

1. *Prepare pie crust:* Combine flour, salt and baking powder. Add butter and shortening and cut into the flour with a fork or pastry blender until the mixture resembles coarse meal.
2. Add cold water 1 tablespoon at a time and stir with a fork to incorporate until dough is formed and can be handled. Do not over mix or knead.
3. Wrap dough in plastic wrap and refrigerate for half an hour.
4. Roll out dough on a floured board to ¼-inch thick. Fit in a 9-inch deep pie dish. Trim excess pastry and crimp the edges.
5. Preheat oven to 350°F before baking pie.
6. *Prepare filling:* In a large bowl mix together eggs, sugar, corn syrup, melted chocolate, butter and vanilla. Add pecans.
7. Pour in prepared pie crust.
8. Bake on middle rack of the oven for 50-55 minutes, or until pie appears barely set. It will solidify when it cools down.

Makes 8-10 servings

## Tips

- *Of the 1½ cups of pecan used in the recipe, I like to use 1 cup of chopped pecans and ½ cup of pecan halves. The pecans halves make the pie look prettier and the chopped pecans make slicing easier.*

# Chocolate Fondue

*A warm chocolate sauce in which pieces of cakes, fruits and marshmallows are dipped.
A sweet ending to a special meal and a fun way to entertain. Who does not like chocolate?*

## Ingredients
A chocolate fondue fountain or a fondue pot
Fondue forks or bamboo skewers

*Dunkers*
Strawberries, hulled and washed
Bananas, sliced
Pears, cut bite size
Marshmallows
Rice Krispies treats, cut bite size
Pound cake, cut bite size
Vanilla wafers

*Chocolate Fondue*
Belgian chocolate specifically for fondue or
24 oz semi sweet chocolate morsels with
¾ cup vegetable oil

## Preparation
1. *Prepare chocolate Fondue:* If you use the chocolate specifically for fondue you do not need to use the oil otherwise combine the chocolate morsels with the oil and glass bowl and microwave for 3 minutes until all the chocolate is melted. Stir until smooth.
2. Turn on the fondue pot to heat, and pour the melted chocolate into the base bowl of the unit. Fill just below the rim. Turn the motor on and watch the chocolate flow down the tiers.
3. Serve with fondue forks or lots of wooden skewers with the dunkers.

*If you do not have a fountain:* Follow the instructions in step 1. Then pour the hot chocolate in a fondue pot that is placed on a canned heat burner or candle to keep the chocolate melted.

Makes 8 servings

## Tips
- *Never add hard chips to a fountain while the motor is running. Only add melted chocolate.*
- *Never add cold liquid to chocolate, it may cause the flow to stop. Add only warmed liquid.*
- *Always check to make sure no chunks of food are in the base bowl. It may clog the flow of chocolate.*
- *If you cannot find Belgian chocolate specifically for fondue in the stores, you can try to get it through the Internet or use any chocolate chips but you need to add the vegetable oil.*

#  Index

7-Bone Roast 122
7-layer Mexican Dip 24
Acknowledgment 5
Almond Bars 289
Almond Cake 253
Amazing Butterscotch Bars 279
Aniseed Biscotti 314
Appelized Tea 50
**Appetizers and First Courses 9-44**
Apple Crisp 346
Apple Sour Cream Coffee Cake 247
Applesauce 344
Apricot and Almond Florentines 288
Apricot Coconut Bars 276
Apricot Jam 340
Apricot Jam Sable Cookies 298
Armenian Eetch Salad 81
Artichoke-Chili Dip 9
Artichokes Stuffed with Shrimp Salad 106
Artichokes with Fava Beans 212
Artichoke-Spinach Dip 10
Asian Steak Marinade 210
Asparagus and Roasted Pepper Salad 85
Asparagus Parmesan 231
Assorted-Nut Crisp Bars 332
Avocado Dip (Guacamole) 23
Austrian Rugelach 309
Baba Ghanoush 21
Baked Quesadillas 30
Baklava 351
Balsamic Basil Vinaigrette 90
Banana Chocolate Chip Brownies 322
Banana Chocolate Chip Loaf Cake 256
Banana Chocolate Chip Muffins 266
Banana Pineapple Coconut Loaf Cake 257
Banana Squash Puree 228
Banana-Walnut Chocolate Chip Cookies 316
Barazik (Sesame-Pistachio Cookies) 302
Barbequed Pork Ribs 146
Barley Mushroom Soup 64
Basic Meat Loaf 116
Basic Split Pea Soup 62
Basic Tomato Salsa 197
Beef 114-129
Beef Roulade 125
Beef Stroganoff 126
Beef Taco 117
Best Hot Chocolate 53
**Beverages 45-55**
Birds Nest 352
Black Olives and Feta Cheese Swirls 13
Blackberry Smoothie 46
Bloody Mary Smoothie 48
Blueberry Scones 273
Bolognese Sauce 206
Bourma 353
Braised Short Ribs 121
Braided Brioche Bread 236
**Breads 234-242**
Brisket Roast 120
Broccoli , Ham and Cheese Strata 233
Broccoli and Bow Tie Pasta 168

Broccoli and Cheese Savory Muffins 271
Broccoli, Cheese and Rice Casserole 186
B'steeya 151
Bulgur Pilaf with Onions, Peppers and Tomatoes 176
Bulgur Pilaf with Vermicelli Noodles 177
Butter Toffee 328
Butterfinger Fudge Brownies 320
Butternut Squash Risotto 184
**Cakes 243-275**
California Rolls 43
Candied Apricots 329
**Candies 327-339**
Cantaloupe Smoothie 47
Caramel Brownies 321
Caramel Pecan Bars 280
Carrot Cake 250
Carrot Crunch 230
Carrot Cupcakes 261
Carrot Puree 229
Carrot Salad 73
Cashew Chicken Casserole 159
Cauliflower and Garbanzo Bean Curry 219
Champagne Sangria 51
Championship Chocolate Chip Bars 281
Cheddar Cheese Bread 240
Cheese Fondue 41
Cheesy Cauliflower 218
Chicken Burger 195
Chicken Enchiladas 161
Chicken Lettuce Wrap 155
Chicken Parmesan156
Chicken Quesadillas with Mango Salsa 29
Chicken Stir-fry with Snap Peas and Cashews 162
Chicken Tikka 150
Chili con Carne 118
Chili Spiced Mango Sauce 199
Chocolate Chip Biscotti 313
Chocolate Chip Cookies 293
Chocolate Chip Cupcakes 263
Chocolate chip Muffins 265
Chocolate Coconut Pecan Bars 277
Chocolate Fondue 365
Chocolate Fudge Brownies 319
Chocolate Graham Break-aways 287
Chocolate Mousse 349
Chocolate Mousse Brownie Cake 255
Chocolate Nut Bars 286
Chocolate Pecan Pie 364
Chocolate Pudding Trifle 359
Chocolate Sable Cookies 299
Chocolate Sour Cream Cupcakes 262
Chocolate Zucchini Cookies 317
Chocolate Zucchini Loaf Cake 259
Cilantro Pesto with Peanuts 205
Cinnamon Seasoned Pecans 333
Classic Margarita 49
Classic Pimm's Cup #1 49
Classic Sangria 51
Cobb Salad 72
Cocoa Krispies Marshmallow Treats 325
Coconut Macaroons 295
Coffee Liqueur 55

Cold Cantaloupe Soup 58
Cold Cucumber Yogurt Soup (Tzatsiki) 56
Cold Papaya Champagne Soup 57
Cold Strawberry Soup 59
Cole Slaw 82
**Cookies 276-326**
Corn and Zucchini Casserole 232
Crab Cakes 107
Crab Stuffed Artichokes 105
Crab Stuffed Mushrooms 26
Cranberry Gelatin Mold 97
Cream Caramel (Custard Dessert) 347
Cream Cheese Cookies 305
Cream Cheese Layer Bars 285
Creamy Baked Cheese Pasta 166
Creamy Cauliflower/Potato Soup 65
Crisp Aniseed Sweet Rings 307
Crispy Oven Fried Potato Wedges 175
Crock Pot Beet Stew 119
Crunchy Broccoli Salad 86
Crystallized Ginger 330
Cucumber Tomato Mint Salad 79
Curried Chicken and Wild Rice Casserole 158
Curried Prawns 102
Custard Dessert (Cream Caramel) 347
Dark Chocolate Truffles 338
Date Bars 282
Date Muffins 268
Date Nut Cake 248
Date Scones 274
Date-Nut Coconut Sticks 310
Daoud Pasha (Meatball Stew) 115
Deluxe Date Squares 283
**Desserts 344-365**
Dhal Makhni (Lentils Seasoned with Butter Fried Spices) 224
Dolma and Sarma 141
Double Chocolate Biscotti 315
Easy Chocolate Truffle Squares 336
Egg Salad Sandwich 192
Eggplant Imam Bayeldi 215
Eggplant Parmesan 216
Eggplant Parmesan Panini 187
Eggplant Stuffed with Meat 142
Eight-Layer Bars 284
Ejjeh (Parsley Frittata) 37
Electric Skillet Roast Chicken 154
English Breakfast Scones 275
Ethel's Kahkes 304
Falafel 44
Falafel Sandwich 196
Fattoush 78
Festive Punch 52
Fish Kebab 99
Fish Tacos 112
Florentines with Milk Chocolate 312
Flourless Chocolate Cake 249
French Dressing 92
Fresh Apple Cake 246
Fresh Blueberry Muffins 268
Fresh Peach Pie 363
Fresh Spinach with Sautéed Onions in Olive Oil 225
Fried Cheese Beoreks 34
Fried Chicken Fingers 28
Fried Eggplant with Basil and Balsamic Vinegar 214
Fried Fresh Sardines 111
Fried Halloumi Cheese (Saganaki) 40
Fried Red Mullet 110
Fried Rex Sole 109
Fudge Ribbon Cake 243
Garlic Sauce 209
Gazpacho 60
Gazpacho Smoothie 48
Ghureybia (Sugar Cookies) 308
Ginger Soy Marinade 211

Grace's Simit 306
Greek Salad 77
Greek Style Leg of Lamb Roast 135
Green Bean Salad 76
Green Beans w/Sautéed Onions & Tomatoes 222
Grilled Bratwurst Sandwich 194
Grilled Chicken Kebab 149
Grilled Chicken Raspberry Salad 70
Grilled Eggplant Salad 84
Grilled Lobster, Avocado and Mango Salad 88
Grilled Shrimp with Pesto 100
Guacamole (Avocado Dip) 23
Hawaiian Ham Savory Muffins 270
Herbed Cheese 17
Honey Mustard Dressing 93
Honeyed Sesame Candy 331
Hot Buttered Rum 54
Hot Port 54
Hot Spiced Cider 53
Hummus 20
Imrig Halva 358
Individual Beef Wellington 124
Introduction 3
Irresistible Peanut Butter Cookies 292
**Jams and Jellies 340-343**
Jello Molds 94-97
Jumbo Raisin Cookies 291
Kadaif 356
Kafta in a Tray 140
Key Lime Cake 251
Key Lime Pie 360
Kibbeh be Saniyeh 139
Killer Shrimp 101
Korean Barbeque Ribs 129
Kung Pao Shrimp (Spicy Shrimp with Peanuts) 104
Lace Oatmeal Cookies 311
**Lamb 130-143**
Lamb Chops with String Beans 130
Lamb Shish Kebab 133
Lamb Stew with Green Peas 131
Lamb Stew with Okra 132
Lasagna with Meat Sauce 165
Lasagna with Spinach and Artichoke 164
Leg of Lamb Roast 136
Lemon Cake 252
Lemon Herb Mayonnaise 208
Lemon Roasted Potatoes 174
Lemon Shandy 50
Lemon Vinaigrette 91
Lemoncello 55
Lemon-Poppy Seed Muffins 267
Lentil Patties (Merjemekli Kufteh) 38
Lentil Salad 68
Lentils Seasoned with Butter Fried Spices (Dhal Makhni) 224
Lentils with Cracked Wheat (Moudardara) 182
Lentils with Rice (Moudardara) 181
Lobster Risotto 185
Lobster Roll 189
Lule Kebab 134
Macadamia Nut White Chocolate Chip Muffins 265
Ma'moul 303
Mamounia 357
Mango and Hearts of Palm Salad 87
Mango Apricot Smoothie 45
Maple Syrup Glazed Salmon 98
Marinated Olives 36
Mashed Potatoes 172
Mayonnaise 208
Measurements and Temperature Equivalents 369-371
Meat Marinades 211
Meat Samosa 32
Meatball Marinara Sub 190
Meatball Stew (Daoud Pasha) 115
Meatballs 114

Meatballs 114
Meatloaf Ciabata 193
**Meats 114-148**
Mediterranean Bean Salad 66
Mediterranean Salsa 198
Merjemekli Kufteh (Lentil Patties) 38
Mexican Chicken Casserole 160
Mexican Wedding Cookies 296
Milk Chocolate Fudge 335
Milk Chocolate Truffles 337
Mimosa 52
Mint Jelly 343
Mock Sou Beorek 35
Mother's Fried Chicken 153
Moudardara (Lentils with Rice) 181
Moudardara (Lentils with Cracked Wheat) 182
Moujadara (Pureed Lentils) 223
Mouhamara 22
Mushroom Risotto 183
Mushroom Sauce 202
Mustard Mayonnaise 208
Mustard Vinaigrette 91
Nutella and Banana Panini 188
Nutella Chocolate Truffles 339
Oatmeal Chocolate Chip Cookies 301
Oatmeal Raisinets Cookies 300
Okra with Cilantro in Tomato Sauce 226
Old Fashioned Peanut Brittle 327
Olive Bread 241
Oriental Chicken Cabbage Salad 83
Orzo Shrimp Salad 103
Oven Fried Cauliflower 217
Oven Roasted tri-Color Potato Salad 75
Paella Valenciana 113
Paella Vegetarian 213
Papaya Seed Dressing 93
Parmesan Cheese Twists 14
Parmesan Crusted Oven Baked Chicken Tenders 157
Parsley Crusted Rack of Lamb 137
Parsley Frittata (Ejjeh) 37
**Pasta 164-170**
Peach Cobbler 345
Peach Smoothie 47
Peanut Brittle Marshmallow Treats 324
Peanut Butter Chocolate Chip Bars 318
Pecan Honey Bars 290
Pecan Shortbreads 297
Pepper Jelly 342
Pesto Sauce 205
Pigs in a Blanket 25
Pineapple Smoothie 47
Pineapple Zucchini Loaf Cake 258
Plain Basmati Rice 179
**Pork 144-146**
Pork Kebob 144
Potato Kibbeh 171
Potato Salad 74
**Potatoes 171-175**
**Poultry 149-163**
Pound Cake with Candied Fruits 244
Puff Pastry Dough Cheese Beoreks 33
Pumpkin Bread 239
Pumpkin Chiffon Pie 362
Pumpkin Pie 361
Pureed Lentils (Moujadara) 223
Quick and Easy Brioche 235
Raspberry Gelatin Mold 96
Raspberry Smoothie 46
Raspberry Vinaigrette 90
**Rice 176-186**
Rice Pilaf with Vermicelli Noodles 178
Rice Pudding 348
Rice Stuffed Grape Leaves (Yalanchi Sarma) 27
Roast Chicken with Herb Butter 152

Rock Cakes 272
Saganaki (Fried Halloumi Cheese) 40
**Salads 66-93**
Salmon Patties with Red Pepper Coulis 108
**Sauces and Marinades 197-211**
Sautéed Green Beans with Red Pepper 221
Savory Cheese Muffins 269
Savory Parmesan Cheese Cookies 16
**Seafood and Shelfish 98-113**
Seared Beef Tenderloin with Mushroom Sauce 123
Seasoned Pita Chips 15
Sesame Marinade 211
Sesame-Pistachio Cookies (Barazik) 302
Sfouf (Turmeric Cake) 260
Sha'abiat 355
Shankelish 18
Shankelish Bread 242
Shankelish Salad as an Appetizer 19
Shitake Mushroom Sauce 203
Shrimp Scampi with Linguini Pasta 167
Skirt Steak 127
Skirt Steak Fajita 128
Slow Cooker Pork Roast 145
S'more Snacks 326
Smoked Salmon and Avocado Timbale 42
Smoked Salmon Bagel Sandwich 191
**Snack and Sandwiches 187-196**
**Soups 56-65**
Spaghetti Sauce 206
Spaghetti with Meatballs 170
Spanakopita (Spinach turnovers) 11
Special Cornbread 234
Spice Descriptions 8
Spiced Candied Walnuts 334
Spicy Indian Marinade 211
Spicy Shrimp with Peanuts (Kung Pao Shrimp) 104
Spinach and Cheese Strata 233
Spinach-Cheese Swirls 12
Spinach Turnovers (Spanakopita) 11
Split Lentil Soup 63
Squash Stuffed with Meat 143
Steak Marinade 209
Sticky Buns 237
Sticky Rice with Mango 350
Stir Fried Chicken and Vegetables 163
Strawberry Banana Smoothie 45
Strawberry Jam 341
Strawberry-Lemon Gelatin Mold 95
Stuffed Kibbeh 138
Succotash 227
Sugar Cookies (Ghureybia) 308
Super Easy Marinara Sauce 204
Swiss Cheese - String Bean Casserole 220
Tabouleh 80
Tahini sauce (Taratour) 207
Tahini Sauce 207
Tangy Lemon Cheesecake 254
Tangy Lemon Triangles 323
Taratour (Tahini Sauce) 207
Tarragon Dressing 92
Tex-Mex Marinade 211
Three Pepper Sauce 201
Tricolor Basmati Rice 180
Tri-color Raspberry Gelatin Mold 94
Tropical Chicken Salad 69
Tzatziki (Cold Cucumber Yogurt Soup) 56
Tuna Salad 71
Turmeric Cake (Sfouf) 260
Twice Baked Cheese Soufflés 39
Twice Baked Potatoes 173
Ultimate Chocolate Chocolate-Chip Cookies 294
Ultimate Chocolate Pecan Bars 278
**Veal 147-148**
Veal Sticks 147

Vegetable 212-233
Vegetarian Samosa 31
Walnut Parcels 354
Watercress, Blue Cheese and Walnut Salad 89
White Chocolate Graham Break-aways
White Chocolate Sour Cream Pound Cake 245
White Kidney Bean and Tuna Salad 67

Whole Cranberry Sauce 200
Wiener Schnitzel 148
Yalanchi Sarma (Rice Stuffed Grape Leaves) 27
Yogurt Soup with Stuffed Kibbeh 61
Zucchini Bread 238
Zucchini Chocolate Chip Cookies 317
Zucchini Pasta 169

# Measurement & Temperature Equivalents

Oven temperatures vary from gas to electric as well as the heat distribution in the oven. It is up to the cook to adjust temperatures at cooking time by closely watching the first time baking or roasting of a new recipe.

I have used standard measuring cups, spoons, and kitchen scales to weigh ingredients. Successful results will depend on using the proper measuring cups and spoons and not coffee cups, teaspoons or soup spoons.

- Use glass measuring cups to measure any kind of liquid.
- Use dry measuring cups to measure flour, farina, sugar, shortening, cocoa powder, etc.
- Use measuring spoons to measure salt and spices.

## Dry Measurements

| | | |
|---:|:---:|:---|
| 1 tablespoon | = | 3 teaspoons |
| 1/8 cup | = | 2 tablespoons |
| 1/4 cup | = | 4 tablespoons |
| 1/3 cup | = | 5 tablespoons + 1 teaspoon |
| 1/2 cup | = | 8 tablespoons |
| 2/3 cup | = | 10 tablespoons |
| 3/4 cup | = | 10 tablespoons + 2 teaspoons |
| 1 cup | = | 48 teaspoons |
| 1 cup | = | 16 tablespoons |
| 16 ounces | = | 1 pound |

## Liquid Measurements

| | | |
|---:|:---:|:---|
| 8 fluid oz | = | 1 cup |
| 16 fluid oz | = | 2 cups |
| 32 fluid oz | = | 4 cups |
| 1 pint | = | 2 cups |
| 1 quart | = | 4 cups |
| 1 gallon | = | 4 quarts |

## Pound Equivalents

| Grams | | Ounces |
|---|---|---|
| 10 gr | = | 1/3 oz |
| 15 gr | = | ½ oz |
| 50 gr | = | 1¾ oz |
| 100 gr | = | 3½ oz |
| 150 gr | = | 5 1/3 oz |
| 200 gr | = | 7 oz |
| 250 gr | = | 9 oz |
| 300 gr | = | 10 2/3 oz |
| 400 gr | = | 14 oz |
| 500 gr | = | 17 2/3 oz |
| 600 gr | = | 21 oz |
| 1000 gr | = | 35 oz |
| 1200 gr | = | 42½ oz |
| 1500 gr | = | 53 oz |
| 454 gr | = | 1 pound |
| 1 egg = 50 gr. | = | 2 oz. |

## Temperatures

| Celsius | | Fahrenheit |
|---|---|---|
| 105 | = | 225 |
| 120 | = | 250 |
| 130 | = | 275 |
| 150 | = | 300 |
| 165 | = | 325 |
| 180 | = | 350 |
| 190 | = | 375 |
| 200 | = | 400 |
| 220 | = | 425 |
| 230 | = | 450 |
| 245 | = | 475 |

| Ounces | | Grams |
|---|---|---|
| ½ oz | = | 14 gr |
| ¾ oz | = | 21 gr |
| 1 oz | = | 28 gr |
| 1½ oz | = | 43 gr |
| 2 oz | = | 57 gr |
| 2½ oz | = | 71 gr |
| 3 oz | = | 85 gr |
| 3½ oz | = | 99 gr |
| 4 oz | = | 113 gr |
| 4½ oz | = | 128 gr |
| 5 oz | = | 142 gr |
| 6 oz | = | 170 gr |
| 7 oz | = | 198 gr |
| 8 oz | = | 227 gr |
| 9 oz | = | 255 gr |
| 10 oz | = | 283 gr |
| 12 oz | = | 340 gr |
| (1 pound) 16 oz | = | 454 gr |

## One Pound Equivalents

2 cups butter
4 cups all-purpose flour
2 cups granulated sugar
3½ cup powdered sugar
2¼ cups brown sugar, packed

## Emergency substitutions

| | |
|---|---|
| 1 tsp baking powder | = ¼ tsp baking soda plus 5/8 tsp cream of tartar |
| ¼ cup dry bread crumbs | = 1 slice of bread (toasted and crumbled) |
| ½ cup soft bread crumbs | = 1 slice of bread |
| 1 cup buttermilk | = 1 cup yogurt or 1 cup milk less 1 Tbsp + 1 Tbsp white vinegar or lemon juice. Let stand 5 minutes. |
| 1 cup sifted cake flour | = 1 cup less 2 Tbsp sifted all-purpose flour |
| 1 cup self rising flour | = 1 cup all-purpose flour plus 1¼ tsp baking powder |
| 1 oz. unsweetened chocolate | = 3 Tbsp cocoa powder plus 1 Tbsp butter |
| 1 cup dried shredded coconut | = 1 1/3 cup dried flaked coconut |
| 1 Tbsp cornstarch | = 2 Tbsp flour |
| ¾ cup cracker crumbs | = 1 cup bread crumbs |
| 2 egg yolks | = 1 whole egg |
| 1 Tbsp flour for thickening | = 1½ tsp cornstarch |
| 1 small clove garlic | = 1/8 tsp garlic powder |
| ¼ oz. envelope gelatin | = 1 Tbsp gelatin flakes |
| ½ tsp freshly grated ginger | = ¼ tsp powdered ginger |
| ½ tsp dried herbs | = 1 Tbsp fresh |
| 1 cup honey | = 1¼ cup sugar plus ¼ cup water |
| 1 tsp lemon juice | = ½ tsp vinegar |
| 1 tsp fresh lemon rind | = 1 tsp dried |
| 1 cup whole milk | = ½ cup evaporated milk plus ½ cup water |
| 1 cup whole milk | = ¼ cup dry whole milk powder plus 7/8 cup water |
| 1 cup whole milk | = 1 cup non-fat milk plus 2½ tsp butter |
| 1 tsp dry mustard | = 1 Tbsp prepared mustard |
| 1/3 cup fresh orange juice | = ¼ cup reconstituted frozen orange juice |
| 1 cup sour cream | = 7/8 cup sour milk or buttermilk plus 3 Tbsp butter |
| 1 cup brown sugar | = 1 cup granulated sugar plus 2 Tbsp molasses |
| 1 cup sugar | = 1¾ cup confectioners' sugar |
| 1 cup sugar | = ½ cup maple syrup plus ¼ cup corn syrup (reduce liquid in the recipe by 2 Tbsp) |
| 1 cup tomato juice | = ½ cup tomato sauce plus ½ cup water |
| 2 cups tomato sauce | = ¾ cup tomato paste plus 1 cup water |
| 1 (3/5 oz) compressed yeast cake | = 1 package or 1 Tbsp dry yeast |

## Abbreviations

| | | | |
|---|---|---|---|
| oz | = ounce | Tbsp | = tablespoon |
| fl oz | = fluid ounce | tsp | = teaspoon |
| qt | = quart | cm | = centimeter |
| lb | = pound | in | = inch |
| gr | = gram | ft | = foot |
| kg | = kilogram | pkg | = package |